S0-DUE-626

REVELATION AND THEOLOGY

VOLUME I

Theological Soundings •

REVELATION and THEOLOGY

VOLUME I

by E. Schillebeeckx, O.P.

translated by N. D. Smith

SHEED AND WARD: NEW YORK

Originally published as parts 1 and 2 of *Openbaring en Theologie* (Theologische Peilingen, I), Uitgeverij H. Nelissen, Bilthoven (1964). This translation is based on the second revised edition of 1966.

Library of Congress Catalog Card Number 67–21907

Nihil Obstat
Leo J. Steady, Ph.D., S.T.D.
Censor Librorum

Imprimatur
† Robert F. Joyce
Bishop of Burlington
July 19, 1967

The Nihil Obstat and Imprimatur are official declarations that a book or pamphlet is considered to be free of doctrinal or moral error. No implication is contained therein that those who have granted the Nihil Obstat or Imprimatur agree with the contents, opinions or statements expressed.

Manufactured in the United States of America

Preface

I am deeply indebted both to my superiors in the Order of Preachers and to my publisher for this opportunity of collecting my already-published articles and republishing them in book form, together with various published and unpublished lectures. For some time past it has been impossible to satisfy all the requests for offprints of articles, and several of the journals in which some of my articles have appeared have ceased to exist. Certain articles have been photocopied and it has thus been possible to supply these articles to those who required them. It is clear, then, that the republication of my articles will do much to rectify this unsatisfactory situation. What is more, this collection is to be thematically arranged so that each volume will contain articles grouped around one single subject. The author himself must, however, accept that there is a certain disadvantage inherent in a collection of his articles written over a long period. For although it may be unusual for him to dissociate himself completely from what he has written in the past, his thought has certainly undergone a process of development and, even if his ideas have not changed in any way, he would undoubtedly express what he wrote ten years ago quite differently now.

The whole series of volumes will include publications extending over a period of some twenty years, the earliest article dating from 1943. Even the earlier articles have been left unchanged, apart from certain points of style and, here and there, the omission or the condensation of a paragraph, in order to avoid repetition. The original place and date of publication has been given in each case, so that the articles may be read against their original historical background, which may, in certain cases, be important. As I have already said, the articles have not been collected in chronological order, but have been grouped under various themes. More recently published material has not been incorporated into earlier articles, since this would have placed this edition in a false perspective and resulted in a loss of the documentary character of the original articles.

After arranging the various articles according to theme, I came to the conclusion that the complete edition would comprise eight main volumes. These main volumes and their themes will be:

I. Revelation and Theology
II. God and Man
III. World and Church
IV. Priest and Layman
V. Jesus, the Christ
VI. Church and Sacrament
VII. Christian "Spiritual Life"
VIII. 1. Religious Life; 2. Dominican Spirituality

Though the series as a whole has the general title *Theological Soundings,* each main volume will appear under its own title. In view of this, and of the fact that there may also be compelling reasons for giving priority to the publication of a particular main volume, the actual order in which the series is eventually published may differ from the order given above. Moreover, several of the main volumes may well, like this first, be further divided into two separate books.

Not all my articles are to be included in this collection. The choice has been determined above all by a desire to allow one article to throw light on the views expressed in another. In this book, for example, the reader will be able to see how a mainly historical article like "The development of the apostolic faith into the dogma of the church" (Part 1, Chapter 4) provides a basis for part of the more speculative article "Scholasticism and theology" (Part 2, Chapter 10). It will thus be to some extent apparent that the study of tradition (and, of course, of scripture) and so-called "speculative theology" are indispensable to each other.

Because these articles have been grouped round one definite theme, this first main volume—that is, this and the second book which together comprise *Revelation and Theology*—may also be looked on as an introduction to theology, even though not all the questions which should arise in such an introduction are dealt with. Each of the two volumes of *Revelation and Theology* includes articles published between 1944/5 and 1962/3—precisely the period, in fact, of the great theological renewal in Europe. The characteristic features of this gradual development should, therefore, be seen mirrored in these books themselves.

In conclusion I should like to thank both my Dominican superiors and my Dutch and Belgian colleagues, especially P. Defever and R. Bromberg, and my assistant, T. M. Schoof, for the help they have given me with all the work involved in preparing a volume for press.

E. Schillebeeckx, O.P.

Nijmegen

Contents

Abbreviations

AAP	St. Thomas Aquinas, *In Aristotelis Analytica Posteriora*
AAS	*Acta Apostolicae Sedis,* Rome 1909ff.
AM	St. Thomas Aquinas, *In Aristotelis Metaphysica*
Ang.	*Angelicum,* Rome 1924ff.
AP	*Archives de Philosophie,* Paris 1923ff.
Bbl	*Biblica,* Rome 1920ff.
Bijd.	*Bijdragen,* Maastricht
BT	St. Thomas Aquinas, *In Boethium de Trinitate*
BThom	*Bulletin thomiste,* La Saulchoir 1924ff.
BZ	*Biblische Zeitschrift,* Paderborn n.s. 1957ff.
Carit.	St. Thomas Aquinas, *De Caritate*
CBQ	*Catholic Biblical Quarterly,* Washington, D.C. 1939ff.
CEG	St. Thomas Aquinas, *Contra Errores Graecorum*
CIC	*Codex Iuris Canonici,* Rome 1918
CLC	*Actorum et Decretorum S. Conciliorum recentiorum Collectio Lacensis,* Freiburg 1870ff.
Conc.	*Concilium,* London 1965ff.
DN	St. Thomas Aquinas, *De Divinis Nominibus*
DR	H. Denzinger, *Enchiridion Symbolorum, Definitionum, et Declarationum de Rebus Fidei et Morum,* ed. Karl Rahner, Freiburg 1953^{29}
DS	H. Denzinger, *Enchiridion Symbolorum,* ed. Adolf Schönmetzer, Freiburg 1963^{32}

DTC	*Dictionnaire de Théologie Catholique,* Paris 1930ff.[3]
DTF	*Divus Thomas,* Fribourg 1886–1953
DTP	*Divus Thomas,* Piacenza 1880ff.
DV	*Dieu Vivant,* Paris 1945ff.
EJ	St. Thomas Aquinas, *Super Evangelium secundum Johannem*
EL	*Ephemerides Liturgicae,* Rome 1887ff.
ER	St. Thomas Aquinas, *In Epistulam ad Romanos*
ETL	*Ephemerides Theologicae Lovanienses,* Louvain 1924ff.
FS	*Franz. Studien*
Greg.	*Gregorianum,* Rome 1920ff.
KT	*Kerk en Theologie*
LV	*Lumière et Vie,* Lyon 1951ff.
Mansi	*Sacrorum Conciliorum Nova et Amplissima Collectio,* ed. J. Mansi, Florence 1759ff. and Paris–Leipzig 1901–27
MM	*Misc. de Meyer*
n.	number (issue)
n.	note (footnote)
NKS	*Nederlandsche Katholieke Stemmen,* Zwolle 1901ff.
NRT	*Nouvelle Revue Théologique,* Louvain 1925ff.
OG	*Ons Geloof*
PG	*Patrologiae Cursus completus, Series Graeca,* ed. J. P. Migne, Paris 1857ff.
PL	*Patrologiae Cursus completus, Series Latina,* ed. J. P. Migne, Paris 1844ff.
Potent.	St. Thomas Aquinas, *De Potentia*
Prd	*Periodica de Re Morali, Canonica, Liturgica,* Rome 1930ff.
QLP	*Questions liturgiques et paroissiales,* Louvain 1910ff.
Quinz.	*La Quinzaine,* Paris 1929–32

Quodl.	St. Thomas Aquinas, *Quodlibeta Disputata*
RAM	*Revue d'Ascétique et de Mystique,* Toulouse 1920ff.
RF	St. Thomas Aquinas, *De Rationibus Fidei*
RHE	*Revue d'Histoire Ecclésiastique,* Louvain 1900ff.
RIP	*Revue International de Philosophie,* Brussels 1938ff.
RMM	*Revue de Métaphysique et de Morale,* Paris 1893ff.
RNP	*Revue néoscolastique de Philosophie,* Louvain 1894ff.
RSPT	*Revue des Sciences Philosophiques et théologiques,* Paris 1907ff.
RSR	*Recherches de Science Religieuse,* Paris 1910ff.
RSR (*US*)	*Revue des Sciences Religieuses de l'Université de Strasbourg,* Strasbourg 1924ff.
RSV	*The Holy Bible, Revised Standard Version,* New York 1946, 1952
RT	*Revue thomiste,* Brussels 1893ff.
RTAM	*Recherches de théologie ancienne et médiévale,* Louvain 1929ff.
SBAW	*Sitzungsberichte der Bayerischen Akademie der Wissenschaften zu München,* Munich 1860ff.
SC	*Studi Cattolici,* Rome 1957ff.
SCG	St. Thomas Aquinas, *Summa Contra Gentiles*
Schol.	*Scholastik,* Freiburg 1926ff.
1, 2, 3, 4 Sent.	St. Thomas Aquinas, *In Quattuor Sententiarum P. Lombardi Libros,* I, II, III, IV
ST	St. Thomas Aquinas, *Summa Theologiae*
StTh.	*Studia Theologica,* Lund 1949ff.
TG	*Theologie und Glaube,* Paderborn 1909ff.
Thom.	*Thomist,* Washington, D.C., 1939ff.
TL	*Tijdschrift voor Liturgie*
TP	*Tijdschrift voor Philosophie,* Louvain 1929ff.
Verit.	St. Thomas Aquinas, *De Veritate*

VT	*Vox Theologica*
WW	*Wort und Wahrheit,* Freiburg 1946ff.
ZKT	*Zeitschrift für Katholische Theologie,* Innsbruck 1877ff.

REVELATION AND THEOLOGY

VOLUME I

I

REVELATION AND ITS "TRADITION"

1 Revelation, Scripture, Tradition, and Teaching Authority[1]

Although it is possible to speak of an anonymous revelation outside the Jewish-Christian religion only in the light of the historical reality which is Christ, and in no other way, I propose to postulate, at least for the sake of this enquiry, which aims at being a synthesis, this anonymous revelation. What is in fact an implication or a consequence of Christianity will be seen here as its general background. It is necessary to state this explicitly at the outset, in order to avoid giving the impression that this preliminary consideration is unbiblical. What I have to say here will moreover be set out schematically, since I aim to do no more than provide a basis for discussion between Catholic and Protestant theologians.

THE BACKGROUND TO AND THE "HEART" OF CHRISTIAN REVELATION: GOD'S EFFECTIVE SAVING WILL

We know, through the divine revelation in Christ, that God intended that all men should be saved in Christ and, what is more, that this salvation not only was a possibility

1 For details of original publication of this and all subsequent chapters, see the table on pp. 259–260 below.

in Christ, but also has actually been brought by Christ, for all men, even though who in fact attains this salvation remains a mystery for us.

That is why it is possible to say that wherever men make history, a history of salvation or of perdition is brought about, because the significance they give their life is always, in acceptance or refusal, a response to the anonymous grace of God, his call to salvation. History is essentially a history made by human freedom. The real place where the human world becomes history is human freedom. If this freedom is confronted with Christ's salvation, though perhaps anonymously, in the universal and effective saving will of God, then this (implicit) confrontation with God's universal will to save—universal because it is concrete and individual with regard to *all* men—de facto causes a history of salvation or of perdition. Seen in the perspective of grace, secular human history is, via human freedom which responds in a negative or positive way (and which makes history), a history of salvation or of perdition. On the other hand, however, the freedom of the individual entering this world and its already formed human history also encounters an already existing history of salvation or of perdition, with the result that history itself has something to tell him, as it were from outside, about the God of salvation.

Included in the perspective of salvation from which God's attentive concern appeals to man through grace, man's situation is also characterised by the dynamic element of this call to salvation. The world, which was offered by God to man so that it should be given human significance, was offered to him concretely by the God of salvation. Thus, within the interior attraction of grace in which God offers the grace of faith to man, the world of creation, which is above all the world of one's fellow men, is a reference not only to the creative God, but also in the concrete sense to the living God, the God of salvation. In this way, creation, secular history, and man's encounter with his fellow men are all brought within the orbit of salvation. Within God's universally effective will to save, the world, as creation, as human history, and as human encounter acquires a special significance which it would not otherwise have of its own accord; it appears to us at the same time as a translation, however inadequate, of God's inward appeal to us through grace, as a means in and through which man is made more explicitly aware of this inward offer of grace, and finally as a sphere within which man may respond, either positively or negatively, to this divine appeal. That is why it is possible for us to say that, at least in the perspective of the saving mystery of Christ, the history of salvation or of perdition is as extensive as the human world itself. In other words, the history of salvation is not restricted exclusively to the religion of Israel or to Christianity, but is, because of Christ, an event of universal significance.

It is, however, also possible to dispute the extent to which we may speak of an authentic revelation in this connection outside the sphere of public revelation. In itself, God's inward appeal to us through grace may only be called revelation in its outward manifestation, for it always comes to us from outside—"from what is heard" (Rom. 10:17).[2] Outside Israel and Christianity there is an anonymous, and therefore vague and ambiguous, though undoubtedly existent, *auditus exterior* ("hearing from outside"): the world of creation as the translation of God's inward communication to man. The whole of secular human life thus somehow makes explicit what God's inward offer of grace means for us, namely, that God is our salvation.

What is brought about in the secular world is the same as

2 *The Holy Bible, Revised Standard Version,* New York, Nelson, 1946, 1952. All scriptural quotations in this book are from this version, copyrighted 1946 and 1952 by the Division of Christian Education of the National Council of Churches.

what is brought about in the concrete appearance of the same saving will of God, that is, in the man Jesus, with the difference that the first is vague, ambiguous, easy to misinterpret and therefore frequently misinterpreted, whereas the second cannot be misunderstood. Only Christ is the absolutely clear saving will of God. Although a presentiment of this saving will was felt outside Israel and Christianity (in grace), its true aspect was only seen in Christ. That is why we refer to a revelation in the whole of human history, a revelation which is truly supernatural but anonymous, and indeed to the anonymous revelation of Christ himself, incomplete and therefore open to misinterpretation. This is not an a priori deduction, but the implication of a twofold (Catholic) Christian truth that the possibility of salvation exists (in Christ) for all men, even if they are historically and concretely not confronted with Christianity, and that salvation is impossible without faith (see Heb 11:6). Faith is man's surrender to divine revelation. On a basis, then, of the absolute necessity of faith for salvation, God's universal will to save includes the real possibility that all men, wherever they live, may accept salvation by (anonymous) faith, and thus be anonymously confronted with God's saving revelation. In other words,

> In past generations he allowed all the nations to walk in their own ways; *yet* he did not leave himself without witness, for he did good . . . [Acts 14:16–17.]

This was said of the concrete and living God.

THE HISTORY OF SALVATION AND THE PROPHETIC MESSAGE

In Israel. Against the background and in the climate of this universal, anonymous invitation to communion with the living God, God began to clarify, as it were in an official manner, the meaning of his saving will, and he did this in Israel. Although we must always take care to assess the phenomenon of Israel as something which is distinct and independent from the religions of the ancient Near East, we must at the same time not use this as a reason for denying all continuity between Israel and the surrounding, anonymously supernatural religions. Anonymous revelation became in Israel a particular, concrete and "public" revelation, deriving the elements through which it found expression from the religious manifestations of "universal revelation." Judgement was at the same time pronounced by the particular revelation of Israel on the non-Israelite religions, in which human religious consciousness had tried to give a concrete but ambiguous form to universal revelation.

Israel's history of salvation is distinguished from the universal history of salvation by the presence of the prophetic message in Israel's history. The word of God which, speaking, makes the history of salvation, became, via the prophets of Israel, a word that interpreted Israel's history as its saving value. By virtue of the critical function of Israel's prophets, who spoke in the name of the God of salvation but also had their roots in Israel's faith, this word brought divine revelation into the history of Israel in an unambiguous manner. It is therefore in the revelation of the word that the formal distinction between Israel's particular and "public" revelation and universal and anonymous revelation is to be found.

That this divine word was heard in Israel and not elsewhere points moreover to a particular election of this people with Christ in view. It is not that the "covenant" as such, the intersubjective relationship of a people with its God, was peculiar to Israel. The religions of Israel's neighbours were also familiar with a kind of "covenant" with their God—it was the will of the living God that all should be saved, and Israel herself was aware that she had not been chosen because of her own merits. Many of the Old Testament prophets recognised that God could have called another pagan people. But the fact that the revelation of the word occurred precisely in Israel points to God's particular concern with the history of this people. Although Israel did not become conscious of the universal saving significance of her election as a mediation for all men until late in her history, the history of her salvation was nonetheless—seen in the perspective of Christ—a veiled pre-revelation of the mystery of Christ. This is so precisely because the history of salvation was "accompanied" in Israel by the message of the prophets, in which salvation became transparent. God's saving activity became visible and tangible as acts of God in history because of the word, and always with Christ in view.

Thus, although revelation is fundamentally situated in Yahweh's activity for the salvation of his people, and therefore in the history of Israel, the saving value of this history was only interpreted by the prophetic message. Israel's saving history gained its full and clear meaning as revelation when Israel listened to the message of the prophets. God's saving activity is not only a divine action, but also a divine interpretation of this action, in and through the prophetic message. The secular event of Israel's exodus from Egypt thus has a real saving significance, and it does not have this only in the theological reflection of the pious. As a secular historical event the exodus itself is a saving act of God, a revelation of salvation. But this saving act only becomes de facto an aspect of *our* history, i.e., a part of our consciousness and reflection, in and through the word. Yahweh said to Moses:

> I have seen the affliction of my people who are in Egypt, and have heard their cry because of their taskmasters; . . . I have come down to deliver them. [Ex. 3:7–8.]

It is in this word that God's saving act, accomplished in the historical fact itself, and his revelation of himself formally became for us revelation. God's saving activity—revelation in reality—and his word—revelation in word—are therefore indissolubly united to each other in the one concept of revelation. Both are essential ingredients of the one divine revelation.

It may be regarded as characteristic that the fundamental saving events of the Jewish people were marked by the appearance, whether before, during, or after these events, of a prophetic figure who interpreted Israel's national history in the light of her consciousness of faith, in which these prophets were themselves involved. The prophetic message threw light on the presence and the content of the saving act and, if the message preceded the events, even brought about the presence of a saving fact. It was precisely because salvation was revealed in a veiled manner in an event belonging strictly to this world, that is, in Jewish history, that the unerring recognition of the fact as a fact of salvation required the prophetic message. The word thus forms an integral part of the manifestation of God's saving activity. It is, of course, true that God did not simply say something about salvation. He also accomplished salvation within history. But, if this history was to be experienced as saving history, he had to interpret its meaning in and through the message of the prophets. The history of salvation, or God's saving activity as revelation, was for this reason an interpreted history, interpreted under a divine guarantee.

In Christ. If divine revelation has an essential bearing upon God's saving love for man, then this divine saving love for man in history of its very nature means promise and faithfulness. (See Deut 7:8–10.) The revelation-in-word therefore stands in the sign of the promise and its fulfilment, and man's temporal and spatial situation is the material with which God shows his love and invites man to respond to this love. As an event consisting essentially of dialogue between God and man, revelation, because of man's position in a world of fellow human beings and things in which he makes history, is of its very nature accomplished in history.

It is therefore impossible to separate God's elective love from man's association with this world in which he makes history. The history of mankind's salvation, in the form in which this became clear for the first time in the history of Israel, was—seen in the perspective of the mystery of Christ—in Israel a problematic reality, since God did not speak his definitive word in Israel. Israel's history merged into the coming of the Son of God into the history of our world. As an act of God in historical form, the whole of Jesus' human life was revelation. From his dialogue with the Father, the Son entered our human history, which thereby became, because of Jesus' human freedom, definitive saving history. But the definitive entry of this salvation in Christ into our history can be historically recognised only in the prophetic message of the same Christ, and only by those who believe in this message. It is only through the revelation of Christ's word that the saving significance of the revelation-in-reality which has been accomplished in the life and death of Christ becomes accessible to us historically in faith. It is precisely because salvation offers itself to us as a supernatural reality in the form of an earthly, secular reality—the humanity of Christ—that this saving reality appears as given and as revealed to us in the word.[3] The manifestation of the historical appearance of salvation in Christ thus includes Christ's prophetic message as an essential element in its constitution.

THE HISTORY OF SALVATION, THE WORD, AND THE SACRED BOOKS

From her history of salvation and the word, there emerged in Israel a consciousness of salvation, a consciousness that it was God's special people. Throughout the course of its his-

[3] See E. Schillebeeckx, *Christ the Sacrament of the Encounter with God,* New York, Sheed and Ward, 1963, 25–33.

tory, the nation became more and more deeply aware of its religious significance and of its being the people of God. In this way, living traditions developed in Israel, and these traditions, together with its history of salvation and the word, formed a single whole constituting Israel as the people of God. Israel, however, frequently interpreted its history wrongly, in an all too human way. The prophetic message therefore acted as a constant critical authority in Israel, sifting what was authentic in these traditions from what was not authentic.

The sacred books of Israel gradually emerged against this background of saving history and traditions, brought about or critically sifted by the message of the prophets, and it was in these books that Israel's consciousness of salvation was reflected via the critical interpretation of the prophets. These books appeared with the divine guarantee that this written expression of Israel's consciousness of salvation was a faithful reflection of the saving plan that God himself wished to realise in his people. The inspiration of these writings was therefore an extension of the divine and interpretative element expressed in the prophetic message, which in its turn was also supported by Israel's consciousness of salvation. In this sense, the inspiration of these books was, on the one hand, a personal charism, peculiar to the sacred writer himself. On the other hand, however, the sacred writer wrote precisely as a member of the people of God and in the service of this people. The inspired written word must therefore be seen, via the prophetic message, in association with Israel's history of salvation. The scriptural message thus had its roots deep in Israel's history. As Renckens rightly says:

> What lay behind the whole of Israel's national life was the inspiration which proceeded from this mystery, and which gave form and shape to the great diversity of material resulting from historical events and the various statements of the people.[4]

[4] H. Renckens, *The Religion of Israel,* New York, Sheed and Ward, 1965, 40.

A similar process occurred in the apostolic church in connection with the salvation brought about by the man Jesus. The saving event and the word of Christ, received, experienced, and heard by the apostolic church, in which the idea developed among the early Christian community that it was the redeemed people of God and the church of the Lord, eventually found their way, via the preaching and the witness of the apostles, into the holy scripture of the New Testament. On the one hand the hagiographers of the New Testament wrote as members of the church which was being built up, but on the other the apostolic message and the literature of the New Testament were at the same time the interpretative element by means of which the saving significance of the mystery of Christ, as this was experienced in the early church, was authentically proclaimed to the world under a divine guarantee.

Revelation-in-reality, revelation-in-word, and holy scripture thus form one single whole. Scripture provides us with an infallible and precise expression of the revelation as this was revealed in God's saving activity in Christ, in a veiled manner in Christ's prehistory in the Old Testament, and indeed even in the remote prehistory of the whole of mankind. Scripture is an essential element of the redeeming mystery of Christ as divine revelation.

THE APOSTOLIC CHURCH AND ITS SCRIPTURE AS OPPOSED TO THE POST-APOSTOLIC CHURCH

The apostolic church read the Old Testament in the light of the event of Christ. In this sense, the books of the Old Testament belonged to the books of the church of Christ. The Old Testament certainly had an independent significance of its own for Israel, but it was the beginning of a work, the last sentence of which was completed in the New Testament, and this final sentence elucidated the initial sentence. In this context, it is important to note that the Old Testament only discloses its full meaning when faced with the saving reality of Christ.[5] Many different biblical meanings in the Old Testament escape notice outside this contact with Christ. We should certainly not assume that the apostolic church read things into the Old Testament that were not there. On the contrary, nothing more was read into the words than they in fact said. It is simply that the deepest meaning of the books of the Old Testament was discovered in the apostolic church—a meaning which was only apparent to those who, in faith and because of the apostolic witness, were confronted with the reality of the mystery of Christ. The words of holy scripture therefore also have a value which transcends their meaning within their contemporary context, since scripture must always be a message for the present time.

What scripture has to tell us is the divinely guaranteed apostolic expression of the single and non-recurrent apostolic contact with the earthly and glorified reality of Christ. It was in the apostolic period, and only in this period, that redemption was definitively brought about, even though the eschatological manifestation of redemption did not end in the apostolic age. Revelation, too, was thus definitively brought about and in that sense closed. The history of salvation of course continued, but the definitive statement of God's plan with the whole of human history had been made. The public revelation-in-word closed with the completion of the great event of the resurrection of the dead Christ. A definitive interpretation of human history was thus provided in scripture. We can expect no other judgement on history than the judgement passed on it by the death and resurrection of Christ and proclaimed in scripture.

5 An interesting analysis of this is provided by, for example: R. Bijlsma, *Schriftuurlijk schriftgezag*, Nijkerk 1959; and C. H. Dodd, *The Old Testament in the New*, Philadelphia, Fortress, 1963.

Clearly, then, the history of salvation that followed the event of Christ's resurrection had a different meaning from that which preceded this event. Revelation—definitively brought about, closed, and therefore brought to fullness—acted as a norm in the life of the church. (This is of course the reason why the college of bishops, headed by the successor to St. Peter, did not assume all the rights of Peter and the apostles.) Scripture is the "covering letter" accompanying the mystery of the redemption brought about by God in the man Jesus, and it is clear that God intended it to be the lasting document accompanying this definitive saving event. In its later life the whole of the church, including the ecclesiastical or hierarchical office of that church, would have to refer to the apostolic church with its scripture. The apostolic church is the canon of the church's faith, the norm of the whole of the church's life, and consequently scripture is also the canon and norm of the church's life of faith because of its apostolic character. The apostolic church together with its scripture is therefore the *norma non normanda*—the norm in its own right—of the whole of the post-apostolic church. Since scripture belongs to the phase in the history of salvation in which the apostolic tradition was constituted, it is, as the written tradition of the college of apostles, the Magna Carta against which the life and the confession of the church must always be verified.

On the other hand, however, it is not possible to give an independent value to this "covering letter," as if salvation were to be found exclusively in scripture. It is generally the case that truth is not to be found above all and formally—I say explicitly, *formally*—in a book, but in the consciousness of a living human community, insofar as this community is directed towards reality, which ultimately is the truth. This is also the case in regard to religious truth. Saving truth is the meaningful content of the life of faith of the entire church, which recognises itself in scripture. The living reality is always richer than the written expression of this reality, at least as far as its literal and explicit meaning is concerned. But this written expression in itself contains a dynamism which embraces an inner reference to the fullness of the saving truth. Scripture is, after all, the word of God in human form. The divine word, thus given human form, transcends the directly analysable sense of these human words, which thus go beyond their purely human meaning and refer objectively beyond themselves: this is the *sensus plenior* of scripture, that is, the deepest meaning of the word of God, which is only very gradually made fully explicit within the life of the church.

The revelation-in-word is directed, through the medium of the history of salvation and therefore through the medium of scripture as well, to the whole of humanity, and inwardly to the heart of each individual, including ourselves, who live in the church today. This means that scripture has, so to speak, a double context: its context within the apostolic church, and its present-day context. For scripture is the record and the fundamental, divinely-guaranteed expression of our present-day faith as well. Thus through the centuries the church, constantly deriving its life and faith from the bible, has always been in process of reclaiming the more implicit meaning of scripture, on a basis of the grace of faith which empowers us to be "sympathetic" to the divine meaning of the bible's human words. This development has never resulted, and will never result, in the discovery of any new dogmas or revelations: any such we should have to find elsewhere than in scripture, as though the apostles had ignored the bible and confided some truths of faith to us in secret. The apostolic tradition which grew into scripture will always be the expression constituting the apostles' own, and thus our own, consciousness of faith, though this can never be adequately put into words or into writing.

This consciousness of faith, which, through the grace of faith, is based on the totality of revelation, leads to a deeper understanding of the divine meaning of the human, scriptural word in direct proportion to the extent to which the church lives in history in the light of the explicit statement of the bible, in faithful contact with the saving reality itself. In this sense, the life of Christianity does not depend exclusively on the *sola scriptura.* Christ does not confront us exclusively with the sacred books, addressing us at the same time, inwardly and personally, through the testimony of his Spirit in accordance with the inclination of the grace of faith. We are also made citizens of the kingdom of God and members of Christ's body in the "sacrament of faith," called by Gregory of Nyssa the "first *traditio.*"

It is clear, then, that the concept *traditio non scripta,* as opposed to holy scripture, is wrongly translated as "oral tradition." This translation is one-sided and incomplete, since it is not primarily a question of an "oral" but of an "unwritten" tradition, and this is first and foremost the handing on of the saving reality itself, through which the Christian comes into contact not just with the apostolic word but with the saving reality which is indicated by the word and can only be experienced reflectively in the power of the word. The celebration of the mystery of the eucharist, the Christian's prayerful contact with the reality of salvation, and his reception into the living charity of the Christian community all form part of the so-called "unwritten" traditions. What has been handed down to us, for example, in connection with the eucharist, is not simply the scriptural account or a doctrine about the eucharistic mystery, but the reality itself of the eucharist. And it is in contact with this reality that Christians are able to come to a deeper understanding of the meaning of the eucharist and to explicate it more fully.

A comparison may help to make this clearer. In the earliest church, the gospel of St. Matthew, read and interpreted in the light of apostolic experience and of association with the mystery of Christ, disclosed the content of this saving mystery by an appeal to the Old Testament, which yielded its deepest mystery in contact with the living and definitive reality of salvation. In the same way, involvement in the saving reality of the glorified Lord living in the church is the only sphere in which the inner meaning of the New Testament can be fully understood. Our association with the reality of salvation is always differently situated in accordance with our changing circumstances. "Alongside" scripture, but never independent of it, we must therefore distinguish an element that, as such, cannot be traced back to the scriptural element. This is our living involvement in the saving reality itself, in the charity of the Christian community, in the worship of the church, in prayer, and so on.

It is true that this living contact is only brought about in faith, and thus when we believe in God's word and in scripture. But this does not mean that there is only contact with Christ in the word. There is in fact a contact in reality, although this only becomes explicitly conscious in belief in the word. Here too, revelation-in-reality and revelation-in-word are indissolubly united, and a denial of the validity of one of these elements makes the other meaningless. The inexhaustible meaning of scripture has always been, and will continue to be, more fully disclosed in the experiential knowledge of the church throughout the centuries in contact with the saving reality itself, of which the scriptures form an essential part. This does not imply that our association with the saving reality results in our reading more into scripture than the words themselves say. It does, however, mean that, in our contact with the saving mystery, the inner significance of the "covering letter" is bound to emerge with greater and greater clarity. This saving mystery is itself the *sensus plenior* of scripture, the "fuller meaning" of which is precisely the saving reality which is indicated in the human words.

There is, however, a difference between the reading and re-interpretation of the Old Testament in the light of living contact with Christ, as occurred in the case of the sacred writers of the New Testament, and our reading and interpretation of the Old and New Testaments in the light of our communion-in-faith with the Lord who is present in the church. The New Testament is the "covering letter" of salvation that has been definitively completed. The possibility of being able to re-interpret this scripture from the point of view of a new phase of salvation is of its own nature excluded, since salvation in Christ is a definitive reality that will never be surpassed. (It is only the eschatological revelation that will go beyond scripture and render it superfluous.) Our association with the saving reality is therefore a communion with the glorified Lord, to whom the scriptures bear witness. That is why the *ephapax,* the unique event of the mystery of Christ, and the apostolic testimony of this event in scripture always act as a norm to the conscious content of our knowledge through contact with the saving reality.

Tradition in the church, which, according to the Council of Trent, should be treated with "equal reverence" as scripture, is an apostolic, and therefore a biblical, tradition. It is, in other words, the *paradosis* itself of the apostles. But this *paradosis* is a handing on both of realities of salvation, such as the celebration of the eucharist, and of the message which grew into scripture. The whole of the church is thus, even in its teaching office, first and foremost an *ecclesia discens,* a learning church, with regard to what is revealed, before it becomes in its magisterium an *ecclesia docens,* a teaching church, for us. Ignatius of Antioch was acutely aware of this when he wrote that the church had constantly to seek refuge in the scriptures "tamquam ad carnem Christi" ("as in the body of the Lord"). (See *Ad Philad.* 4, 1.) And in the words of Augustine, which were repeated again and again through the Middle Ages,

> Everything that we need for our life of faith and our moral life can be found in what is stated explicitly in scripture.[6]

The whole of the church's life—in other words, ecclesiastical tradition—must refer at all times to the apostolic church with its scriptures as to its norm, if it is to remain pure in its living growth, if it is to be revived and even if its theological expression is to be reformed and its perhaps one-sided religious experience is to be re-orientated. In this connection, Reformed Christianity, drawing its sustenance from the explicit testimony of the bible, is a constant admonition to us Catholics, and often a legitimate protest.

SCRIPTURE AND TRADITION IN THE CONTEXT OF THE ECCLESIASTICAL OFFICE

Revelation in word and deed is not handed down within the church in a mechanical way, like a dead thing passed on from hand to hand. It is, on the contrary, essentially linked with its living subject, the church, consisting of the living people of God headed by the ecclesiastical office, both of which are under the guidance of the Spirit of the heavenly Lord. The entire church is subject to tradition—the church which prays and lives in faith, hope, and love, the church which celebrates the liturgical mysteries, the church which is apostolically effective in its office and in its people and the church which reflects on its faith. The entire church carries out this tradition, but each part of the church does this in its own place and in its own way, the laity as the people of God

6 *De doctrina christiana,* II, 14 (*PL* 34, 42): "In iis quae aperte in scripturis posita sunt, inveniuntur illa omnia quae continent fidem moresque vivendi."

and the office of the church in its hierarchical leadership. In addition, the ecclesiastical office as a whole also has a critical function. Everything that comes about and is brought to light within the life of the church must be carefully considered according to its apostolic and biblical content.

It is true that this consideration is also the task of everyone in the church, both laypeople and those holding office, but it is the exclusive function of the teaching office of the church finally to judge whether we are faced, in connection with any definite reaction on the part of the people of the church, with an infallible, apostolic, and biblical reaction, or with a human—and perhaps all too human—reaction.[7] In this sense, the church's teaching office is the judge of our faith, but it is this because it is itself governed by the norm of scripture. The magisterium of the church does not, therefore, stand above scripture, but it does stand above our interpretation of scripture. According to the Catholic view, then, scripture has a critical function with regard to the concrete and empirical appearance of the church. It is fundamentally Christ himself who interprets scripture through his Spirit, active in the entire church and in a special way in the office of the church.

The infallibility of the church's faith—an infallibility in which the church's faith, the charism of the college of bishops, and the official charism of the pope as the head of this college form an indissoluble unity—is based upon the *ephapax,* the definitive character of the Christian mystery of salvation with its accompanying document, scripture, beyond which we can never go. In other words, this infallibility has an eschatological basis.

The word of the Lord abides forever. That word is the good news which was preached to you [in the gospel]. [1 Pet 1:25; see also Is 40:8.]

[7] See the Pastoral Letter of the Dutch bishops, Christmas 1960, French translation: *Le sens du Concile,* Bruges and Paris 1961.

The word of God abides forever in Christ, the *eschaton.*

I am sure that he [i.e., Christ] is able to guard until that Day what has been entrusted to me. [2 Tim 1:12.]

[And] when the Spirit of truth comes, he will guide you into all the truth. [Jn 16:13.]

Those holding office in the church are only in the service of the faith of the redeemed people of God:

"I am a fellow servant with you and your brethren who hold the testimony of Jesus . . ." For the testimony of Jesus is the spirit of prophecy. [Rev 19:10.]

In Israel it was possible for the people of God as a whole to be unfaithful to God, because salvation had at this time still not been brought about definitively. But against the background of the eschatological accomplishment of salvation in Christ, it is, in the Catholic view, impossible for the redeemed people of God, the church, to falter as the church, since, if this were to happen, the eschatological character of accomplished salvation would be brought into desperate straits. In the perspective of this imperishable or unfailing quality of the "faith of the church" ("the powers of death shall not prevail against it"), we may regard the charism of infallibility of the whole office in the church as an implication of the eschatological, definitive salvation (reality, word, and scripture) for the time between the resurrection and the parousia of the Lord.[8] This eschatologically based infallibility of the church's faith is also parallel to the so-called *opus operatum* character of sacramental sanctification, of which the imperishable foundation of the church as the primordial

[8] This infallibility is thus based on Christ's word itself, both horizontally, as an *anamnesis* with regard to the scriptures, and vertically, as borne by the living Lord. See Chapter 2, "The Lord and the Preaching of the Apostles," on pp. 25–32 below

sacrament is the eschatological basis. Christ situated the fullness of the diaconate of sanctification in the church, the fruit of his redemption. The imperishable quality of this diaconate, on a basis of the definitive accomplishment of salvation, is given concrete form in the unfaltering saving efficacity of the church's sacraments for those who believe in Christ. The word and the sacraments endure because of their eschatological foundation. What is called the "jurisdictional power" of the ecclesiastical office—really a "service"—only refers to the manner in which the word and the sacraments are legitimately administered in the Catholic Church.

The infallibility of the "faith of the church" (and all the mutually interacting elements implied in this, especially the infallibility of the church's office in "matters of faith and morals") may therefore be traced back, not to a fixed possession of the church on its own account, but to the power of Christ as the Lord who holds the church definitively in his hand. This infallibility is therefore a grace which visibly manifests itself in the church.

The limits of the infallibility of the church's authority will also be clear from this. This infallibility is a charism that preserves the whole deposit of faith throughout the entire life of the church on earth until the *parousia*. It is, however, no guarantee that the church will experience all the aspects of the faith at their precise hierarchical value at all periods of its life. The imperishable existence of the church, of which this infallibility is an implication, should not be regarded as something static. Whenever attention is directed in the church to one particular detail in one definite period of the church's existence rather than to the dynamic inviolability of the whole treasury of faith, the limits of this infallibility begin to reveal themselves. Although I cannot go into a detailed analysis of these limits here, I should like to indicate at least one of the functions of the church's teaching authority: its function in the definition of dogma.

This function is subordinate to the formal mission of the teaching office of the church (Mt 28:18–20) to preserve and to hand down the testimony of the apostles in a pure, living form which will appeal to men at all times. The situation frequently necessitates a more precise definition, but here the apostolic tradition, the *paradosis,* acts as an objective norm to the church's magisterium, and the carrying out of this function of defining dogma is subordinate to the church's task of preserving the apostolic testimony itself. The definition of dogma is never an isolated activity—dogma is not defined for the sake of the definition! There is, moreover, always a danger present in any definition of dogma, however necessary and beneficial it may be in certain situations, in that a precise definition of one aspect of faith may lead to the obscuring of another, complementary aspect. History provides evidence of the fact that one definition frequently requires another at a later period, the second definition integrating the "one-sidedness" of the first into a more perfect whole. Hilary, for example, alluded to the awkward situation into which the church was often forced whenever it was obliged to define a datum of faith dogmatically in order to combat error.[9]

Conclusion

It will consequently be clear that I regard as alien to Catholicism both any exclusive assertion of the *sola scriptura,* the *sola traditio,* or the *solum magisterium,* and similarly any affirmation of two or three parallel and independent sources. Both the scriptures and tradition are necessary to the life of the church. But, on the other hand, scripture and tradition also need the church and each other if they are to be recognised as canonical scriptures and as authentically apostolic tradition. Apostolic scripture is not scripture as, for example,

9 *De Trinitate,* II, 2 (*PL* 10, 51).

Marcion interpreted it, but as it is interpreted in the church of Christ. The church's supervision of scriptural exegesis does not place it above scripture, but merely points to the church's recognition of the exclusively apostolic principle as the norm of Christian faith and of life in the church. And this recognition of the apostolic authority with regard to our faith means in the last resort a recognition of the *auctoritas*, the power and authority, of God as the only and the exclusive criterion of Catholic faith—the Father sent his Son and manifested himself in him, and Christ sent his apostles, who became the foundation of the church.

2 The Lord and the Preaching of the Apostles

Revelation is both a saving event and a preaching which bears upon this event. In the *kerygma* (proclamation) of the apostles, the reality of salvation appears as something that is given to us. The completion of revelation in Christ therefore includes a completion and a closing of the apostolic message as the lasting foundation and the norm of the post-apostolic church. From the Catholic point of view as well, the apostolic *kerygma* has to some extent to be accepted as a unique and non-recurrent event with regard to the apostolic preaching of the church, which has to refer to it as to its norm.

If we are to provide a satisfactory answer to the question of what the apostolic preaching as characterised by Christ's dignity as Lord is,[1] and what the method and the means of this preaching are, then we are well advised to divide this question into two parts, and consider firstly the preaching of the apostles themselves and secondly the preaching of the church.

THE KYRIOS IN THE "KERYGMA" OF THE APOSTLES

The consequence of the mutual implication of saving event and preaching was that the completion of the mystery

[1] This was the theme discussed in January 1959 at the annual congress of the Union of Students in Theological Faculties in the Netherlands. This

of Christ—on the appointment of the Suffering Servant of Yahweh as Kyrios—inaugurated the closing of divine revelation, and was at the same time the foundation of the preaching which bears upon the mystery of Christ. In other words, the preaching of the apostles belongs to the constitutive phase of revelation. It is, together with the saving reality which it passes on to the church, the lasting norm for the whole of the church's further life.

Nonetheless, an unmistakable growth can be discerned between Christ's ascension to the Father and the end of the early apostolic period of the church with the sacred writings produced at this time. The two possibilities that may have occurred or that did take place then can be ignored here.[2] The very fact of this growth in itself forces us to consider the question of the vital relationship between the activity of Christ as Lord and the *kerygma* of the apostles, a relationship which was both horizontal and vertical.

The Apostolic Testimony of the Historical Christ Who Became the Kyrios

The condition that was laid down when a successor was found to the apostle Judas indicates that an immediate encounter with Christ was the basis of the preaching of the apostles.[3]

---

paper aimed to provide the congress with a schematic outline of the perspective in which this question may be answered from the Catholic point of view.

[2] These are, firstly, that not everything had been revealed with Christ's ascension (those who maintain this thesis base their argument on Jn 16:12–14 and 14:25–6); and secondly that the whole of revelation was completed with Christ's departure, with the result that the growth of the mystery of faith in the early church is on a par with a development in tradition or dogma. This second claim is based on Jn 15:15; Acts 1:3; Mt 28:19–20.

[3] Acts 1:21–3; 13:31; 1:8; 2:32; 3:15; 5:27–32; 10:39, 41–2; Lk 24:48; 1:2; Jn 15:27; 1 Jn 1:1–3.

We are witnesses to all that he did both in the country of the Jews and in Jerusalem. [Acts 10:39.]

The climax of this encounter with Christ was in the apostles' immediate experience of Christ's dignity as Lord, in other words, their experience of the risen Christ who appeared to them. Testifying to the power and the *parousia* of Christ, the apostles did not resort to cleverly-thought-out fairy tales, but to the fact that they had witnessed Christ's glory with their own eyes.[4] The essence of this is that they had been immediate witnesses of the risen Christ. Their association with the earthly Christ established above all the continuity between the historical Servant of God and the Kyrios who appeared to them. The Kyrios to whom they bore witness was identical with the Son of Man who had been known to many men and who had been crucified by Pilate. (This is the basic plan of the apostolic *kerygma.*) It was this witness, based on personal experience, that made the *kerygma* of the apostles unique and gave a distinct meaning to the whole of the early apostolic church as such, borne up as it was by an apostolic office that had, until this point, been called in a special way.[5]

Viewed horizontally, then, the *kerygma* of the apostles was directly linked with the Kyrios, that is, with the appearances of the risen Messiah within the ealiest church.

The Direct Activity of the Kyrios in the Apostles' Preaching

Vertically too, there was a vital link between the Kyrios and the preaching of the apostles. Christ's "sitting on the right hand of the Father" was the very heart of the early

[4] 2 Pet 1:16; Jn 1:14; 1 Jn 1:1–3.

[5] I do not propose to deal here either with the problem of the relationship between the "Twelve" and the other apostles such as Paul, or with the question of the other apostles' witness of the resurrection.

Christian confession of faith. For the early church, Christ was a personal and present reality, and not simply someone who had brought about redemption in the past, nor even simply the person whose eschatological *parousia* was impatiently awaited. For the first Christians, Jesus was, on the contrary, a person living in the present who came into contact at the present moment with those who believed in him. It was precisely because they felt Christ to be present in this way that the early Christians longed for the full presence of the *parousia*. They experienced daily the Lord's personal leadership of the young church through his Spirit, whose constant and active concern they experienced vividly in their midst.

Being therefore exalted at the right hand of God, and having received from the Father the promise of the Holy Spirit, he has poured out *this which you see and hear.* [Acts 2:33.]

It was only as the Kyrios that Christ was to send the Spirit of whom it was said that "he will teach you all things, and bring to your remembrance all that I have said to you" (Jn 14:26).

The Unity of These Two Moments

What the apostles did in their capacity as apostles, they brought about together with the Spirit of the Lord. "It has seemed good to the *Holy Spirit* and to *us* . . ." (Acts 15:28).[6] What did the apostles do in connection with the "proclamation of the mystery of salvation"? This may be summed up schematically under three main categories—the preaching, or proclamation, of the apostles (*kerygma*), their witness or testimony of salvation (*martyrion*) and finally their teach-

[6] See also Acts 3:9; 4:31; 5:3–4; 6:3–5; 7:55; 8:29, 39; 10:19; Jn 14:26; 15: 26–7; 16:13–15; Mt 10:18–20; Mk 8:11; Lk 21:13ff.

ing (*didachē*). The *kerygma* was the proclamation of the good news that God had, in Christ, intervened as a redeemer. The *kerygma* was the proclamation in the Spirit of the saving event, one of the integrating elements of the constitutive phase of the revelation of salvation. The *martyrion* had a juridical nuance, and was the apostolic act in which the apostles bore witness to what they had seen and heard to the forum of history and the world.[7] This testimony was not a kind of photographic reproduction, but a result of the apostles' dialogue with what was revealed; in other words, it was a revelation that had been reflected on. (Hence the difference between the vision of the synoptic gospels and that of the Johannine gospel.) Finally, the *didachē,* proceeding from the mystery of Christ and the developing church, disclosed the meaning and the consequences of this revelation of salvation—its implications, its elucidation in the light of the Old Testament, the limits dividing it from false teaching, and so on. Light is also thrown on the demands of life in the world by this being in Christ. The *didachē* included the entire incarnation of the apostles' faith in the concrete world of their time, together with the *paraclēsis* of the "holy commandment delivered them" (2 Pet 2:21)—the ethics of the gospel.

This multifarious apostolic work of preaching was, on the one hand, a fully human activity and, on the other, an activity carried out by the living Kyrios himself. It was the Lord who spoke and acted in the active *paradosis* or tradition of the apostles, their *kerygma, martyrion,* and *didachē*. This is why St. Paul was able to say that what he had received from others—from other apostles, that is—was identical with what he had received from the Kyrios. This does not, however, mean that there was only a horizontal link between the *kerygma* and the Kyrios—there was also a vertical link with the living Lord. The encounter

[7] Jn 1:14; 15:27; 19:35; 1 Jn 1:1–3; 1 Pet 5:1; 2 Pet 1:16; Heb 2:3.

with the earthly and glorified Christ, as the point at which the apostolic church began to exist, had the same meaning and content as the present speaking and acting of God in the Kyrios. In other words, the tradition of the apostles included both the meaning of the mystery of Christ which had been completed in history, and with which the apostles had been directly confronted, and the meaning of the Lord's present speaking in the hearts of the apostles and in the church.

In the constitutive phase of revelation, then, the apostles mediated in the making present of the saving mystery that had been accomplished in Christ. The Lord's hidden activity in and through the preaching of the apostles established, together with the apostles' immediate testimony of the mystery of Christ that they had seen and heard, the inviolable deposit of faith that acted as a norm to the later church. Both the inward speaking of the Lord and the external material from the apostolic tradition—which in its turn came from the apostles' direct association with the earthly Christ and the risen Christ who had appeared to them—together formed the preaching of the apostles. The Lord himself spoke in the apostolic preaching, and this was consequently not merely an *anamnesis* of the words of the earthly Christ and the risen Lord during his appearances to the apostles. In this *anamnesis* the living Christ spoke here and now to the apostles. The apostles' handing down of what they had previously heard and experienced of the Christ event took place while they were listening to the living and active words addressed to them in the present by the invisible Kyrios. The apostolic *kerygma* is therefore the historical form in which the Lord's actual inner speech appeared, as the glorified continuation of Christ's preaching.[8]

[8] The "witnesses" were not only the apostles, but also the Spirit of the Lord; see Jn 15:26–7; Lk 24:48–9; Acts 2:8; 1 Jn 1:1–3; Acts 5:30–2; 1:8; 4:31–3; Jn 16:8. Heb 2:3–4 speaks of a "cotestimony of God" (*synepimartyrountos tou Theou*).

THE KYRIOS IN THE "KERYGMA" OF THE CHURCH

The early apostolic church had a certain unique and non-recurrent quality, but this quality is also to be found in the structure of the post-apostolic church. Here too, a process of human tradition is taking place—a process which is at the same time the expression in time and space of the speaking here and now of the living Lord. Christ's present speaking in the church's preaching of the word on the one hand and inwardly in our hearts through grace on the other is not a double address, but one and the same address, in which what was said at an earlier time is really included in what is said here and now. Christ's power as Lord is revealed first and foremost in the church and her preaching.

The whole life of the church, from the early apostolic period until the *parousia,* is ruled by the Kyrios, who "builds up the body of the church" through the mediation of his Spirit and of the church's apostolic office. The preaching of the church is a manifestation of both forms of mediation in their coincidental activity. This preaching in word and deed is the manifestation in time of the revelation already completed in the Kyrios.

The distinction between the preaching of the apostles and that of the church (*kerygma, martyrion,* and *didachē*) is not a difference in authority, infallibility, and value as a norm. They differ in that the outwardly proclaimed fact of faith, which is the content of what is said here and now by the Lord, originated in the apostolic church in the apostles' direct and personal testimony of Christ's earthly humanity and of the Kyrios who appeared to them. This immediacy, which was intended by God, gave a unique and non-recurrent character to the preaching of the apostles, and thus came within the constitutive phase of revelation. As such, the apostle was a historical figure within the plan of salvation. As invested with plenary powers by Christ, and from his own historical experience—and thus from his association and dialogue—with the Christ who lived and died on earth, but who also rose and appeared to the apostles on earth, the apostle bore witness here and now to the speaking Kyrios, while at the same time he bore co-testimony to the true meaning and content of what took place for our salvation. It was this fundamental apostolic preaching, prepared by the Spirit, that acted as a norm for the post-apostolic church. The apostles were, therefore, in a very distinctive way, the "pillars of the church." Their witness was part of the *ephapax* of revelation.

Spoken to here and now by the Kyrios, the apostolic office of the post-apostolic church does not derive the externally provided facts of the historical mystery of Christ from its historical and immediate experience, but from the reality of the early apostolic church. The church's apostolic office acts as a norm for our life of faith only as ruled itself by the norm of the apostolic church, and it is in this way that the church's preaching gives visible form to a continuous speaking here and now by the living Lord. In this latter respect, then, the post-apostolic church is in no way different from the apostolic church. Because of the immediacy of the apostles' experience, the preaching of the apostles formed part of the deposit of faith which is the church's norm in its preaching. The church's preaching thus makes use of the testimony of the Lord both horizontally and vertically. It is in this preaching that the Kyrios continues to bear witness through his Spirit. The Lord's guarantee thus applies not only to the apostolic church, but also to the post-apostolic church. In this way, both the preaching and the whole of the history of salvation of the church is at all times based on the historically past, external revelation, to which the apostolic church bore witness in its life and its scripture, and the church continues to be addressed here and now by the living Kyrios and to be orientated by him towards the *eschaton*.

3 Revelation-in-Reality and Revelation-in-Word

For some Christians, Christianity is first and foremost a revelation by the word of God. For others, however, its essence is above all to be found in the deification of man through sacramental togetherness with God in Christ. I propose in this chapter to go more deeply into these two complementary aspects of the Christian plan of salvation.

THE WORD OF GOD AS THE MEDIUM OF REVELATION

The "Word of God" as the Old Testament Expression for the God Who Addressed Man Personally

It is a remarkable fact that Israel made no distinction between the word and the event or thing that was expressed in words. The Hebrew *dābhār* meant both a spoken or written word and an event in nature or in history. The phrase "after these words" often meant "after these things,"[1] for words were not only spoken, but also done.[2] Thus, the story of Solomon's life was expressed in scripture by the term, "the words of Solomon."[3] A person's life in the Old Testament

1 See, for example, Gn 22:1.

2 Gn 24:66.

3 1 Kings 11:41.

was the word that he spoke—he *was* that word. The word was the full manifestation of a person or a thing.

Furthermore, no distinction was made in Israel between the word and the person speaking. Speaking was a mode of being of the person himself. The expression, "Thus says Yahweh," contains a heavily charged dynamism. The power of the word was the power of the person who spoke the word, and the power of the word of God was particularly great.[4] God's word was truth and reached its target unerringly, whereas the words of the false gods were lies and ineffectual.[5] A word of God that was not realised was, for Israel, an impossibility.[6] The word of God consequently made history:

> The Lord has sent a word against Jacob, and it will light upon Israel; and all the people will know. [Is 9:8–9.]

The prophetic word, as the word of God in the mouth of man, in a certain sense caused history. As an expression of God's will—"For he commanded and they were created,"[7] or, more simply, "He spoke and it was"—the prophetic word called the future into being.[8] At the same time, it explained the meaning of history—it was the divine interpretation of a natural or historical event in the midst of the people of God. That is why it sometimes happened that the prophecy took place after the event. Whenever the primitive belief, common among Israel's neighbours, that the word possessed a magic power, gained ground in Israel,[9] it evoked a sharp reaction on the part of the prophets, who constantly ascribed

4 Is 55:10–11; Wisd 18:14–15, etc.

5 Is 41:22–4.

6 Deut 18:18–22.

7 See, for example, Ps 148:5.

8 Is 9:7; 49:2; 55:10–11; Jer 5:14; 23:29, etc.

9 Among the many studies devoted to the "word" among the Semites, see especially L. Dürr, *Die Wertung des göttlichen Wortes im Alten Testament und im antiken Orient,* Leipzig 1937.

the power of the word to the personal power of Yahweh.[10] It was only because the prophet was a "man of God" that his words were efficacious.[11]

The word of God was the incarnation of God's saving will; that is to say, it coincided with the historical events themselves, and with the natural events that were ordered and guided by God himself for the benefit of the people of God. Nature and history came about through God's word. "Man lives by everything that proceeds out of the mouth of Yahweh" (Deut 8:3): that is, we live from the word of God.[12] The "word of God" included every divine activity connected with man and the world. The world, created by Yahweh's word and disrupted by man's sin, was to be re-created by Yahweh's word.

This Old Testament theology of the *dābhār* (or word) has a deep significance—it points to the personal relationship between God and man. It is not only the God of creation who shows himself, but also the God of salvation and of the covenant. The "word" showed not only that creation and history were brought about by a creative God and that they had to be interpreted "theistically," but also, and especially, that they had to be interpreted in the context of man's personal relationship, his dialogue with God. All these events were an invitation on God's part to man, whom God addressed personally in them. The world and history were no longer simply a subject for philosophical analysis, they were the subject of a personal dialogue between God and man. This "word of God" was God himself, insofar as he was calling man to a living communion with him. The word was at the same time the existence of man and the world, viewed as a task and a vocation for man and as a "notifica-

10 See, for example, Ex 22:18; Lev 20:6, 27; Deut 18:9–14; 1 Sam 15:23; 28:3.

11 1 Sam 9:6; 1 Kings 17:24.

12 See Jer 17:16; Ps 89:35.

tion" to him in his personal relationship with the living God.

Revelation itself is, in this sense, a revelation-in-word, a dialogue. But this dialogue was accomplished both by events in history and by the prophetic utterances that threw light on its meaning. Revelation-in-reality and revelation-in-word are both aspects of one and the same divine speaking, or of the "word of God." Although revelation consisted primarily of God's saving activity, and thus of the history of the Jewish people, this history only acquired the full and pregnant significance of revelation when it was understood by the people of God in their awareness of salvation. The divine saving activity, within which history became a history either of salvation or of perdition, was illuminated by the word of the prophet, in whom this dialogue of action met with a clear response. The word revealed to God's people the presence and the meaning of the divine saving activity, and explained the natural and historical event as a personal address on God's part. Because of its supernatural mystery concealed within a profane, or rather a secular, event, this divine saving activity inwardly *demanded* a complementary word. It was therefore only in the prophetic word—the word of the man who heard and understood the inward speaking of God in the historical event—that saving revelation became full self-awareness in the chosen people. The accomplishment of salvation in history was a speaking on the part of God, but the precise meaning of this divine dialogue—in other words, the worldly event as a dialogue with God—had to be interpreted by a human word on the part of the prophet:

Surely Yahweh our God does nothing, without revealing his secret to his servants the prophets. [Amos 3:7.]

New things I now declare; before they spring forth I tell you of them. [Is 42:9; see also 1 Pet 1:20.]

The Old Testament theme of the "roaring of the lion"[13] refers to the prophetic proclamation of future historical events as a judgement of God. Within the general dialogue between God and man through nature and history (which is not simply worldly happenings with a theistic background, but worldly happenings which have their principle in the God of salvation who seeks a living communion with man), God's particular speaking in and through the human word finds a place. It is because dialogue, or the word, plays a part of primary importance in human relationships that Israel called God's disclosure of himself to man in nature and history a "word," a dialogue. This speaking of God, which might in the Old Testament have been to some extent anthropomorphic, acquired its full and pregnant significance in the complete revelation in Christ.

The Man Jesus—God Speaking in Human Form

Christ among us was, in and through his historically situated and conditioned humanity, the revelation of God. He was thus God's word—God himself, the Son, addressing us personally in the man Jesus. God the Son was a personal fellow man who dealt with us as man to man, at the personal level. Every truly human act on Christ's part was therefore, even more strongly than in the history of the Old Testament, a word spoken by God to man. Moreover, here the dialogue in the proper sense acquired its fullest significance. If Jesus' humanity was the medium of divine revelation, then this implies that Jesus' human word literally acquired a constitutive significance in this revelation.

It is clear from the study of anthropology, and in particular from the study of the various phenomena associated with aphasia, that speech is an essential part of a person's in-

[13] See, for example, Jer 25:30; Amos 3:4–8; Joel 3:16; Hos 11:10.

carnation in this world.[14] The human word is the human reality itself as this is manifested in outward expression. It is a mode of human existence. "Venir au monde, c'est prendre la parole" ("to come into the world is to acquire words, a language").[15] The word is one of the most characteristic modes of human encounter. What man is is expressed in language, and it is in language that man turns to others. Language is essentially man's self-disclosure to others, revelation. If language is essential to man's "incarnation," then we may expect the human word of Christ to have a constitutive significance in the incarnation of God as redemptive revelation. All anthropomorphism in God's speaking ceases here—God himself personally speaks in the man Jesus, in Jesus' human word. The revelation in reality, which is the person of Christ himself in the totally human form in which he appeared, allowed its meaning and content to emerge clearly in the human word that this man addressed to us. We must now consider this word of Christ.

Jesus' word was God's word, in the form of a human and historically conditioned word. We must consider it in its full human and personal value and power if we are to throw light on the theandric value of the word of Christ.

The word, as an essential element of dialogue, is the means by which the inner world of two persons is opened to each other. It is an expression of the freedom which aims to communicate its concealed value to others and thereby surrender itself. According to Buehler, three principal aspects can be distinguished in human dialogue.[16] (1) *The content:* something is said. The speaker communicates some-

14 G. Gusdorf has, for example, made out a very plausible case for this in his book on phenomenology, *La Parole,* Paris 1953. It is, however, difficult to agree in principle with this writer's view of the human person, in which he follows Merleau-Ponty.

15 Gusdorf, 8.

16 K. Buehler, *Sprachtheorie,* Jena 1934.

thing, explains something, testifies to something, and so on. (2) *The invitation:* somebody is addressed. Speaking is an act directed towards a fellow person. Speaking is addressing someone. The thing with which the speaker is concerned is the matter with which he appeals to or questions his partner in the dialogue. When he speaks, he expects a reaction. Speaking itself is a call to this reaction, an invitation to a definite response. The reaction can take as many different forms as the address itself. The minimum response required is attentive listening. If, however, I express a command when I speak, then what I say is at the same time an appeal to obedience. If I speak suppliantly, then I appeal to my partner's goodwill and expect a favourable response. Among the many other forms of address and response is speaking which bears witness. If I testify to something that the person to whom I am speaking knows nothing or can know nothing about, then my address is an appeal to surrender in faith to my testimony, an invitation directed to my partner in the dialogue, so that he will have faith in me and take me on trust. Speaking which testifies or bears witness therefore contains an invitation to believe. Finally, dialogue also contains a third aspect: (3) *Self-unveiling*—speaking is not only a speaking about something, it is also an expression of oneself, a revelation of oneself and a giving of oneself.

The word of the man Jesus which testifies is also like this —it essentially contains an "invitation to faith." But, if the power of the human invitation, directed towards the freedom of a fellow human being, is limited because it is human speaking, this is not the case with Christ—the invitation here is the incarnation of a divine invitation which can address human freedom in its inmost core. The anthropological fact of the effect of the human word retains its full validity, but gains an unsuspected depth because the speaker is now God himself—the Son, God in a human form. The human word of invitation that is addressed to us has the relative value and the impotence of a human influence which is only superficial and powerless before the core of personal freedom. The human word of Christ, on the other hand, penetrates to the most intimate core of our personal freedom, which opens itself to receive it, because Christ's word, his invitation, is a personal act on the part of the Son of God. His human word is de facto able to bring about in us the obedient response in faith.

This listening with assent to Christ's word transcends our human powers. When his word de facto arouses in us this response in faith, it at the same time brings about in us the existential basis from which we, still as human beings, can make our theologal[17] act of faith in his word. The "invitation to faith," which is inherent in all human testimony, acquires a deeper meaning in Christ's speaking in testimony. Aquinas called this invitation the very essence itself of the light of faith (*lumen fidei*)[18] that is given to us as grace by means of Christ's word. It is only by this inward grace of faith that I know myself, in and through what is spoken by Christ, to be addressed by the living God, and I make an act of faith and trust in Christ's invitation which is the incarnation of the word of invitation, the grace of faith.

De la Potterie has, in a painstaking study, indicated the scriptural basis of this Thomist view of faith.[19] The "balm" or chrism is (in some scriptural texts) the word of Christ himself (*fides ex auditu,* "faith from hearing") as this is brought to our minds by the Holy Spirit (*locutio interna,* "inward address"). The inward unction is essentially connected with the *ex auditu*. This applied to those who heard the word of

[17] For the use of *theologal* see *Christ the Sacrament,* 16 *n.* 14.

[18] "An inward instinct of the God who invites" (*ST* II–II, q. 2, a. 9, ad 3; *Quodl.* II, q. 4, a. 1). Thomas often elaborates this doctrine in connection with a scriptural, and especially a Johannine, text. See *EJ,* c. 6, lect. 5: "instinctus interior impellens et movens ad credendum" ("an inward instinct urging and inducing man to believe").

[19] I. de la Potterie, "L'onction du chrétien par la foi," *Bbl* 40 (1959), 12–69.

Christ directly. This word was human, but it was also the incarnation of an inward grace. Given the inner efficacity of the human saving acts of Jesus, there is no reason at all to give a different explanation for the effect of his speaking, and simply to refer to an accompanying activity of grace. It is really a question of the inward power, which is no different from the power of divine grace itself, that addresses us humanly in the manner of the saving word. The invitation to faith as the inward element of Christ's speaking is the inviting power of a divine grace in human form. In this sense, Christ's word has a sacramental value just as much as his saving acts. His word is no less a saving act than a physical contact that healed the sick. In both cases it is a question of an effective act of God, although in human form.

It is only on this christological basis that the saving mystery of the church's proclamation of the word, especially in the eucharistic service of the word, can be understood.

The Church's Proclamation of the Word

The apostles did nothing other than simply pass on the word of Christ—they preached the "word of God."[20] This does not mean that they proclaimed the word *about* God, but that they proclaimed the word that God himself spoke in Christ,[21] that is, the gospel, the word of salvation and redemption that Christ himself spoke in dialogue and in deed. At the same time, Paul called the word of God "my word." This means that what the apostles said was at the same time Christ's speaking through the apostle:[22]

20 See 2 Cor 2:17; 4:2, etc.

21 H. Schlier's studies throw considerable light on the idea of the "word of God" in the New Testament. See "Die Verkündigung in Gottesdienst der Kirche," *Die Zeit der Kirche,* Freiburg 1956, 244–64; *Wort Gottes. Eine neutestamentliche Besinnung,* Würzburg 1962.

22 See 1 Thess 1:5; 1 Cor 2:4; Rom 2:16; 2 Cor 4:3, etc.

When you received the word of God which you heard from us, you accepted it not as the word of men but as what it really is, the word of God. [1 Thess 2:13.]

We are ambassadors for Christ, God making his appeal through us. [2 Cor 5:20.]

This identity of the word of Christ and that of the apostles (*qua* apostles) is based on the plenary powers and the mission which the apostles received from Christ—they were given the task and the power to speak the word of God in Christ. For this reason, the proclamation of the word was a *diakonia,* a service and a mission—the "ministry of the word" (Acts 6:2–4). This ministry of the word is therefore an act of the office of the church.[23] The church's ministry of the word thus implies that the word proclaimed is the word of Christ himself, in the form of the apostolic word. The church's ministry is the self-revelation of Christ, which continues to be alive and effective through the revealing power of the Holy Spirit in the word of the apostles. This is why the church's word is also a power.[24]

It follows, therefore, that just as the word that was spoken personally by Jesus while he was still on earth possessed an inward divine fruitfulness of grace, so also does the church's ministry of the word possess an inward power of grace. The church's word is the personal word of the heavenly Christ in the form of the apostolic word; it is, in other words, the personal word of Christ *in forma ecclesiae* ("in the shape of the church"). The analogy with the sacraments of the church is thus quite clear. The immediately expressive gesture of love of the man Christ is his glorified body. This made Christ's word objective; it was his final word, which through

23 Besides the official ministry of the word, there is also a place for a charismatic proclamation of the word. See, for example, 1 Cor 12:28f.; Eph 2:20; 3:5; 4:11.

24 Rom 1:16.

the ages speaks to us of the resurrection from the dead.[25] Since the ascension, however, we have not been able to see or hear this heavenly sign of love. Within the environment of our life on earth, this effective heavenly expression of love is made visible and audible by Christ in the sacraments and the word of the church. Christ's saving intention, perfectly expressed in his heavenly body, has been made incarnate in the church since the ascension in the church's sacramental rites and in her word.

Christ's personal will to save and his personal speaking to man thus form a unity with the church's sacramental act and the word of the church. As the incarnation in the church of a personal word of the God-man, the ministry of the word is also inwardly effective. Here, too, there is much more than simply an accompanying activity of grace—the church's proclamation of the word possesses, as the incarnation of Christ's personal word, a divine saving power. We acknowledge this, for example, after the reading of the gospel at Mass: "Through the words of the gospel may our sins be wiped away"; or when listening to the reading of the Divine Office: "May the reading of the gospel be for our salvation and protection." These are not simply the expression of a pious hope—they express a reality of grace.

But the objection will immediately be raised: have I not equated the proclamation of the word and the reading of scripture with the efficacity of the sacraments, and thus made the word of the church, the church's preaching, and the Divine Office an eighth sacrament? Many Catholics find this objection a stumbling-block and tend, therefore, to minimise the dynamism, the inward saving power, of the ministry of the word. But their objection is based on a misunderstanding. They are forgetting the sacramental structure of the whole

25 I have attempted to analyse the structure of this in my article "Godsdienst en sacrament," *SC* 34 (1959), 267–83. This study throws some light on the subject under discussion here.

church and of its specifically ecclesial[26] acts, which are all visible signs of grace. The church is the focus of Christ's visible presence of grace on earth. It is the great sacrament from which all kinds of dynamic sacramental movements proceed. The eucharist, the focal point of Christ's real and active presence among us, is at this centre of the sacramental church. The other six sacraments radiate clearly from this focal point.

It is only the preaching of the church that can disclose this mystery to us and enable us truly to believe in it. Illuminated by this word, we see a broad wave of sacramental activity continue to flow outwards—grace is visible for us in all the church's activities, and in the Christian life of the faithful as a power attracting others. But, although less pronounced and already flowing away, these sacramental waves still continue to surge in the sacramentals. Finally, this sacramental life ebbs away in the reality of the material and historical world of men, which is equally under the influence of Christ, the Lord.

All these factors are, *each in its own way,* "sacraments," that is, true, visible realities, of which the Lord makes personal use in a richly inspired and varied manner in order to orientate men towards God in Jesus Christ. All this means that the grace of Christ does not only come to us inwardly. His grace approaches us, in many different variations, visibly as well. This is the lasting consequence of the incarnation. Through the Son of God's becoming man, the world of men has been included into the personal relationship of God to man and man to God. In union with the inward grace, the whole world of creation has thus become *gratia externa,* the exteriority of grace, that is, grace itself in visible efficacity. The word of the church and the church's ritual sacraments are simply the burning focal points of this world-embracing manifestation of the Lord in what is the concentration of

26 For the use of *ecclesial* see *Christ the Sacrament,* 48 *n.* 3.

the visible presence of grace—the church, in whom, thanks to the eucharist, Christ is truly *sōmatikōs,* somatically—that is, physically, and therefore personally—present.

It is possible to define the limits of the sacramental nature of the church's word as opposed to those of the ritual sacraments against the background of this broad sacramentalism of the church. "The word" is the church itself in one of its essential activities. In the manner of the word it thus shares in the essentially sacramental structure of the church. Both the word and the seven sacraments are a personal address on the part of the living Lord through human forms. In both cases, the response can take the form of acceptance or of refusal. But the proper nature of the word and the proper nature of the sacrament will indicate the proper efficacity of these two activities of the church. Leaving aside the special case of the eucharist, the presence of Christ in the word and in the sacrament is not a question of "more or less," but of a difference in manner. The manner in which the Lord is present in the word and in which he is present in the sacrament differs according to the proper sense and meaning of *word* and *sacrament.* There is a clear difference between the manner of Christ's presence in his own humanity (*in propria carne*) on the one hand and the manner of his presence in the sacrament on the other hand,[27] and finally the manner of his presence in the word, although there is, in all three cases, each in its own manner, a real and active presence of Christ himself.

Both the modern science of the phenomenology of language (as, for example, in Gusdorf) and the Old Testament show clearly that the word cannot be separated from the person speaking—the word, dialogue or conversation, is a manner of being and of being present of the person himself. The

27 A further distinction must, of course, be made here between the sacramental presence of Christ in the six sacraments and his real eucharistic presence.

word of Christ is a word of testimony. Consequently it brings us face to face with the presence of Christ himself, but as one bearing witness and inviting us to believe. The real efficacity, then, of the ministry of the word is our obedience in faith,[28] which is impossible without our being raised up by grace, since it is God alone who can make us capable of believing. Christ is therefore present, and actively present, in the word of the church, but in the manner of the word that invites us to believe. This invitation is a divine invitation (although it is made in a human form) and because of this it confers on us the power to accept it freely. The church's preaching of the word of God thus possesses an inward power of grace, but—and this must be emphasised—in the manner of the word of testimony, a manner which is of quite a different nature from the efficacity of the ritual sacraments *which presupposes this faith,* although the same basic pattern and the same sacramental structure (a structure which is perceptible in all the specifically ecclesial acts of the church) are present in both.

The inward efficacity of the church's word is the "dynamism" of the person speaking. In this case, it is that of Christ himself, in the form of the word of the church. The divine invitation to believe which is essentially implied in the word of testimony acquires a human incarnation here. This does not, however, invalidate the divine power, but makes it visibly present and active among us in the word that is spoken by the church or in the word of scripture that is read within the church.

Obedience in faith, the fruit of the ministry of the word, is presupposed in every fruitful reception of a sacrament which, of its very nature, must be a *sacramentum fidei* ("sacrament of faith").[29] Without the saving power of the

28 "Faith comes from what is heard" (Rom 10:17).

29 I have already analysed this tradition in *De sacramentele heilseconomie,* I, Antwerp and Bilthoven 1952. Since then, however, a scriptural study has

word, a sacrament cannot in fact be fruitful. This structure points to the inward link between the ministry of the word and the ministry of the sacrament. Since the sacrament is completely fruitful only in the person who is intimately associated in faith with Christ's giving of himself in the sacrament of the church, the ministry of the word is of necessity related to the ministry of the sacrament. Thus, what is commenced in the word is completed in the sacrament. Faith is the *initium salutis,* the beginning of salvation. In the sacrament, salvation is given to us in full. The sacraments confer or intensify "sanctifying" grace, whereas the church's preaching only confers immediate or "actual" graces which bring us to obedience in faith. Faith, aroused and made meaningful by the ministry of the word, is the space in which the sacraments must live. That is why Christ entrusted both the ministry of the word and that of the sacrament to the same office.

This, however, is not all. Just as the prophetic word, which pointed to God's personal invitation contained in the saving events, formed part of the inner constitution of the Old Testament revelation in reality, so too is the church's word necessary to the inner constitution of the sacrament. No one has so far formulated this idea more successfully than Aquinas, who elaborated one of Augustine's suggestions.[30] Just as God, the *logos* or word—Aquinas reasoned—became incarnate in an outward form, perceptible to us, so too did the "word of faith" (*verbum fidei*) become incarnate in the ritual actions, through which these actions became sacraments or *verba incarnata* ("incarnate words"). The theological doctrine of the *forma sacramenti* ("the form of the sacrament"), which at first sight seems to say so little and which was moreover also suspect on account of its later con-

---

appeared which shows clearly the scriptural basis of this teaching: L. Villette, *Foi et sacrement,* I, Paris 1959.

30 *ST* III, q. 60, a. 6; see the following footnote.

nection with Aristotelian hylomorphism, thus contains a profound reality. This is that the *forma* of the sacrament, in other words, what makes the ritual action formally a sacrament, is a "word of faith," a word that proceeds from God, is accepted in faith by the church, and finally, borne up by the church's faith, becomes incarnate in a rite, with the result that this word becomes the essential core of the sacrament and of its sacramental saving effect.[31]

The ministry of the word is consequently not simply presupposed in the ministry of the sacrament, but penetrates to its very heart. Just as the prophetic word in Old Testament times called forth and brought about the saving event in history, precisely because it was a divine word, although spoken in a human form, so too does the sacramental word, the *forma sacramenti,* cause the saving appearance of Christ's redemptive act in the sacrament. Thanks to the ministry of the word, a ritual act becomes the manifestation in mystery of Christ's heavenly act of salvation. The word itself thus becomes a sacrament, namely in the seven sacraments which are an incarnation of the *verbum fidei.* The word of God *in forma ecclesiae* is not an eighth sacrament, but it makes the seven sacraments sacraments and has, as the word of God, a distinctive meaning and saving power—the power to arouse that obedience in faith which is the condition of the fruitful reception of any sacrament and the very pivot of the Christian life.

These basic principles enable us to define more precisely the significance of what is usually called the "first part of the Mass" within the whole celebration of the eucharist. It will be clear from what I have already said that the phrase "first part of the Mass" is in some respects not altogether unfortunate—it is the Mass itself, but does not have the last word in the sacrifice of the Mass.

31 An analysis of these Thomist ideas will be found in *De sacramentele heilseconomie,* I, 378–80.

Before considering this question, however, I should like very briefly to emphasise the unity that must exist between the ministry of the word and the personal Christian life. I cannot hope to deal exhaustively with the whole question of the ministry of the word in this article, but I feel that it is important to say something about the harmony between the testimony of the word and the Christian life, in order that what I have already said in the preceding sections should not be misunderstood.

The sacraments have a saving power which is independent of the personal holiness of the one who administers them. In the concrete, however, the holy manner in which the sacrament is administered does contribute considerably to the fruitful reception of the sacrament. Thus the ministry of the word is in a sense a reality which is objective in its effect, but this does not exclude the sense in which personal holiness and intelligence play a very special part in the ministry of the word, even more than in the sacraments. "We believe, and so we speak" (2 Cor 4:13). The ministry of the word must be a confession of this faith and it must form a harmonious whole with the preacher's Christian life. It is for this purpose that the charismatic gifts of grace are given to each according to his state in life. It is then that Christ is fully present in the word of the church, for he is then present in a special way in this personal surrender in faith to the word. And that personally spoken word then refers, in the whole of its human form, to the action of grace that is present in the holy testimony of a believing person. This presence of Christ in the word is doubly effective. What is more, the sense of Christ's presence in the ministry of the word will prevent the minister of the word himself from making foolish attempts to allow his own understanding—or lack of understanding—to prevail instead of allowing God to speak through the word. This question really requires a separate study. All that I have done here is to draw attention to it.

THE SERVICE OF THE WORD IN THE CELEBRATION OF THE EUCHARIST

Just as every sacrament is introduced, surrounded, and enclosed by the ministry of the word, which awakens in us a grateful obedience in faith to the saving reality that is accomplished in us in the sacrament, so also is the celebration of the eucharist of its very nature a ministry, or service of the word, which is especially prominent in the opening part of the Mass known as the "liturgy of the word." If we are to understand this fully and at the same time refute the obvious objection that there are, in this part of the Mass, not only a service of the word, but also a confession of faith, a confession of guilt, prayers, and supplications, then we must go more deeply into the New Testament teaching about the "word of God."

Schlier has correctly pointed to the implications of the word of God according to primitive Christianity.[32] Because it was given to the church—that is, to the apostolic office of the church—the gospel, as the word of God spoken by men, acquired many different new shades of meaning. The place of the ministry of the word is, in principle, the assembled people of God, the faithful community which unites for the purpose of worshipping and praising God. The assembled people of God is thus the inward situation in which the word of God resounds. But the form of God's word is influenced by this situation and many different aspects of this one service of the word are thus brought out. The word is addressed to people who, because of their baptism, have already given themselves in faith to Christ and to catechumens who are being strengthened and instructed in their faith. Thus the "service of the word" automatically also acquires the form of a confession of faith—a confirmation of the word of God that has been accepted through the power of the ministry of the word,

32 *Wort Gottes.*

or a consolidation of the incipient faith of the catechumens.

The same situation—the fact that the word of God resounds in the community of those who already believe and in the community of the catechumens—brings out even more shades of meaning in the word of God. It is not only proclaimed as an apostolic *kerygma* or as an apostolic *didascalia,* admonishing and announcing. It can also be a "word of prayer," a "word of hymn" or song of divine praise, a doxology, an acclamation, or a priestly blessing. All these variations—these typically liturgical elements—are so many different forms of the one word of God. They are all to be found especially in the first part of the Mass—the scriptural readings,[33] the sermon, the supplications, the acclamations, and the confessions of faith and of guilt. Thus both the apostolic office and the faithful, praying church are prominent in the "service of the word," in instruction and confession of the word which flow naturally into the *oratio communis* ("common prayer"). Christ is personally present in this part of the Mass—on the one hand in the community that prays and confesses its faith and guilt, and on the other in the word of scripture that bears witness and in the church's official preaching. But Christ is present there bearing witness, instructing, and admonishing in order to bring us to the more profound obedience in faith that is necessary if we are to offer *his* sacrifice with him under the visible forms of bread and wine. The "service of the word," which evokes our response in faith, strengthens it, and gives meaning to it, has to arouse in us a faith in the reality of what is about to take place—the reality that is of vital importance to all of us. The first fruit of the celebration of the eucharist is thus given to us already in the first part of the Mass: obedience and surrender in faith to Christ's sacrificial act of love—an obedience which flows over into praise, thanksgiving and rejoic-

[33] For the importance of this immediate contact with scripture itself, see Part II, Chapter 6: "The Bible and Theology," on pp. 167–195 below.

ing, into confession, and into acceptance of the demands of morality and religion and into supplication. This sacrificial disposition which is aroused by the word is not something extra to the sacrifice of the Mass, but something that enters into the full significance of the sacrifice through the active participation of the faithful.

This is not all. It would be wrong to call the first part of the Mass the "liturgy of the word" *in contrast to* the sacrificial service. The *anaphora,* with the words of consecration as the central point, is itself a service of the word in the form of the ancient Jewish *b^{e}rākhāh,* or blessing. According to St. Paul, we "proclaim the Lord's death" in the celebration of the eucharist (1 Cor 11:26). In the view of many exegetes and liturgical historians, Paul is referring here not only to a proclamation in and through the ritual act itself, but also to an accompanying proclamation of the word of Christ's death and resurrection. The phrase: "Let us give thanks to the Lord our God," means: "let us bring the *b^{e}rākhāh* to the Lord our God"—that is, praise *and* thank him because he has redeemed us through his death and resurrection. The Jewish *b^{e}rākhāh* (in Greek, *eucharistia*), which was at the same time a "sacrifice of praise," undoubtedly influenced the structure of the Christian eucharist—a praise of God, the *anamnesis* or proclamation of the reason for this praise ("praised be God who has redeemed us from Egypt, who . . . , who . . . , etc.") followed by a doxology and, encouraged by what God did in the past, a supplication, asking him not to be slow to respond in the future. This praise of God for the "signs and wonders" that he has performed in nature and in history for his people, ending with a suppliant "be mindful, O God" became, in the Christian *eucharistia* of the consecrating preface, a praise of God for the miracles accomplished by him especially in the death and resurrection of Christ. The "Amen" (or "bravo") of the faithful confirms this "proclamation of the Lord's death."

But this proclamation of Christ's death by the *word* cannot be dissociated from the liturgical *action* itself of the eucharist. The word is not simply an interpretation of what takes place in the action. It forms a single liturgical whole with it, with the result that this proclamation even becomes the *forma* of the eucharist.[34] In the celebration of the eucharist, the word makes Christ appear not only in the manner of speaking in testimony and not only even in the manner of the sacramental sign, as in the case of the other sacraments, but also in the special manner of the eucharistic presence, by virtue of the dialogue of transubstantiation, through which the "sacrifice of praise" at the same time becomes an offering of expiation—that is, the sacramental sacrifice of the cross. Thus, taking up one of Schlier's ideas, we may truthfully say that the service of the word is in fact only a "foreword"[35] to that which is accomplished in the eucharistic sacrifice itself—the word of the proclamation is a foreword to the decisive word of the eucharist. The whole celebration of the eucharist is thus a service of the word, and the whole eucharist is a sacramental event.

But it is here—that is, in the very core of the *anaphora*—that the word reveals its supreme saving power and, as it were, transcending itself, becomes *compressed*[36] into a personal reality, Christ himself in the form of sacrificial bread and wine. Subject to the word of the covenant—"calix Novi Testamenti"—the sacrificial forms of bread and wine are the

[34] It is not relevant to this study to consider to what extent the whole of the *anaphora* was the *forma* of the eucharist in the course of the history of the church, and to what extent only the words of consecration are now this *forma,* at least in the west.

[35] See *Wort Gottes.*

[36] This word (*verdichten*) is borrowed from Karl Rahner: "When is the *most compressed,* the most effective word spoken? Which is *the* word of the priest, of which all the others are only expositions and variations? It is the word that the priest speaks when, quite absorbed into the person of the *Word* of the Father become flesh, he says softly, 'This is my Body . . . This is the chalice of my Blood' "; *Schriften zur Theologie,* I, Einsiedeln 1956[2], 362.

real presence of the sacrificed Christ, the Lord. The spoken word finally gives way here to the pre-eminent word, the person of the living Christ. But, as is the case elsewhere, the proclamation of the word is especially demanded here by the presence of Christ, so that it is possible for us to believe truly in the presence of this unfathomable reality and to experience its awesomeness and its fascination. An Old Testament image that is perhaps unfamiliar to us in the west acquires its full meaning in the eucharist—the "service of the word" is truly the "roaring of the lion," announcing a great event that will be a judgement to salvation or to disaster. It is only when the service of the word is taken quite seriously, and we encounter the testifying Christ in it, that we shall be able to encounter and receive him (in the full sense of the word) in his presence in the eucharistic sacrifice, "until he come"—until we are with him at the resurrection.

It will therefore be clear that the sermon, following the gospel, in no way "interrupts" the celebration of the eucharist, but forms an integral part of the service of the word, and as such shares in its saving power. In the sermon, the word of God sounds in the manner of the apostolic word of the church. All that I have said about the service of the word applies equally to the sermon in the Mass. In this sermon, the word of God is associated in a special way with the concrete people who are taking part here and now in the celebration of the eucharist. The sermon is therefore an extension of the first part of the Mass—it belongs to this rather than to the sacrificial part. It is even possible to say that the whole of the first part, dogmatically speaking, grew out of a sermon of the church, with the result that, if the concrete historical development of the liturgy of the Mass is disregarded, at least the essential core of the Christian *b^{e}rākhāh* (or blessing) on the one hand, and of the church's preaching, to which the faithful give their consent in prayer and in confession, on the other hand, have been preserved.

The sermon thus, so to speak, forms an element of the proper of the Mass, of its changeable part. The concrete content of the sermon is not, however, laid down in the missal, but is left to the inspiration of the priest, the servant of the word. It is impossible for the word of the sermon to be laid down because it is directly concerned with the actual day-to-day life, in the Christian sense, of Christian people. We might speak, then, not only of the *commune* (the "common") of the Mass and of its *proprium* (the "proper"), but also of its *propriissimum*—that is, the sermon, which is the most individuated, most special part. The whole is a service of the word, culminating in the *forma* of the eucharist. We may therefore say that the sermon ends in what makes the eucharistic celebration the eucharist—the *forma* of the whole liturgical event, the "word of God." We have already seen that the event itself was called a "word of God" in the Old Testament, insofar as this event formed the essential content of the dialogue between God and man. As the content of such a personal relationship of dialogue with God, the eucharist is a *mysterion* which requires an initiation or, to use a patristic phrase, a "mystagogical catechesis." This does not mean that the sermon always has to be a sermon about the eucharist, or that it must be directly related to the proper or the common of the Mass. The good news, in whatever form it is proclaimed, always leads us to Christ's redemption, of which the eucharist celebrates the memory.

To conclude, then, Gusdorf called the word "un engagement de la personne parmi les choses et les personnes."[37] This is pre-eminently the case with the word of God, which "came over to our side" in Christ and entered our human world of things and persons. Christ gave an ultimate meaning to things and to people by his word. He fully expressed himself in the world of things and people to the Father, so

[37] *La Parole*, 32. "A commitment of the person to and among things and other persons."

that we might listen to this word. It sometimes happens that the partners in a dialogue become different people after a conversation—they are enriched, having discovered a new world, and even the things around them are changed. In dialogue, the word has a truly "creative" function. But such a human word is only a pale reflection of the divine word addressed to us in the man Jesus. This divine word inwardly seizes hold of us in our innermost being and inwardly changes the things that surround us. Because of this divine dialogue, the bread is no longer purely human bread, but Christ's body in the sacrificial form of bread. Thus we may see that the whole of the life of grace—concrete human life itself—is nothing but a relationship in dialogue with the living God within the communion of the "saints." The whole of our human and Christian condition can be understood in the light of the prologue to St. John's gospel:

> In the beginning was the Word, and the Word was with God. . . . And the Word became flesh. [Jn 1:1, 14.]

This is the eucharistic word—it is always the same word of God, that forms the "object" of a dialogue which begins with God himself, and in which we are invited to participate so that we may finally share in the divine life that is expressed in the "word" so that it can communicate itself to us and become reality in us.

4 The Development of the Apostolic Faith into the Dogma of the Church

There are two distinct phases in the tradition of faith. The first is the *constitutive* phase, which includes the whole of the reality of revelation and which closed with the end of the early apostolic church, that is, with the death of the last apostle, as the last authentic witness of the mystery of Christ.[1] The second is the *interpretative* phase, during which nothing new has been added to the content of faith, but its hidden wealth has been more sharply defined since the closing of revelation with the death of the last apostle.

Although the closing of revelation is not a dogma that has been solemnly defined, it has been universally accepted by the normal teaching authority of the church. This teaching is also closely connected with the doctrine about the unchangeable nature of dogma. This closed and unchangeable

1 See the decree *Lamentabili,* esp. DS 3421 (= DR 2021). See also DS 3020, 3459 (= DR 1800, 2059), and DR 2080 (omitted in DS).

(For the convenience of readers, references to H. Denzinger's *Enchiridion Symbolorum* are throughout given according to both systems of numeration. "DR" refers to Karl Rahner's 1953 edition, as representative of editions published between 1908 and 1957; and "DS" refers to Adolf Schönmetzer's 1962 edition, which was the first to employ the new numeration system. Further bibliographical details are given in the list of abbreviations on pp. xiii–xv above.—Tr.)

nature of revelation must be respected throughout the interpretative phase, which includes the growth of dogma in the whole course of the church's history up to the *parousia.* This development, within fixed limits or in the tradition of the original content of revelation, is not only a historical fact, but also an authentic doctrine of the church.[2]

These two facts confront us with the problem of the essence of the bond between closed revelation and the later stages in the development of the faith. The question is: how can a recent definition of a dogma be implied in a revelation closed twenty centuries before? How can we speak of there being a new pronouncement *for us* in revelation without in effect appealing to a new revelation? In other words, how can the development or gradual maturing of tradition (which is to be found not only in the faith of a particular part of the church, but in that of the whole church) be reconciled with the church's doctrine of the closed nature of revelation and the unchangeable character of dogma?

A HISTORICAL SURVEY OF THE PROBLEM

In the Fathers and the Middle Ages

In its present scope, this problem is of very recent date. It is, in fact, scarcely a century old. The unchangeable nature of dogma and the need to keep to the *paradosis,* that is, to what was handed down, was stressed by the fathers. More attention was given, from the third and fourth centuries onwards, to the development of Christian doctrine, as the result of the necessity to combat heresies. Vincent of Lérins wrote a treatise in which he set out the principles of a continuous development. In the patristic period, it was basically only a

2 See DS 3020 (= DR 1800); and *Pascendi,* esp. DS 3483 (= DR 2079) and DR 2080 (omitted in DS).

question of expressing in a more explicit form what had previously been less adequately formulated.

The theologians of the Middle Ages did not consider the development of dogma as a dynamic process, but they did study the various phases within objective revelation and before its closing as a static situation.[3] Their basic thesis was that faith was substantially the same at all times, both before and after Christ. Because of the inward, objective, and organic structure of the truths of faith, belief in one article of faith implied, by way of a necessary, assumed, or consequential connection, belief in all the truths of faith. The minimally explicit content of faith embraced the existence of the "God of salvation," in which the whole content of revelation was implied. This was a consequence of the supernatural character of faith as the "beginning of eternal life." The objective revelations up to the death of the last apostle were only an explicitation of what had already been implied in the faith of the first human beings. A second kind of explicitation came into operation after the explicitation of revelation itself had been closed. This later process aimed only to formulate more explicitly what had previously already been formulated "sufficiently explicitly" by the apostles.[4] The problem was limited to a consideration of the relationship between the different creeds, and the actual development of dogma was only indirectly touched on to a limited extent. The competence to formulate more explicit confessions of faith was reserved for the teaching office of the church,[5] but theology fulfilled a fundamental, subservient function here.[6]

Basing their view on patristic texts,[7] the medieval theologians were of the opinion that the apostles had a more com-

3 See, for example, Aquinas, *ST* II–II, q. 1, art. 7 to 9.

4 Aquinas, *ST* II–II, q. 1, a. 10, ad 1.

5 Aquinas, *ST* II–II, q. 1, a. 10.

6 "Per studium sanctorum": Aquinas, *3 Sent.* d. 25, q. 2, a. 2, sol. 1, ad 5.

7 Especially Gregory the Great, *In Ezech.* lib. II, Hom. 4, § 12. (*PL* 76, 980); see Aquinas, *3 Sent.* d. 25, q. 2, a. 2, sol. 3.

plete knowledge of the content of revelation than later Christians. This doctrine has remained influential in theology until the present time, but the necessary distinction between the assertion that the apostles had a very profound awareness of the essence of Christianity and the assertion that they also had a more explicit intellectual knowledge of all Christian dogmas is often not made. If this distinction is not made, it is difficult to reconcile this doctrine with the fact of the development of dogma. The church fathers, on whom these theologians based their view, meant in the first place that revelation ended with the apostles and that attempts to add new elements to the apostolic tradition were heretical.

In the Later Scholastics

No further progress was made with this problem in the fourteenth and fifteenth centuries. It is at present widely believed in scholastic circles that theologians placed a dogmatic value on the theological conclusion in these two centuries—in other words, that theological reasoning would guarantee the evolving continuity of dogma. This interpretation is, however, unhistorical. Even in Aquinas *fides* (faith, or belief) had a wider meaning than purely dogmatic faith.[8] All the truths which, if they were denied, would threaten dogmatic faith proper were included under "faith." The medieval view was, then, that whoever believed the *prima credibilia,* the central truths or articles of faith, was consequently bound to "accept" all the truths connected with these central truths. The question as to whether these other truths were accepted with or without supernatural faith was, however, not asked at this time. It was purely a matter of a consistent moral attitude.

This problem remained unchanged for several centuries

[8] See Part II, Chapter 5: "What Is Theology?" on pp. 87–166 below.

after Aquinas. The only difference was that not only the articles of faith, but also those truths which were not articles, became "theological principles." This resulted in the distinction (not made by Aquinas) being made between what was "formally revealed" and what was "virtually revealed," which included the "conclusions of faith." Whether these conclusions were also revealed remained outside the theological problem of this time. Every true theological conclusion was called a *creditum* ("a thing believed"), not in the theological sense, but in a noetic sense. In other words, the theological conclusion did not have the scientific value of a *scitum* ("a thing known"), but was of a lower noetic order. It was not evident; it was *non scitum, sed mere creditum* ("not known, but rather believed"), that is to say, it came under *fides,* halfway between the Aristotelian *epistēmē* (knowledge) and *doxē* (opinion). Supernatural faith was left completely out of account.[9] Whether a theological conclusion was revealed or was not revealed was therefore an unknown problem in the fourteenth and fifteenth centuries.

Gradually, however, attempts were made to classify the various "Catholic truths" more accurately. It was in the sixteenth century that this tendency first resulted in the question being asked as to whether the theological conclusion had a dogmatic value. Melchior Cano still denied that these conclusions could become dogma, but maintained that the church could confirm them as truths, though not as truths of faith.[10] Vazquez was one of the first to teach that the theological conclusion had to be accepted with divine faith by those who accepted the syllogistic method of reasoning, and, after being defined by the church, by all Christians.[11]

9 See A. Lang, "Die conclusio theologica in der Problemstellung der Spätscholastik," *DTF* 22 (1944), 270–1; E. Krebs, *Theologie und Wissenschaft nach der Lehre der Hochscholastik,* Münster i. W. 1912, 8*.

10 See A. Lang, "Das Problem der theologischen Konklusionen bei M. Cano und D. Banez," *DTF* 21 (1943), 87–9.

11 G. Vazquez, *In I Partem,* q. 1, a. 2, disp. 5, cap. 3.

Molina rejected such rationalism.[12] Suarez sought a compromise, and maintained that what had been formally revealed could be either explicit or implicit, and that the implicit conclusion could, by discursive reasoning, be deduced from the explicit. Such conclusions had, in Suarez' view, dogmatic value. It was only what had been virtually revealed that could not have a dogmatic value.[13] John of St. Thomas, using different terms, put forward very much the same teaching as Suarez, but emphasised that the definable truth was not really a conclusion, but was only presented in the form of a conclusion.[14] The Salamanca school formulated the theory that became classic in the scholastic period, namely that if a theological conclusion was reached by strict deductive inference (*illatio*), it could not be the object of divine faith. If, however, the conclusion was based on two premisses of faith, it had to be accepted in faith, not as a conclusion, but in itself.

This entire scholastic controversy, however, was not really concerned with the problem of the development of dogma. The problem is rather: how can we explain the fact that we can give our assent in faith to truths which we establish by means of theological reasoning? This doctrine implies the view that the more recent definitions of faith were *logically* contained in the earlier stages of the development of the faith. When the problem of the development of dogma was really stated later on, in our own time, mainly as a defence against modernism, an appeal was made by the modern scholastics to the doctrine outlined above in an attempt to find a solution. This "logical type," which I shall consider later on, can therefore not be regarded as a traditional thesis. It is rather the scholastic thesis of the dogmatic value of certain theological conclusions seen in a new perspective

12 L. de Molina, *Comm. in I Partem,* q. 1, a. 2, disp. 1.

13 P. Suarez, *De fide, Disp.* III, sect. 11.

14 John of St. Thomas, *In I Partem,* q. 1, disp. 2, a. 4.

that was quite alien to the earlier problem. It is only with this formal reservation in mind that I can accept the appeal made by the modern scholastics to the earlier scholastic teaching.

In the Modern Period

The various solutions to this question that have been provided in the modern period, since the problem of the development of dogma has in fact been stated, can be broadly divided into three types—the historical, the logical, and the theological type.

1. *The historical type.* Some theologians believe that it can be established from historical research that there has been, throughout the centuries, a fundamental and unchangeable identity between the various phases in the church's awareness of the truths of faith. They claim, for example, that it should be possible to show, from historical documents, that Mary's assumption into heaven was, in one way or another, confessed in apostolic times.

This thesis is, however, contradicted by historical research itself, which—because of the lack of evidence—does not, in many cases, allow us to establish with any certainty, on purely historical grounds, the continuity of any datum of faith. This is of necessity implied in the historical method itself, which can only reconstruct explicit thought in all its historical situations, while a great deal of human thought takes place implicitly. Historical research can, in many cases, show that there was no contradiction between earlier and later stages of faith, and even point to some connections, but it can do no more than this.[15]

[15] See also H. D. Simonin, " 'Implicite' et 'explicite' dans le développement du dogme," *Ang.* 14 (1937), 126–45.

2. *The logical type.* As I have already observed, present-day Thomists make use of the scholastic views about the dogmatic value of theological conclusions in order to elucidate the problem of the development of dogma. They claim that it is possible, by means of discursive reasoning and logical analysis, to lay bare the implicit and virtual richness of the truths of faith that have long been recognised as explicit, and thereby to deduce the more recent explicit definitions of dogma. The dogmas that have been defined more recently are thus regarded as logically equivalent to the primitive Christian data of revelation that were not in those days precisely defined. Theological reasoning is thus the principle both of the unchangeable character of dogma and of its development. Conceptually there is an advance, since the implications of the primitive truths of faith, which were not explicitly recognised at the time, are deduced from these early truths. On the other hand, however, there is also an objective, factual identity between the theological conclusion and the premisses of faith.

Three different tendencies can be distinguished in the logical type. According to R. Schultes,[16] a logical connection can only be the norm of a true development of dogma if it is not a strictly deductive connection: that is, if there is no *illatio* (strictly deductive inference), but rather a *syllogismus explicativus* (a syllogism in which the conclusion in effect "draws out" a proposition already "contained" in the major premiss). It is therefore only when the conclusion is a clearer, but essentially equivalent, expression of the same datum of faith that a process of theological reasoning can be the criterion for a true development of dogma. M. Martin-Sola,[17] however, went much further. He maintained that the norm of a true development of dogma is that the theological con-

[16] See especially his *Introductio in historiam dogmatum,* Paris 1922.
[17] *L'évolution homogène du dogme catholique,* two parts, Fribourg 1924.

clusion is reached by reasoning according to which there is both a conceptual advance and a factual identity between the conclusion and the premisses. The theological reasoning is thus, according to Martin-Sola, the sign and the guarantee of the continuity of the various stages of faith. But it is only after a conclusion of this kind, which as such comes within the category of virtual revelation, has been defined by the church that it can be accepted as contained in formal revelation. In itself, the conclusion is directly revealed. *Quoad nos* (in respect of us), however, it is only indirectly revealed. The church's definition, however, changes the indirect *quoad nos* into a direct *quoad nos,* by virtue of the fact that the truth is in itself directly revealed even though it was only discovered by means of reasoning. Because of the factual identity of the concepts, despite their distinction, Martin-Sola calls this development homogeneous: that is to say, we do not, with the conclusion, step outside the original datum of revelation that served as the premiss of the reasoning.

The most extreme thesis was, however, advocated by M. Tuyaerts.[18] In his view, every true theological conclusion has, even before it is defined by the church, to be accepted with divine faith, because God in his revelatory activity not only knew all that revelation included virtually, but also knew in advance all that we can and must conclude from this, with the result that he himself vouches for these conclusions as such by his authority as revealer. The limits of theological reasoning are therefore also the limits of the development of dogma. In other words, it is only theological speculation which causes dogma to evolve.

The logical type was at one time greatly favoured, but there is less support for it now, mainly because of its thesis that theological reasoning provides the *only* explanation for the development of dogma. Those modern authors who ac-

18 *L'évolution du dogme,* Louvain 1919.

cept the dogmatic value of theological conclusions[19] in no way intend to define the nature of the development of dogma. Van der Putte is opposed to any attempt to identify the problem of the development of dogma with the theological conclusion.[20] In this, he is completely at variance with the logical type proper, and he explicitly affirms that those definitions of dogma that can be historically established do not come anywhere near to showing the character of a speculative development. On the other hand, he claims that "all perceptible development and growth must be able to show a logical connection with the previously given doctrine,[21] with the result that the "homogeneity of the development of dogma demands that every justified theological conclusion should be credible both objectively and subjectively."[22] To prove this, van der Putte uses the same argument as M. Tuyaerts.

Against the theory of the logical development of dogma, it is possible to put forward the following argument. On the one hand, relatively strict logical connections between the various stages of faith must be accepted, and in establishing these connections Christian reasoning plays an *instrumental* part within the greater complex of the development of tradition. On the other hand, it is not possible to regard logical connections as the principle of a development of a supernatural faith. A development of faith can only have a strictly supernatural principle, whereas consent to the conclusion of a theological argument, in whatever way it is presented, is not entirely dependent on the light of revelation, but also on human reason. Theological reasoning as such can

19 See, for example, J. C. M. van der Putte: *De dogmatische waarde van de theologische redenering,* Nijmegen 1948; and "Dogma-ontwikkeling en theologische redenering," *Jaarboek 1950 Werkgen. Kath. Theol. Nederl.,* Hilversum 1950, 163–80.

20 "Dogma-ontwikkeling," 163–4.

21 *De dogmatische waarde,* 227.

22 *De dogmatische waarde,* 252.

therefore be the principle of a *theological* development, but not the principle of a *dogmatic* development.

There is, however, an even more radical objection to the logical type. Its exponents tend to confuse the psychological and the logical aspects of reasoning. They identify the structure of the logical connections in a syllogism with discursive thought as a factual, *psychological* activity, and regard the definition of the logical structure of this as the definition of the discursive reasoning itself. Newman pointed this out when he made a distinction between "implicit" and "explicit" reasoning. From the psychological point of view, discursive thought is merely the totality of experiential knowledge—in other words, it is continuously growing experience controlled, not by subjective factors, but by the objective itself that becomes more and more completely contained in explicit knowledge. Thus discursive reasoning is a gradually increasing appropriation and taking possession of something that was already previously present in the total consciousness, but not yet fully an explicit possession. The syllogism is therefore only meaningful when it is used as an element of experiential knowledge, since the concept can only grasp reality as an element of experience. Logical thought only controls the explicit aspect of human thought. In expressly conceptual thought, which assumes experiential knowledge, it is the noetic structure of experience that is revealed and critically tested. In explicit reasoning, the original datum is seen in the light of the implications that are discovered by experiential knowledge and reflective analysis. These implications then show themselves as *consequences* or *conclusions,* but they were present from the very beginning in the consciousness, although unnoticed. Development is, then, always a transition from implicit to explicit consciousness. Seen in this light, the function of the connection within the mystery of faith is firmly established and at the same time more soundly situated in a psychological whole that includes strictly supernatural elements.

3. *The theological type.* Defined negatively, this modern tendency explicitly or implicitly denies the two preceding theories. Those who support the theological type therefore emphasise that revelation is not simply a number of truths, but one complex saving reality, of which the intellectual is merely one aspect. The doctrinal development is simply the intellectual aspect of a much larger developing whole. This modern trend of thought stresses the religious contact with the reality of revelation itself as the breeding-ground for the growth of the revelation-in-word, either by postulating a preliminary implicit stage of knowledge of the faith (J. H. Newman, the Tübingen school, M. Blondel, De la Barre, H. de Lubac, etc.), or by disregarding such a comprehensive implicit awareness, or at least by defining it less precisely (L. Charlier, N. Sanders, etc.). All these authors regard the final pronouncement of the church's teaching office as the ultimate criterion for the development of dogma (especially R. Draguet).

After the Tübingen school (especially Drey and Moehler), and also independent of it, as is now generally accepted, it was above all Newman[23] who formulated and attempted to solve the problem. It is, however, a remarkable fact that, although Newman is frequently quoted by modern authors, the recent attempts to solve the problem of the development of dogma are not supported by a sufficient knowledge of Newman's ideas. This is due to the fact that Newman did not expound his views systematically, but expressed them in various different fragments and sermons, with the result that they can only be properly grasped if his ideas are studied

[23] J. H. Newman, *Essay on the Development of Christian Doctrine,* London 1845; *Fifteen Sermons,* London 1898. See also the correspondence between Newman and Perrone, *Greg,* 16 (1935), 403–44.

at greater depth. Since the appearance of J. H. Walgrave's masterly synthesis,[24] however, we can no longer plead ignorance. Because of the importance of Newman's ideas on the development of dogma, I propose, with the help of Walgrave's study, to summarise these views here. The appearance of Christ aroused in the apostles' consciousness of faith a comprehensive intuition of the essence of Christianity. There are, in addition to explicit aspects, also implicit orientations and unexpressed elements in this initial "impression" or "idea," which constitute a knowledge that is experienced rather than consciously thought out.[25] According to Newman, the comprehensive intuition of the apostles was handed down by and in the church. Once an idea is alive within a group, it creates an atmosphere in which the Christian idea is transferred to and impressed upon the new members of the group. The "impression" or idea is the link between unsystematised revelation and systematic theology with the definitions of dogma. The whole of the development of dogma begins with a comprehensive intuition which is in many respects implicit and continues, through implicit and explicit thought, to the point where the dogma is explicitly formulated. The initial truths of faith that have not yet been consciously reflected on, are, according to the psychological and sociological laws of growth of the human mind, driven forward under the impulse of the Holy Spirit and, in the course of time, projected more and more sharply onto the explicit consciousness of the church.

According to Newman, thought has an important part to play in this development. The guiding principle of this development, which has its basis in a human nature that is by

24 J. H. Walgrave, *Kardinaal Newman's theorie over de ontwikkeling van het dogma,* Antwerp 1944; and *Newman the Theologian,* New York, Sheed and Ward, 1960.

25 "The absence, or partial absence, or incompleteness of dogmatic statements is no proof of the absence of impressions or implicit judgements in the mind of the church" (Sermon xv, Fifteen Sermons, 323).

definition evolutionary, is to be found in human reason. In this context, Newman called "reason" or "reasoning" the real principle of development, and by this he meant reasoning in the widest sense of the word. He distinguished between two aspects of reasoning in this sense. (1) *Implicit reasoning* is, according to Newman, spontaneous, non-technical, non-reflective, and unconscious experience as an aspect of the whole of the personal Christian life. This form of reasoning is a slow maturing which is subject to many different influences and whose results are personal and cannot be communicated. (2) *Explicit reasoning,* on the other hand, is either purposeful, or reflective, technical, and logical thought. In explicit reasoning, implicit reasoning is re-thought in a logical form. It is, in other words, a later logical arrangement of the growth of experiential knowledge. The syllogism, therefore, does not give us a new truth, but exposes the logical structure of the process of development along which we have already come, in our spontaneous experience, to this truth. Although it does not measure up to the wealth of implicit thought, this logical interpretation is nonetheless a homogeneous extension of the implicit preliminary stage. The fact that living experiential knowledge and reflective thought are not proportionate to each other means that a certain latitude is left for what Newman called "the illative sense." In view of the fact that logical, reflective thought is an inadequate expression of experiential knowledge, a theological syllogism—according to Newman—can give only probability. The illative sense which, in matters of faith, is a gift of God at least in its origin, is a synthetic function of the judgement by means of which we, through intimate contact with and affective experience of the reality of faith, obtain a selective sense of judgement, so that we can, despite non-apodeictic reasoning, come to the right conclusions.

But, in this world, which always threatens to level down dogma, dogma would not be safe unless God's providence supported it infallibly. This, for Newman, formed the basis of the inner need for a visible church with infallible teaching authority. According to Newman, then, neither logical thought nor history could be the ultimate criterion for the development of dogma. Nor indeed could the illative sense of the faithful and of the theologians of the church be the ultimate criterion, since this sense is strictly personal and cannot be communicated. Only the church's authority to teach was therefore, according to Newman, the ultimate principle of the continuous development of dogma.

Even before Newman, similar views were expressed by the Tübingen school (Moehler and Drey) and by Scheeben, and after Newman by the Jesuit De la Barre.[26] M. Blondel also put forward a similar view,[27] but, in making a distinction between the comprehensive implicit Christian experience (the "implicite vécu"), and what is explicitly known (the resulting "explicite connu"), appealed to the Christian life itself as the source of a deeper knowledge of the truth. According to Blondel, dogma in practice—Christian life and activity—gives us an "intuition" of the whole reality of faith. This intuition in turn enables us, in new situations, to "sense," by spontaneous, sympathetic reaction, where the truth of faith is situated and where it is not. H. de Lubac also maintained that, when revelation was closed, everything had already been given to, and was present in, the Christian consciousness.[28]

Charlier[29] insisted on the fact that the church herself is the reality of revelation and that the development in knowledge of the faith is only the complement of the development of the church herself. The laws of growth of this development are,

26 A. De la Barre, *La vie du dogme catholique,* Paris 1898.

27 M. Blondel, "Histoire et dogme," *Quinz.* 56 (1904), 145–67, 349–73, and 433–58.

28 H. de Lubac, "Le problème du développement du dogme," RSR 35 (1938), 130–60 (esp. 157f.).

29 L. Charlier, *Essai sur le problème théologique,* Thuilles 1938.

in Charlier's view, concealed in God, but, since factors of human development must be taken into account in connection with these supernatural laws, we can, by means of these human factors, gain some insight into the laws governing the definition of dogma. Only the church's teaching office can, however, establish the identity between an earlier stage of faith and its present position. Sanders[30] also made a similar distinction, but stressed the revelation-in-word as the real revelation of the reality of salvation. By virtue of the life itself of the church as the reality of salvation, there is, according to Sanders, a transition from implicit to explicit in our knowledge of the revelation-in-word.

According to Draguet,[31] a development can be recognised as authentic only by the fact that the church's teaching office declares it infallibly to be a dogma. On the other hand, in common with the logical and the historical type of theory, he concedes that this theological principle of the church's magisterium only has a supplementary function, especially in those cases where the logical and the historical arguments do not produce a satisfactory result. He explains the fact that revelation has been closed by saying that at least "all the principles of Christianity" were established from the very beginning.[32] He does not, however, admit to an implicit, but real, awareness concerning all the data of revelation at the close of revelation.

It will be clear from this historical outline that both the unchangeable nature and the development of dogma must take place within the Christian consciousness of faith. Revelation *quoad se*—that is, revelation which is unrelated to the church's awareness of faith—is not really revelation. All the

[30] N. Sanders, "Openbaring, traditie, dogma-ontwikkeling," *SC* 15 (1939), 1–12 and 111–29.

[31] R. Draguet, "L'évolution des dogmes," in M. Brillant and M. Nédoncelle, *Apologétique,* Paris 1948², 1097–1122.

[32] "L'évolution des dogmes," 1108.

data of revelation must be given *quoad nos*—given, that is, with respect to us—at the close of revelation.

If we consider the most valuable elements in all these attempts to solve the problem together with the medieval, and especially the Thomist, doctrine of the "light of faith," we should at least be able to obtain a clear perspective within which a more fully worked out solution should be situated. The elaboration of this solution will of necessity be personal in character, since there is no traditional view here. The problem of the development of tradition, in all its dimensions, is essentially a modern one.

PERSPECTIVES FOR A SYNTHESIS

On the assumption that there is, because of the transcendence of grace, a real discontinuity between the natural and the supernatural, we may affirm that the supernatural is of significance for the natural, and indeed that this significance has its point of contact in the natural. At the same time, since there is only one divine providence, the natural consequently gains its ultimate significance from the supernatural. The entire structure of the natural development of man, both individually and socially, is therefore bound to *serve* the development of grace and consequently also that of dogma. The whole of man's active equipment—active, that is, in the mental and spiritual growth of man—will have its function in the human life that has entered the reality of revelation. At the same time, however, transcendental dimensions must also be taken into account. The natural factors, which also influence the development of dogma, therefore merge again and again into mystery, and are thereby adjusted or definitively defined. The spontaneous Christian experience of life, both individual and collective, "implicit" Christian thought, and explicit analysis and synthesis thus play an indispensable part in the development of dogma, a function which can, however, only determine a development of *faith* when it is subject to the guidance of strictly supernatural principles.

The Function of the Light of Faith

It is important to stress that revelation is not only revelation-in-word, but also revelation-in-reality, a *mystērion.* It is, in other words, a historical event in which God himself accomplishes a deeper saving mystery—that is, the appearance of Christ "in the flesh," in a visible earthly form. The Old Testament prepared for this event, and the visible, sacramental church brings it to us. Christ himself, both in his actions and in his words, is revelation. "Etiam factum Verbi verbum nobis est"[33]—the acts of the word speak to us and, on the other hand, the revelation-in-word is only one aspect of the total appearance of the mystery of Christ. It is therefore preferable to speak of the development of tradition rather than of the development of dogma. What has been handed down to us, for example, in connection with the eucharist is not simply the *doctrine* of the eucharist, but also—and above all—the reality itself of the celebration of the eucharist, the meaning and content of which are expressed in conceptual terms in the doctrine. The tradition itself is both kerygmatic and sacramental.

The reality and the doctrine of revelation, which continues to live in the church, cannot be recognised or assimilated as a *mystērion*—that is, as a visible appearance of divine realities of immediate concern to us—unless God himself inwardly prompts us to accept them in faith. *Vidit et credidit,* "he saw *and* believed": in other words, we do not come into contact with the act of revelation and its supernatural saving content in the revelation-in-word and revelation-in-reality unless God addresses us inwardly. Aquinas

[33] Augustine, *Tract. in Joa.* XXIV, 2 (*PL* 35, 1593).

called this inward divine impulse towards faith the *lumen fidei,* the "light of faith" or "inner illumination," which is an "inner *instinctus* of God [i.e., an instinct implanted by God] which prompts us to believe."[34] It is through this inward attraction proceeding from God that the subject who encounters the church in the course of his life is inwardly adapted to the supernatural dimension of the mystery of revelation. In other words, this light of faith enables me to grasp more in the mystery of revelation than is said about it in conceptual terms and than history tells us about it. The material objects of faith enter our conscious minds by way of the church's proclamation of the word (*fides ex auditu,* or "faith by learning and listening") and the historical saving fact of the living church herself. We do not, however, come into contact with the formal object of faith in this way, but in a purely supernatural way, "through the inner impulse of the grace of faith" or light of faith. The affective contact in which we know God is in us the result of the *locutio interna* (inner address") or of the light of faith. Its meaning and content, however, come from objective, public revelation.

This meaning is not explicitly known from the very outset, but is preceded by an implicit stage, which may be called —in Newman's terminology—the sphere of implicit "impressions." Both the explicit stage and the preliminary, implicit stage thus provide the content, the *determinatio,* of the light of faith.[35] It is by the light of faith that we recognise this content as revealed by God. This inner illumination is not a new revelation, but an inward impulse through the grace of faith whereby we are able, in a supernatural way, to

[34] *ST* II–II, q. 2, a. 9, ad 3. This idea is expressed even more clearly in *EJ* c. 6, lect. 5; *Quodl.* II, q. 4, a. 1, ad 1; *3 Sent.* d. 23, q. 2, a. 1, ad 4.

[35] Aquinas, *4 Sent.* d. 4, q. 2, a. 2, sol. 3, ad 1: "Fides principaliter est ex infusione . . ., sed quantum ad determinationem suam est ex auditu" ("Faith is in principle by infusion . . ., but in respect of its content it is by hearing and listening").

judge whether we are or are not confronted with a datum of faith—*credibile et credendum* (something at once capable of and requiring belief).[36] The light of faith is the confused inner sense, "lost" as it were in the consciousness, that tells us what we should believe and what we should not. The explicitation of all that the grace of faith prompts us to believe was made by God himself, through the whole constitutive phase of revelation up to the point where revelation was closed. The explicitation within the sphere of the *determinatio fidei*—that is, the transition from the preliminary, implicit stage to the stage of explicit knowledge—is, however, the real sphere of the development of dogma.

This basic, inner structure of the act and the life of faith is therefore of its very nature also the principle of the continuity of the development of faith, since the inward impulse of the light of faith or grace of faith is only effective in the context of the real meaning and content of revelation. Faith is an act which is essentially and intrinsically directed towards the reality of salvation. Essentially the act and the content of faith correspond to each other. The content of faith is not infused into our minds by way of "illumination." There is, therefore, no "anticipation" of the act of faith with regard to its content. The light of faith is infallible in its operation.[37]

Since the data of faith are present in the living community of the church, these data will naturally be received by a mind that is subject to psychological and sociological growth. The light of faith will therefore, of its own nature, not be the principle of *development,* but the principle of the continuity and the unchangeable character of this development of faith —the principle which, in a supernatural way, establishes the connection between the different phases of a datum of revelation. The light of faith thus furnishes us with a formal super-

[36] Aquinas, *ST* II–II, q. 2, a. 3, ad 2; q. 1, a. 4, ad 3; and q. 1, a. 5, ad 1.
[37] Aquinas, *ST* II–II, q. 1, a. 3.

natural principle that, without recourse to a new revelation, guarantees that a developed truth has been revealed by God. Since, according to Thomas, the light of faith is an "inner instinct [or impulse] of the Holy Spirit," and thus an effect of the Holy Spirit, we are bound to conclude that it is the guidance of the Holy Spirit in and through the light of faith which is the principle of the continuity of the development of dogma. This view coincides with the general feeling of the fathers of the Council of Trent, who had intended, in a later session, to define the part played by the church and the Holy Spirit in the sphere of dogma. Circumstances, however, prevented the council from issuing a decree. But the *Acta* of the council give us a good idea of the general feeling among the council fathers:

> Since the Son of God was not to remain always physically among us, he sent the Holy Spirit, who is to reveal the mysteries of God in the hearts of the faithful and *daily,* until the end of time, instruct the church in all truth and settle all doubts that may arise in the minds of men.[38]

This opinion has a sound and firm foundation in the teaching of the light of faith.

The Light of Faith in the Community of Faith and the Church's Teaching Office as the Highest Judge

This does not, however, entirely solve the problem, since, although the reaction of the light of faith is infallibly accurate, it is in fact possible that an individual may err and, because the impulse of the grace of faith is essentially confused in its operation, may erroneously affirm something as a revealed truth.

[38] *Conc. Trid.,* Goerres edn., v, 11.

It is indeed possible for a believer to hold something, as a result of human considerations, erroneously as a truth of faith, but it is impossible for this to happen by virtue of the light of faith.[39]

We can, therefore, never know with absolute certainty whether an individual reaction is the result of the light of faith or not. The intermixture of factors that are influenced by human judgement and the pure impulse of the light of faith means that factual certainty is quite impossible, except insofar as questions about the "necessity of salvation" are concerned.[40] This does not mean that the light of faith ceases to function properly when confronted with the less central truths of faith. What it does mean, however, is that this modest function which operates in a non-reflective way, is, so to speak, lost in the concrete human psychology, within which many different forms of resistance, prejudices, social influences, and so on can give a new interpretation to and even neutralise the pure effects of the light of faith.

Human psychology and the process of human development, which are subject to so many different contacts with the reality of revelation and with its incarnation in this world, provide the affective judgement of the light of faith with the material to which this reacts *per modum inclinationis (gratiae fidei)* ("according to the measure of its inclination to the grace of faith"). But it is always possible for this attraction of faith to be overwhelmed or to be diverted from its course by dynamic human tendencies or possible philosophical prejudices and, as it were, thrust into depths of the human mind. This is why theologians, for instance, may show initial resistance to popular devotion when this anticipates their enquiries and boldly accepts a datum of faith. The light of faith does, in other words, continue to fulfil its function faithfully, but it is possible for centuries to pass

[39] Aquinas, *ST* II–II, q. 1, a. 3, ad 3.
[40] Aquinas, *3 Sent.* d. 25, q. 2, a. 1, sol. 4, ad 3.

before its voice is heard in purity. The light of faith is confused with all the various implicit and explicit factors of the human mind, the influence that these have on each other, and their affective emphases and reticences. This is the explanation of the gradual nature, the ups and downs and the tentative and hesitant progress, of the development of dogma. Nonetheless, it is along this capricious path that the inward *illustratio fidei* ("illumination of faith") makes its affective judgement heard more and more safely and clearly.

It will therefore be evident that the *individual* light of faith cannot function as the principle of the continuity of the development of the church's dogma. In holding this, we should be guilty of Pallavicini's error—his view of the *discerniculum experimentale* was correctly condemned by the church.

This analysis refers us to the faith of the church as a believing community. Although it is in the first place deeply influenced by strongly religious personalities, the growth of the church's faith is still a communal work. The development, according to which dogma grows from an implicit preliminary phase to the explicit stage is a very slow process of maturation in the bosom of the church, within which all kinds of influences throw light on each other—within which opinions, conjectures and theological conclusions are offered to the community and exposed to the reaction of its other members. This is a constant process of friction and purification, in which all members of the church community play a part. Their activity is apparent at the level, for example, of popular devotion, of sacramental practice, and of various social and liturgical movements within the church. Certain members of the church—for example, the eastern Christians—tend automatically to emphasise different aspects from those stressed by others—for example, western Christians. Open to everything that is happening here and elsewhere in the church, theologians naturally speculate about recently introduced "living" material and study the ancient theological sources in the light of the new problems that are raised. The light of faith is "working" in all this activity. At first, its operation is tentative and "unconscious." Gradually, however, in and through the implicit and explicit process of development, the light of faith makes itself more and more strongly felt, until all the various voices eventually converge and the firm conviction grows in the bosom of the church that a definite statement is indeed the explicitation of something that has for a long time been *experienced* in the church and that has been governed by the norm of, or has derived its meaning from, the word of God's revelation in Christ.

The *inclinatio fidei* ("inclination to faith") as the *sigillatio primae Veritatis in mente humana* ("the imaging of divine Truth in the human mind"), can come into operation more purely because the counteracting factors in the slow process of fermentation are gradually eliminated, while at the same time the most suitable theological argument is found after a long process of theological reflection. The new pronouncement is then like a fortunate word suggested to us for the purpose of formulating one of our most intimate insights and convictions, but a word that so far we were simply unable to find! We had it in our possession, but were unable to express it. The collective reaction of faith, struggling towards theological understanding, thus prepares the way for the church's definition of dogma. "The faith of the universal church . . . cannot err."[41] The collective reaction of the whole of the church as a believing community, on a basis of the never-ceasing dynamic force of the light of faith, which is, in a confused manner, operative among all the members of the church, is infallible not only as a matter of principle but also in fact. Both essentially and intrinsically, this factor of continuity needs, however, to be supplemented by the

41 Aquinas, *ST* II–II, q. 2, a. 6, ad 3.

church's teaching authority. This is not only because the constant support and the continuous guidance and correction of the teaching office of the church unceasingly influences the collective reaction of the faithful in an authoritative manner, both explicitly through the magisterium and implicitly through the governing office and the pastoral office of the church. It is also because the church's teaching office, because of its charism of infallibility, is the only authority which can authentically declare whether a collective reaction on the part of the whole community of faith took place in fact by virtue of the light of faith (*ex habitu fidei*) and not just on a basis of human factors. The teaching authority of the church is thus, as the "teacher of the object of faith," not only the "immediate norm of faith," but also the immediate and *ultimate norm* guaranteeing continuity in the development of dogma.

History also bears witness to the fact that the church's teaching office solemnly declares a truth of faith to be a dogma only when the collective reaction of the believing community points clearly and explicitly in that direction and the community of theologians puts forward convincing arguments. By this, I certainly do not mean that the sole function of the magisterium is to confirm at a later stage the reactions of the Christian community.[42] The teaching office of the church has a decisive function not only in the actual definition of dogma, but also in the whole development of dogma. The subject of the church's active tradition is certainly the whole of the church's believing community, but this according to its inner, hierarchical structure. The ordinary members of the church form part of this active tradition, but they do so as ordinary believers—the hierarchy does so as a hierarchy, in and through its teaching, governing, and pastoral office. These last two functions of the hierarchy are, im-

[42] For this point, see my article "Overlevering," *Theologisch Woordenboek*, pt. 3, Roermond and Maaseik 1958, esp. cols. 3691–2.

plicitly or in experience, also an exercise of the teaching office itself. In addition, the church's teaching authority is the ultimately authentic and infallible instrument of the interpretation of tradition, of which the church's hierarchy as such and the ordinary believers, as the non-qualified members of the church, are the active subject. The hierarchy is therefore in an exceptional position not only because it is a special, qualified, and active instrument of tradition—as is the believing community in a non-hierarchical manner—but also because the teaching authority of the church is the exclusive *regula* of the tradition of faith. It is important therefore not to confuse the whole subject of active tradition in all its diversity of structure with the subject of the instrument that is the norm and the judge of this tradition.

We may therefore conclude that the converging activity of the light of faith in the community of faith of the church together with the church's infallible teaching office is the single structural principle of the unchangeable character of the faith throughout all its different phases of development. The laws and factors which cause any human ideology to mature, including implicit thought and reflective reasoning, thus play an active part in the development of dogma. As such, however, they cannot make a datum of faith develop in its properly *supernatural* element. For this reason, they only play an instrumental part with regard to the activity of the light of faith and the teaching authority of the church. The light of faith is, however, not revelation and has therefore no creative function which might, of its own accord, put forward new truths. It is then through external stimuli, the rhythm of universally human progress and self-consciousness, theological investigation, and so on that the critical activity of the light of faith and of the church's teaching office is provided with material. This is why human evolution is so closely interlaced with the development of dogma, why certain dogmas were defined at such a late stage, why most are formulated in the language of the period, and so on.

It is also important to stress that the power of assimilation of the light of faith does not make itself felt only *after* an implicit datum of faith has been made more fully explicit, but that its discreet activity is discernible throughout the whole process of development and maturity, and that the Holy Spirit himself, in and through this active grace of faith, both governs the unchangeable nature of dogma and guides its development according to the Father's saving intentions. Moreover, the light of faith possesses, in and through sanctifying grace, an inwardly finer, selective ability to react, since the gifts of the Holy Spirit inwardly complete what was already present as a germ in the act of faith as such. In this way, the critical faculty of the light of faith is made more pure, accurate, and penetrating. Finally, the only ultimate criterion of a true development in dogma is the teaching authority of the church. The light of faith, with its vague sense, almost lost in the human consciousness, of being drawn by God to faith, is the fundamental principle of orientation in this development.

II

THEOLOGICAL REFLECTION ON REVELATION

5 What Is Theology?

Prefatory Remark Concerning Terminology: Development of the Meaning of the Word "Theology"

The term *theology* has, in the course of time, been applied with various meanings to different realities.

1. Initially, the word was used with reference to the mythical stories of the gods.[1] Theologians in this sense were the ancient poets, such as Homer and Hesiod, who wrote theogonies and told the myths of the Olympian gods. Theology, again in this sense, was contrasted with meteorology, which dealt in a more scientific manner with the divine heavenly bodies. Aristotle also on several occasions spoke of theology as poetic myths about the gods.[2] The view gradually became accepted, however, that these myths about the gods were simply a mythological form concealing true reference to God. Plato consciously dissociated the essential content of these myths from their mythological content. Aristotle also used the word *theology* with a new meaning, or at least changed its field of application. Making a threefold division of science or scientific knowledge (*epistēmē*) into physical, mathematical, and theological,[3] he raised theology to the level of a philosophical science, and indeed made it the "first" or supreme form of philosophical thought.[4] This

1 Plato, *Republic* 379A.

2 Aristotle, *Meteorologica* 2, 1, 2; *Metaphysics* 2, 4, 12; etc.

3 *Metaphysics* 10, 7, 9.

4 *Metaphysics* 10, 7, 7.

"first philosophy" was concerned with the highest causes of the visible divine astral world. Both meanings of the word —the older theology of the theogonies and "myths of the gods," and the newer "philosophical" theology—continued to exist side by side, and the first remained the generally accepted meaning in the language of the people.

The first sense lay behind Aristotle's use of the cognate verb *theologein,* too: it meant "to speculate about the gods" in the "myths of the gods" sense.[5] Much later, in the Hellenistic period, the word meant—in the context of emperor worship—"to venerate as a god."

Though the word *theologia* did not acquire a wholly new meaning in the pseudo-Aristotelian work *De Mundo,*[6] it did nevertheless acquire a new application in view of the swing towards cosmic religion. The deities were no longer the gods of Olympus, but the cosmos itself—the *meteora,* or astral bodies. Meteorology had now become the sphere of theology.

2. These ideas persisted up to the patristic period. Augustine was to adopt Varro's classic definition:

> There are three kinds of theology, that is, of the discipline which is concerned with the gods: one of these is the mythic, the second is the physical, and the third is the civil.[7]

In this definition, the "civil" kind of theology (*theologiae genus civile*) means the theology of public worship—in other words, the worship of the emperor as god. The term *theology* was Christianised only very late because of the initial fear and reluctance on the part of Christians to use pagan terminology. The Greek fathers used the word *theologians* only in

[5] *Metaphysics* I, 3, 6.

[6] That is, so long as we may accept the view of A. J. Festugière, *La révélation d'Hermès Trismégiste, II: le Dieu Cosmique,* Paris 1949, 598–605 (Appendix III).

[7] "Tria genera theologiae sunt, i.e. rationis quae de diis explicatur: eorumque unum mythicum, alterum physicum, tertium civile" (*De Civitate Dei* VI, 5). See also Aquinas, *ST* II–II, q. 94, a. 1; *ER* c. 1, lect. 7, fin.

the sense of the ancient poets who wrote about the gods. The concept was, however, gradually accepted into Christianity. Although Origen still continued to use the word *theologians* in the pagan sense, he did refer to theology as a "teaching about God and Christ."[8] Even the word *theologein*—to worship the emperor as god—was Christianised, and came to mean "to confess Christ truly as God." It was perhaps Eusebius who played the greatest part in the Christianisation of the term *theology,* in a sense contrary to the pagan meaning. This is clear from the phrase "the theology according to Christ,"[9] "sermo de Christo Deo." The frequent use of *theology* in the *corpus dionysiacum* finally consecrated the word, although it was used there with many different shades of meaning, in accordance with the way in which we know God—*theologia mystica, theologia negativa,* and so on. It was only from the fourth century onwards that the Greek fathers used the word theology in the sense of the *sermo de Deo vero* ("treatise on the true God"). Under the influence of the Byzantine theologians of the fourth century, the concept came to have a special meaning—*theologia* was contrasted with *oikonomia,* or the theology of the mystery of Christ. Theology meant the *Sacra Doctrina de Trinitate,* that is, everything concerned with the doctrine of God as opposed to the Christian plan of salvation.[10] This twofold division into *theologia simplex* and *oikonomia* is still preserved in present-day Graeco-Russian theology.[11] At a later stage, especially in the writings of Evagrius and Maximus

8 *Contra Celsum* VI, 18.

9 *De hist. eccl.* I, 1, 7.

10 See J. Haussleiter, *Trinitarischer Glaube und Christusbekenntnis in der alten Kirche,* Gütersloh 1920, esp. 358–60; see also G. L. Prestige, *God in Patristic Thought,* London 1963³. In the case of certain authors, for example, Tatian and Tertullian, *oikonomia* has the meaning of the intercommunication of the divine persons—the "monarchy" or unity of the three divine persons is preserved by the *oikonomia.*

11 See M. Jugie, *Theologia dogmatica christianorum Orientalium ab Ecclesia catholica dissidentium,* Paris 1926–35, II, esp. 26–7.

Confessor, theology acquired the meaning of the sublime "mystical knowledge of God."

3. The word *theology* was not adopted quite so readily by the western church. Although Augustine occasionally, and by way of exception, referred to the *vera theologia,* as opposed to pagan theology, the word was by no means generally accepted. Abelard was the first in the west consistently to use the word *theology* in the Christian theological sense.[12] In the tradition of Abelard, as in the Byzantine theology, the word *theology* tended to mean a treatise about God himself, rather than the theology of the mystery of Christ, which was called the *beneficia* (lit. "benefits"). The term *theology* was not in fact fully adopted by the medieval theologians subsequent to Abelard. To express the *sacra doctrina,* the Augustinian term *doctrina Christiana* was preferred from the twelfth century until after Aquinas.

Aquinas himself seldom used the term *theology,* and whenever he did so he used it in a very different sense from the sense in which we should use it now. The Aristotelian influence is, of course, especially marked in Aquinas' thought. For him, metaphysics was *scientia divina sive theologica* ("the divine or theological science").[13] He sometimes contrasted *theologia philosophica* ("philosophical theology") with *theologia Sacrae Scripturae* ("the theology of holy scripture").[14] He was not here distinguishing between what we should now call "theodicy" and "theology," but rather between the teaching of the pagan philosophers about God and the Christian

[12] See J. de Ghellinck, *Le Mouvement théologique du XIIe siècle,* Bruges 1948², 83 and 92; J. Rivière, "Theologia," *RSR(US)* 16 (1936), 47-57.

[13] *AM,* Proem.; *BT,* q. 5, a. 1.

[14] *BT,* q. 5, a. 1, 4: "theologia quae in S. Scriptura traditur" ("the theology handed down in holy scripture") (according to Decker's edition, p. 195), as opposed to "theologia quam philosophi prosequuntur" ("the theology pursued by the philosophers"). See also *ST* 1, q. 1, a. 1, ad 2: "theologia quae pertinet ad S. Doctrinam" ("the theology which pertains to sacred doctrine"), as opposed to "theologia quae pars philosophiae ponitur" ("the theology which is posited as a division of philosophy").

teaching about God—which, in the case of Aquinas, also includes what we should now call "theodicy."[15] A theological study was therefore, for Aquinas, a study concerned with the "first cause" of things, whereas a philosophical study was concerned with things in their own value.[16] Thus, the study of the human soul, because of its direct relationship with God, was called by Aquinas a theological study, whereas the study of the human body was not.[17] Nonetheless, Aquinas gave the Aristotelian term *theology* his own distinctive shade of meaning,[18] since, on a basis of man's experiential insight into divine things, his intelligence is defective,[19] and revelation in fact comes to his assistance to a great extent in the case of natural truths about God.

Aquinas seldom used the word *theology* as an exact synonym for *sacra doctrina*,[20] and whenever he did so he generally used it in the etymological sense.[21] It will therefore be clear that the term theology did not have the full meaning in the scholastic period that it has today.

4. It was in the period between Aquinas and Duns Scotus that the word theology came to be used as the technical term for what had previously been known as *Sacra Doctrina*. At the same time, it lost the shade of meaning that it had had in the writings of Abelard. It was especially speculative theology that was influential in bringing about this change from *Sacra Doctrina* to "theology." The wide meaning which theology had had as *Sacra Doctrina* was thrust into the background by the discursive procedure or *modus argumentativus* which had been adopted by theology, with the result that

15 See *SCG* I, 4.

16 *ST* I–II, q. 71, a. 6, ad 5.

17 *ST* I, q. 75, Prol.; see also 2 *Sent.* Prol.

18 See, for example, *ST* I, q. 1, a. 1.

19 *SCG* I, 2.

20 See, for example, *1 Sent.* Prol., 4, obi. 2 in contr.; *ER* Prol.; *BT*, q. 2, a. 3, ad 7.

21 Theology is the "sermo de Deo" ("discussion or treatise on God"): *ST* I, q. 1, a. 7, sed c.

theology became (in a certain restricted sense: see below) a *scientia conclusionum* ("science of conclusions"). The older name for the theologian, *Magister in Sacra Pagina* (lit. "Master in Holy Writ"), was also changed at this time to *Magister in Sacra Theologia* (lit. "Master in Sacred Theology"). There is no question, then, but that the classic term *theology* was placed under the sign of speculative theology from the very moment of its birth.

5. This, of course, had unfortunate effects later. The single *Sacra Doctrina* of the Middle Ages was divided in the modern period into all kinds of virtually independent disciplines. The first form of theology to develop outside the scholastic theology was the *ascetica et mystica,* and the term *mystical theology* was originally used in contrast to the term *scholastic theology.* Then, towards the end of the sixteenth century, moral theology, which had become increasingly concerned with casuistry, was separated from the one *Sacra Doctrina.* The "back to the sources" movement of renaissance humanism then gave rise to the distinction between "positive" and "scholastic" theology. The seventeenth century also saw the emergence of "apologetic" theology.[22] The part which remained after all these divisions, was christened "dogmatic" theology. The word *dogmaticus* had been used, in contrast to *ethicus,* even before the seventeenth century, but it was at this period that the terms *dogmaticus* and *scholasticus* were first used in contrast to each other.[23] In this context, "dogmatic" theology, as a division of positive theology and in contrast to scholastic theology, meant the theological discipline that aimed to define precisely the limits of revealed religion as distinct from all the questions discussed by the scholastics. This accounts for the expression: "[intellectus] in dogmaticis

22 See H. Busson, *La pensée religieuse française de Charon à Pascal,* Paris 1933, esp. chapters XI and XIII.

23 See O. Ritschl, "Das Wort dogmaticus in der Geschichte des Sprachgebrauches bis zum Aufkommen des Ausdruckes Theologia dogmatica," *Festgabe J. Kaftan,* Tübingen 1920.

captivus, in scholasticis liber" ("the intellect is captive in dogmatic theology, but in scholastic theology it is free"). It is also only in the light of this distinction that it is possible to understand the title of certain manuals of the period: *Theologia Dogmatico-Scholastica*. It was only later that dogmatic theology came to mean what it means today.

It is not possible even to give an outline of the origin and development of theology in the limited space available in a dictionary. Historical notes will be given at appropriate points in the following synthesis, in which an attempt is made to show what theology really is.

In order to establish the concrete structure of theology and its distinctive methodical procedures, it is not possible to proceed from the natural data of what scientific work is, whether these are the data of the Aristotelian scientific concept or those of the modern, positive, phenomenological, and "humane" sciences. The structure of revelation itself and of the act of faith associated with it must suggest the type of reflection to which faith in Christ can lead. Only then shall we be able, at the same time by appealing to the human sciences, to throw light on the scientific structure of theology in all its many activities. This at the same time vindicates my division of this outline of the nature of theology into the following sections.

FAITH IN THE GOD OF REVELATION AS THE POINT OF DEPARTURE FOR AND THE CONSTANTLY FERTILE BREEDING-GROUND OF THEOLOGY

Faith as the Basis of Theology as a Science

Religion is essentially a personal communion between God and men. This personal contact with the living God cannot be established by human effort. It can only be established by the initiative of grace with the divine revelation that is implied in it. *Salvation* is the very act of the encounter between God and man, in which the first fundamental contact is established by faith. This divine revelation makes history. It would take us too far from our subject to discuss this question fully, and I must be content to summarise briefly the theme of saving history (or history of salvation). The history that is made by men becomes itself the material in and through which God makes saving history and through which he accomplishes his revelation. God's saving activity is revealed by becoming history, and it becomes history by being revealed. The prophetic word throws light on this saving activity and makes it present for us *as* an act of God. All this was ultimately expressed scripturally—in writing—in the bible, under the divine guarantee that it was a faithful reproduction of the consciousness of salvation that God himself wished to realise in the whole of mankind in and through his chosen people, Israel and the church.

There are distinct phases in this historical self-disclosure of the God of redemption. The first was the *constitutive phase of revelation,* the *revelatio publica constitutiva,* the stage in which Christ appeared in human form as the public revelation of God, both in his prehistory of the Old Testament and in his personal completion in human action—the *mysteria carnis Christi* ("the mysteries of Christ's humanity"). In this phase, which closed with the end of the apostolic period, God revealed himself definitively and the eschatological age dawned: we are redeemed. This constitutive phase was followed by the saving history of the church, living from the constituted phase of salvation. Expressed in terms of revelation, it is usual to refer to this as the *explicative and continuing phase of revelation.* It is in this period that what has taken place for all of us in Christ as our prototype and representative is accomplished within humanity in and through the church, on the basis of the completed mystery of Christ.

Faith is conditioned by this revelation, in which we are addressed by God. Faith is therefore a way of knowing. This knowing has a distinctive character in that it is a knowledge which comes about by our being addressed, by our being confidentially informed, through God's mercy. God speaks to us inwardly through the inward grace of faith, the *locutio interior,* and at the same time we are addressed from outside by the God of revelation—this last is the aspect of *fides ex auditu.* This "external address" is the Old Testament history of salvation, accompanied by the prophetic word, and its climax: the human appearance of Christ himself in word and deed as addressed to the apostles. Finally, it is the life of the church, in her activity and in her kerygmatic word, by which man living now is addressed and in which the glorified Christ really lives. Within the church, we believe in the mystery of Christ as the revelation of God—we believe in the Christian historical plan of salvation in which the trinitarian mystery of salvation which transcends history is realised for and in us. The entire theological method is determined by this structure of revelation. First of all, however, we must ascertain how faith in this revelation gives rise to a reflection which we have called theology.

Faith as an Inner Demand for Theology

The act of faith is incipient theology both in its subjective aspect, that is, as seen from the point of view of the believing subject, and in its objective aspect, that is, the content of faith. Both of these aspects implicate each other, but I propose to deal with them separately for the sake of clarity.

1. The subjective aspect. Because of its inward nature as a consent in faith to a mystery, this act of faith contains an aspect of rest and an aspect of unrest, with the result that both Augustine and Aquinas defined the act of faith as a synthesis of firm consent and intellectual speculation: "credere est cum assentione cogitare" (to believe is to reflect with consent).[24] Consent in faith permits of no vacillation. It is not irresolute and unstable, but of its very nature a firm consent on the part of the human mind to the content of revelation, a consent which leaves no room for doubt. It is, however, not given either on a basis of intellectual understanding or on a basis of the inward evidence of what is offered to us for our consent—the reality of salvation. On the contrary, the human mind is conditioned by a divine impulse by grace of the will, which thereby "desires" the reality of salvation that presents itself.[25] The intellect assents to the truth and consents to it, as it is included in the impulse by grace of the will. Believing is an existential attitude of the whole man confronted by the ultimate meaning of his life. Despite the inward non-evidence of the reality of salvation that presents itself, intellectual consent in faith can be understood if viewed in this light. But, precisely for this reason, the human intellect, which is essentially attuned to the inward evidence of reality, is in principle not satisfied. The intellect does not accept the mystery for intrinsic reasons. At the level of intelligibility, absolutely certain consent to the object of faith is therefore essentially associated with a natural quest on the part of the mind, because of the mind's natural objectivity. Consent and a desire for understanding are thus both essential aspects of man's act of faith.[26]

[24] Aquinas, *ST* II–II, q. 2, a. 1; *Verit.* q. 14, a. 1.

[25] Aquinas, *ST* II–II, q. 2, a. 9, analyses the process thus: "Ipsum autem credere est actus intellectus assentientis veritati divinae ex imperio voluntatis a Deo motae per gratiam" ("But believing itself is an act of the intellect assenting to divine truth at the behest of a will moved by God through grace").

[26] See Aquinas, *ST* I–II, q. 67, a. 3: "Imperfectio cognitionis est de ratione fidei, ponitur enim in eius definitione" ("Imperfection of knowledge is of the essence of faith, for it is posited in the definition of faith").

This need causes an extreme tension in the human mind, because the reality of salvation presents itself as the sublime meaning of human life. However slightly and in whatever way this need to reflect may show itself in people, according to their different characters, there is always an incipient theological reflection present in the act of faith which is at the same time a *fides quaerens intellectum* ("faith seeking understanding") in germ. Faith is, in germ, virtually theology. The human openness to the evidence of reality is therefore, from the point of view of the believing subject, the basis of the possibility of theology.

It is important, however, to note in this connection that this intellectual orientation of the human mind is not a kind of intellectual curiosity. The meaning of the reality that presents itself is at the same time revealed as the *value* for human life, in other words, as that which makes life worth living.[27] That is to say, it is in the total reaction of the human person to the mystery that the origin of theological reflection is to be found—the element of knowledge in this is only the formal aspect, but as an element of an integrally human activity and reaction.

2. *The objective aspect—the content of faith.* If speculation were not possible from the objective aspect of the act of faith, then theology would itself be impossible, since it is the objective possibility which provides the basis for the subjective.

Although the content of faith may be a mystery to the

27 See Aquinas, *ST* II–II, q. 4, a. 2, ad 3: "Veritas prima, quae est fidei obiectum, est finis omnium desideriorum et actionum nostrarum" ("That supreme truth, which is the object of faith, is the end of all our desires and actions"); hence, *ST* II–II, q. 2, a. 10: "Cum enim homo habet promptam voluntatem ad credendum, *diligit* veritatem creditam et super ea excogitat et amplectitur si quas rationes ad hoc invenire potest" ("For when a man has a will that is quick to believe, he *values* the truth believed, and on the basis of it he looks for and welcomes any arguments he can find to support the belief").

human mind, this does not imply a belief in something that is devoid of meaning. The revealed mystery of salvation presents itself as something *meaningful.* If this were not so, then every act of faith made in respect of this mystery would be impossible.[28] Mystery and inner contradiction are two totally different things. Wherever reality is present and wherever it announces itself to the human consciousness, even though it may be transcendent and therefore a mystery, then it can necessarily be assimilated by human thought. The mystery of salvation, however transcendent it may be, must also to some extent be clear to the human mind. A mystery is not an entirely unknown quantity. Enough of it is revealed in a veiled manner for us to be able to live from it. What is more, the content of faith is an answer to a problem of human life. Man himself is unable to unveil the ultimate meaning of his life and is therefore confronted with an insoluble problem. The content of God's initiative in grace, which is voluntary and not owing to man, is therefore a priori meaningful with regard to the already existing problem of human life. Whenever God thus reveals himself as the meaning of our existence, this humanly unsuspected and transcendent answer to the problem of human life, which is meaningful in itself, must inevitably be experienced as meaningful by the human mind. In other words, the content of faith implies a certain intelligibility, and is therefore open to reflection.

Moreover, in fact the reality of revelation is offered to us as saving history. It has entered human history and makes use of concepts, images, and words drawn from the normal human experience of life. The God of revelation has accomplished a deeper mystery in this history, which is ac-

[28] *ST* II–II, q. 8, a. 8, ad 2: "Non enim posset homo assentire credendo aliquibus propositis, nisi ea aliqualiter intelligeret" ("For a man could not assent by believing certain particular arguments unless he understood them in some sense or other").

cessible to us, and in these human concepts and images. It is, of course, true that we can only understand the supernatural dimension—the mystery of this history and these concepts—in and through faith. But the transcendental content of faith at the same time discloses a perspective onto its own inner intelligibility. The infinite is disclosed in the finite, without destroying it. And in this way, the human desire to reflect can be directed towards the content of faith. Faith itself is consequently an inner demand for theology.

The Scientific Extension of the Reflection that Is Inherent in the Life of Faith

The reflection that is inherent in the life of faith can take two forms. The first of these forms can be encountered in all the faithful: it is the spontaneous, undeliberate reflection on faith which all Christians pursue. But it can be extended to a deliberate, methodical, and systematic reflection, and this is precisely theology. Theology, then, is something that is inwardly present in the life of faith, but extended to the level of critical—that is, of scientific—reflection. This provides an indication of the scientific character of theology. But this is not all. Theology as a science is concerned with reality itself, in contrast to the purely positive sciences, which are concerned only with the study of phenomena as factual data, and in contrast to the formal sciences, such as mathematics. Theology attempts to throw light on the reality of revelation itself in its inner intelligibility. But in this we are directly confronted with this most important idea, namely, that the basis of the scientific nature of theology—that is, of its task of throwing light on the reality itself of revelation—is nothing less than faith itself. Without faith there can be no scientific theology. The capacity of this science to grasp reality can only be based in the supernatural cognitive aspect of the act of faith, because it is in this only that contact is made with the reality of revelation. It is possible to study Christianity scientifically outside this faith, and even to study its dogmatic content (as, for example, Buddhism is studied in comparative religion), but in that case we shall be concerned with a purely "humane" activity, and not with theology proper, which is concerned with pronouncements about the supernatural reality as this *is* in itself. It was for this reason that Aquinas could say that "faith is as it were the condition of theology."[29] It is important, therefore, to stress the *religious* character of theology as a science.

This does not mean that the specialised scientific activity of theology itself is a religious act—I shall deal more fully with this point later on—but it does mean that theology is a science that is concerned with a *religious reality,* with the result that to live in this religious reality, which is possible only through faith, remains the basis of the scientific value of theology, that is, its concern with reality. In this respect, theology is really the scientific, conscious evaluation and expression of the content of the church's experience of faith. Theology is then "fides in statu scientiae" ("faith at the level of a science"). Since, however, theology is a science of faith, a science that is concerned with mysteries, this special tension between "intelligibility" and "mystery" will determine the whole method of theology.

THEOLOGY AS A SCIENCE OF FAITH: ITS DISTINCTIVE FIELD OF VISION

Theology is Christian faith *in* human reflection. This is really all there is to it. The law of faith becomes visible in human thought. The material datum of theology is thus precisely the same as that of faith—the content or revelation. But the attitude of mind of faith towards this reality is different from the attitude of mind of theology. Faith regards

29 "Fides est quasi habitus theologiae," *BT,* q. 5, a. 4, ad 8.

the content of revelation as *credibile,* that is, as the object of faithful assent to God's testimony—it is the act of encounter with God in its fundamental contact. Theology presupposes this act of faith, but considers the reality of revelation as *intelligibile,* that is, as something whose content is to be understood, as something with an intelligible inner meaning and value—*credibile prout intelligibile* ("the object of faith according as it is the object of understanding"). As a result of this, the immediate subjective principle of theology, or the theological subject, is the human mind, embraced and illuminated by faith—the organic working unity of the light of faith and the light of the intellect.

The First Vatican Council spoke of "reason . . . illuminated by faith,"[30] while Aquinas had spoken of "reason led by the hand of faith"[31]—faith itself *in* human thought. In this way, theology is formally distinguished from faith, in which it nonetheless has its constant breeding-ground. It is precisely because of this distinction that it is possible for the material object of theology to be wider than that of faith. For, although this material object is, in the first place, the content of revelation itself, many secondary objects are also—because of the formal point of view from which this content is regarded—included within theology, with the result that truths which are perhaps also studied by other sciences contribute to the interpretation of the content of faith. In this connection, it is also clear that theology, although based on faith, is a formal science and not a religious act.[32] It is a *study,* even though it is a study of religious realities. It is therefore in itself a *natural activity,* flowing from the act of faith and serving the life of faith, but it may not become something devotional. For this reason, it may not even be

30 "Ratio . . . fide illustrata," DS 3016 (= DR 1796).

31 "Ratio manuducta per fidem" (*1 Sent.* Prol., a. 3, sol. 3).

32 See Aquinas, *ST* 1, q. 1, a. 6, ad 3: "per studium habetur" ("it is maintained by study").

claimed that theology is impossible without a personally experienced religious life.[33] The probable explanation for this modern tendency is that it is a reaction against a theology which had become divorced from the reality of faith, but it can be of little use to a properly conceived theology. A certain affective penetration of faith in and through a well-practiced Christian life undoubtedly exists alongside scientific reflection on faith—"an understanding [of faith] deriving as it were from the state of grace."[34] But this is on an entirely different level—it is, in fact, the Christian life itself.

Furthermore, a disregard of scientific theology will not ipso facto bring about this affective knowledge of faith. On the other hand, it must be recognised that this pure experience of faith, which can give a saint a deeper "feeling" for the divine than ten great theologians may possess between them, creates the optimum atmosphere in which—presupposing the scientific nature of theology research—theology can come to an increasingly pure and trustworthy judgement. The Christian experience of life harmonises the mind with the reality of revelation, which is precisely the field of the theologian's work. This unity of intimate Christian life and theological acumen was precisely what formed the deep "theological sense" of which those saints who were also theologians were so often living witnesses. But we must be careful not to confuse these issues. The influence of the personal spiritual life on theology is formally only an inspirational power, the most suitable sphere from which to enter the field of theology. But it cannot replace the scientific work of theology and, from the theological point of view, it is of no value unless these affective insights are translated into

33 Vague and imprecise ideas of this kind can be found, for example, in the otherwise interesting work by T. Soiron, *Heilige Theologie,* Regensburg 1935.

34 "Intelligentia [fidei] quasi ex habitu gratiae" (Aquinas, *ST* II–II, q. 9, a. 3 ad 3).

theological terms. However much they may influence each other, it would be wrong to identify such different levels of life. The great contribution made by Aquinas, in making for the first time the necessary distinctions here and in giving to everything its proper place, should not be ignored, and theology once again be treated as an undifferentiated stage.[35] In brief, then, to claim with Casel, Soiron and others that theology is impossible without *habitus caritatis* ("the condition of charity"), is a fundamental misconception of the real function of theology and a confusion of theology with other tasks of the life of the church. If this proper function of theology is misunderstood, there is every likelihood that theology will not be able to produce precisely what the church expects of it. To conclude, then: theology, although it proceeds from faith, although it constantly presupposes this faith and serves it,[36] is formally a question of scientific activity and insight, of research and of methodical precision.

Historical Note: So-called "Virtual Revelation" as the "Lumen Quo" of Theology

The organic co-operation between faith and intellect was, in later scholasticism, related in a one-sided way—based on the Aristotelian model—exclusively to the discursive function of theology, and this co-operation and its object were called "virtual revelation." This meant that theology was from the very beginning defined as a *scientia conclusionum,* a science of conclusions only, and that the other aspects of theology were in fact devalued to the level of pre-theological activi-

[35] See Part II, Chapter 10, the section "Truth or Relevance for the Christian Life in Scholastic Theology," on pp. 242ff. below.

[36] See H. de Hannibaldis, *In I Sent.* q. 1, a. 2: "tota theologia ordinatur ad fidem nutriendam" ("Theology is directed wholly to the nurturing of faith").

ties. We shall see that the discursive function of theology does, in a very special sense, form a genuine part of theology, but that it is not the only aspect. Although it is possible, from an Aristotelian point of view, as far as this discursive function is concerned, to call the light in which theology regards everything "virtual revelation"—that is, the co-operation of faith and intellect in the discursive function of theology—this means that theology is limited to only one function. That is why this term is not to be found in Aquinas, although the idea, at least in the context of theology as a *scientia conclusionum,*[37] is certainly present—but nevertheless it is quite clear that the light of *sacra doctrina* was never called "virtual revelation" by Aquinas. The later scholastics were misled by the word *revelabile* in Aquinas, although, as far as I can estimate, he used the word only twice.[38] Just as the words *scibile, sensibile,* and *credibile* have the meaning of "the object of . . . ," so the term *revelabile* clearly has no other meaning than that of "the object of (formal) revelation." It cannot, then, mean "what is virtually revealed."

This is also clearly borne out by Albert the Great who, in his own *Summa,* written after Aquinas's *Summa,* alluded to this article of his former pupil and clearly conceived *revelabilitas* in the sense of formal revelation.[39] The later scholastic interpretation overlooked the very first question in Aquinas's *Summa.* It is clear from this question that Aquinas was not aiming to define theology as science rather than faith, but to situate *sacra doctrina* as a distinctive type, in contrast to the human, natural sciences which are completely outside the sphere of revelation.[40] He also showed, in this question, that revelation is the illuminating principle of

37 This was for Aquinas only one function of *sacra doctrina.*

38 *ST* I, q. 1, a. 3, c., and ad 2.

39 *Tract.* I, q. 3, m. 2.

40 See *ST* I, q. 1, a. 1.

this new type of science.[41] Consequently, everything that is studied in any way in the light of the truths of revelation forms part of the study of theology, whether these truths belong to the *praeambulum fidei,* whether they are deduced from it as conclusions, or whether they are themselves revealed. All the interpretations of the word *revelabilia* that have been suggested therefore seem to me to be one-sided. For E. Gilson, it was ultimately the Christian philosophy.[42] For J. Bonnefoy, it was the natural truths which did not need to be revealed, but which were in fact revealed.[43] For L. Charlier, the *revelabilia* were exclusively the truths of faith, or the *praeambula fidei* and the interpretations of faith.[44] For M. Gagnebet, as for the older scholastics, it coincides with the *virtualiter revelata,* that is, with the content of "virtual revelation."[45] All these theologians have in fact thrown light on only one aspect of *revelabilia* as seen by Aquinas: for him, on the other hand, *revelabilia* implied all these things. Both Charlier and Bonnefoy misunderstood the meaning of the first question of the *Summa,* and interpreted Aquinas as saying that formal revelation was the light of theology as a science, with the result that the light of theology was identified with the light of faith. I cannot analyse Aquinas's first question in detail here, but the result of an analysis as far as the term *revelabilia* is concerned is this. It is precisely because holy scripture or *sacra doctrina* is concerned with truths which are formally revealed that all those truths that belong in one way or an-

41 *ST* I, q. 1, a. 6, ad 2: "Propria autem huius scientiae cognitio est per revelationem" ("but the distinctive mode of learning of this science is by means of revelation").

42 *Le Thomisme,* Paris 1948[5] (introductory chapter).

43 *La nature de la théologie selon saint Thomas d'Aquin,* Paris and Bruges 1939.

44 *Essai sur le problème théologique,* Thuillies 1938.

45 "La nature de la théologie speculative," *RT* 43 (1943), 1–39, 213–55, and 645–74. See also R. Guelluy, *Philosophie et théologie chez Guillaume d'Occham,* Louvain 1947, 41 *n.* 1.

other (either directly or indirectly, previously or consequentially, or even purely factually and pragmatically) to holy scripture, or are in some way connected with it, also belong to the science that regards these as the object of its study. The *revelatum,* or that which is formally revealed, is the principle of their unity, and in this way it is clear that the "discipline in accordance with divine revelation and over against the philosophical sciences"[46] forms a distinctive type which is different from the other sciences. It it clear that the question of the light of theology as distinct from that of faith is not even raised here—it was not Aquinas's aim to investigate it in this context. His view is entirely based on the Aristotelian idea:

Despite the fact that there are certain distinctions in the objects of knowledge in accordance with their natures, they nevertheless pertain to a single science provided that they are known through the same principles, since they will not be distinct insofar as they are objects of knowledge.[47]

THE POSITIVE AND THE SPECULATIVE FUNCTIONS OF THE ONE THEOLOGY

Revelation is accomplished in and through history, and we live now from this revelation-in-word and revelation-in-reality—in and through the sacramental reality of the church and through the church's service of the word. The history of salvation and the word give us, by virtue of the light of faith, a view of the revealed reality, with which we associate ourselves in faith. As we have based the possibility of a theology in the objective and the subjective aspect of the

46 "Doctrina secundum revelationem divinam praeter philosophicas scientias" (*ST* 1, q. 1, a. 1).

47 "Quantumcumque sint aliqua diversa scibilia secundum suam naturam, dummodo per eadem principia sciantur, pertinent ad unam scientiam, quia non erunt iam diversa in quantum sunt scibilia" (*AAP,* c. 28, lect. 41 *n.* 11).

act of faith, so too are the positive and the speculative functions of theology justified in these two aspects.

The structure of the human mind possesses a double, complementary orientation. The human mind seeks first to become conscious of the data that present themselves purely as data, but in addition it seeks to understand the sense, the intelligibility or the *quidditas*, of these data—it seeks to know what *is* reality. This positive and speculative orientation of the human mind—two aspects of one and the same fundamental orientation towards reality—finds its corresponding point of contact in the structure of revelation. This should become clear from the following analyses.

The Positive Theological Function of the One Theology: Positive Theology

With reference to the bible, I said that theological reflection about the content of revelation required a positive examination of the way in which God allowed his divinity and the meaning of our humanity to be experienced by men in his saving activity. If we wish to know what God is saying to us and how he has addressed this invitation to salvation to us, we cannot do this without making an extensive examination of Israel as the people of God and of the man Jesus who appeared in concrete form among us as the Son of the Father and to whom his apostles bore witness. It is consequently the task of theology to subject to close examination this living sense of salvation on the part of ancient Israel and of the new Israel which was expressed under divine guarantee in scripture, and which lived on, increasingly illuminated on the basis of this constitutive revelation, in the post-apostolic church.

The content of revelation is defined by the teaching authority of the church as dogma only in certain points. A great deal of this content of revelation is still not dogmatically defined and, although such a definition is itself adequately true, it cannot exhaust the defined truth. Theology, the science of the integral content of revelation, must therefore diligently study first the Old and New Testaments and then the writings which have testified to the faith throughout the course of time. It must moreover study all these writers—men who have themselves tried to explore and understand the content of revelation—from the fathers of the church down to those of the present day, without neglecting a single period, since God has never failed to keep his promise. It is not only the fact that something has been revealed that is of great importance for a deeper understanding of the intentions of the God of revelation. It is also important to know how it was revealed and how it was made explicit in terms of faith. Insight into the growth itself of the revelation of the Old Testament, of the living mystery of Christ, and of the datum of faith towards dogmatic definition provides us with an initial insight into the content of faith.

The theologian does not, however, carry out this whole positive task formally as a historian. Positive theology is not a historical science, although it has to make use of strictly historical methods as an aid. But the theologian does this as a theologian—from the vantage-point of the church's life of faith today, and guided by the teaching authority of the church, he studies the sources of revelation and the various testimonies of the faith throughout the centuries. Faith and the teaching office of the church thus guide his positive study, in which he makes use of the historical and scientific method. He therefore studies biblical theology, patristic theology, and symbolic theology (the study of the *symbola,* or authoritative confessions, of faith and of the documents of the church's teaching office) in order to understand what God has intended to be the content of revelation as purely and as integrally as possible. He has therefore to determine—in a scientific, and consequently in a fallible, manner, with the result that he is ultimately subject to the criticism of the church's teaching authority—whether a given proposition has in fact been revealed; whether it has in fact already been presented as such by the church, or has only lived in the universal preaching of the church, or is merely a constant datum of tradition (for example, as something unanimously affirmed in the patristic writings); whether it is an authentic doctrine of the church or only a natural truth which is, however, so closely connected with faith that, if it were not accepted, faith itself would suffer; and finally, whether it is only a *theologoumenon* (theological conclusion), a question which can be freely discussed.

The positive theologian also has to determine what is no more than the "clothing" of the affirmation of faith in, for example, a given scriptural or patristic datum, and therefore what there is in this datum that is restricted to the human view of the world and of life at a particular period of history. It is, however, of paramount importance in this connection that positive theology achieves an initial synthesis which is suggested by the content itself of revelation. This synthesis should indicate how, in and through the temporal plan of salvation, the trinitarian mystery of God appears more and more clearly as salvation for mankind, and at the same time that this totality of revelation is echoed in every partial truth of the faith and in what way it is thus echoed. All this is not in the first place a question of speculative construction, but of a faithful study of the history of salvation of Israel and of the church. The real life of faith of ancient Israel, the historical appearance of Christ, the apostolic tradition, and the whole life of the church thus unmistakably show themselves to be the fundamental data of the theologian. It is an insight into all these that theology has to seek.

It is clear therefore that the function of positive theology is not just a pre-theological preliminary stage of speculative theology. It is quite simply theology itself, and as such is subject to the same light *(lumen quo)* of the intellect in close and lasting association with faith. Positive and speculative theology are not two types of theological thought, or two distinct theological disciplines, but two equally essential functions of one and the same science, the unity of which consists in the close co-operation between the light of the intellect and the light of faith, the latter always assuming the leading function. Positive theology, then, does not aim to bring "proofs" from the past that will establish the claims of a present-day speculative proposition. Recourse is made to the past in an attempt to achieve a deeper insight into the mystery of salvation from the vantage-point of the various phases of the objectively growing revelation of the Old Testament and from the perspective of the phases of development in the history of dogma in the dynamic yet consistent life of faith of the church.[48] Every period is marked by its own characteristic point of view, its own emphases and its own reticences. That is why it is only a broadly based positive theological examination—one which does not neglect any single period of the whole tradition of faith—that can safeguard us against one-sided syntheses.

Positive theology, then, does not simply provide us with useful pieces of information with which a speculative theology can be embellished or into which a prefabricated speculative theology can be fitted. Speculative theology is powerless without contributions from positive theology—theological reflection aims at the inner intelligibility of what positive

48 See Pius XII, *Humani Generis* (DS 3886 = DR 3014): "sacrorum fontium studio sacrae disciplinae semper iuvenescunt; dum contra speculatio, quae ulteriorem sacri depositi inquisitionem neglegit, *ut experiundo novimus,* sterilis evadit" ("by study of the sacred sources the sacred disciplines are continually re-invigorated; while, on the other hand, speculative theology which fails to make any further examination of the sacred deposit [of faith] turns out, *as we know from experience,* barren and lifeless").

theology is able to dig up of the wealth of revelation. In this sense, in positive theology speculative theology has already begun. It is not possible to separate these two functions into two successive stages of theological thought. For, although positive theology makes use of purely historical methods, in this historical investigation it is concerned with the reality of faith itself. It aims at attaining a better understanding of the mystery of salvation in which the bible, the patristic period, the scholastic period, and all the other periods of the church were interested. Everywhere and at all times the mystery of salvation discloses something of its inner, integral content. But every expression and every synthesis of the faith is the exponent of limited possibilities of expression and points of view. Even in scripture it is possible to find variously orientated views of the mystery of Christ, with the result that, within the unity of the one faith, a synoptic, a Pauline, and a Johannine image of Christ can be distinguished. One of the functions of positive theology is to distinguish the thematic differences reflected in these various views so that speculative theology may achieve an integral synthesis in which all these aspects of the faith receive their proper emphasis.

It will at the same time be clear that a pure *théologie du magistère*—a theology which has as its point of departure only that which has been dogmatically defined by the extraordinary teaching office of the church—will inevitably be an incomplete theology. The church's definitions, which have generally been occasioned by heresies and false teaching, are only a few crystallisations of a far richer life of faith. What is more, it has often happened that only those aspects that were attacked by heresy were dogmatically defined and that there was no more accurate definition of the truths of faith which the heretics shared with the whole church, although this, in certain aspects, also formed part of our deposit of faith. Thus, as a temporary result of the definition of a dogma, a certain shift of emphasis has frequently taken place, in which certain aspects of the faith have been pushed into the background. Moreover, if the sense of a dogmatic definition is to be evaluated according to its precise content, this must also be viewed in the light of the entire tradition which preceded it and in which the dogma matured to self-expression. It must, however, be admitted that the whole of theology, up to and including biblical theology, can, in one respect, be called a *théologie du magistère,* as the final norm of faith in the interpretation of holy scripture and of every witness of the tradition of the church is the church's teaching authority. But in that case it is a question of a critical authority in the matter of scientific research—a norm which presupposes research and never replaces it.

Finally, it should be noted that theology has, among its positive functions, the task of investigating not only earlier expressions of the life of the church, but also those of today. Examples of such current expressions are the lay institutes and the growing consciousness of the place of the layman as a Christian in the world and as a layman in the church, the liturgical movement, and the noticeable swing on the part of the religious life towards the world. All these present-day expressions of the life of the church form a *locus theologicus,* a theological forum, for theological reflection. Wherever a possible witness to the authentic faith is to be found, the theologian can be rightfully employed in his own sphere of work. Positive theology may therefore be defined as *fides-ex-auditu in statu scientiae*—"faith as listened to and heard, but at the level of a discipline."

Historical Note: Aquinas and Positive Theology

It has frequently happened that Aquinas has been falsely interpreted because of his differently orientated terminology. Aquinas was a great theologian above all because of his positive theological output. It was astonishing for his period, especially as he was often unable easily to obtain certain positive works—such as, for example, the commentaries of a father of the church. I have already pointed out in the introduction to this article that it is characteristic of Aquinas that he seldom used the term *theology,* but usually employed the term *sacra doctrina.* And for him, *sacra doctrina* included very much more than pure speculative theology. Every scientific activity that was concerned with "holy scripture" was, for Aquinas, genuine theology. I have no need to outline here the development of the medieval concept of *sacra doctrina.* This has already been dealt with in an excellent manner.[49] Holy scripture was really the centre of all theological activity. But the method of dealing with it was always dependent on the new techniques of thought, as these came to be used in the *facultas artium* ("arts faculty"). As the growth of human awareness brought about a renewal of this method, there was at the same time a renewal of the theological method, until finally the Aristotelian technique of the *scientia conclusionum* came to be used, when the discursive function of theology was stressed in addition to all the other theological functions.

When Aquinas asked the question, "utrum S. Doctrina sit scientia,"[50] what this *quaestio* meant was whether theology, in addition to its many other functions, also possessed a discursive function. His affirmative answer meant that, in addition to the many other *scientific* activities of theology (here taken in the modern sense), theology also had a definite function in which it realised, in accordance with the medieval view, the Aristotelian concept of *scientia.* It was very far

49 See especially the article referred to above by J. de Ghellinck, and the great works of M. D. Chenu: *La théologie comme science au XIIIe siècle,* Paris 1957[3]; *Introduction à l'étude de saint Thomas d'Aquin,* Ottawa and Paris 1950; *La théologie au XIIe siècle,* Paris 1957.

50 Lit. "whether holy doctrine is a science" (*ST* I, q. 1, a. 1).

from Aquinas's mind to define the whole of theology in this answer. He did not see the drawing of conclusions as the most important function of theology (I shall discuss later what he meant by this); for him the most important function was quite simply the *intelligentia fidei,* the understanding of the faith:

> Reason led by the hand of faith develops to the point at which it more fully takes hold of the objects of faith and then in a certain measure understands *them.*[51]

The master in theology was, then, a *magister in S. Pagina,* a biblical theologian par excellence. He was also a patristic theologian, because scripture was studied in the light of the fathers' study of the bible. The church's pronouncements were also studied in this perspective, and *consuetudines Ecclesiae* ("usages of the church") were looked for—these had a normative value for Aquinas. A good example of this broad view of theology can be found in articles 8 to 10 of the *Summa Theologiae* I, q. 1,[52] in which Aquinas examines the procedures of theological study. It is clear from these articles that the science of theology included—for Aquinas—in addition to the speculative aspect, everything that we should call positive theology. It was only after Aquinas that the division occurred between positive and speculative theology. A relic of this pernicious division still persists in the organisation of programmes of theological study, in which separate courses exist in speculative theology and in the history of dogma. The grave danger inherent in this system is that speculative theology tends to become sterile, while positive theology tends to become pure history.

51 "Ratio manducta per fidem excrescit in hoc ut credibilia plenius comprehendat at tunc *ipsa* quodammodo intelligat" (*I Sent.* Prol., q. 1, a. 3, sol. 3).

52 See also *I Sent.* Prol., q. 1, a. 5, in which these three articles still form one single article.

Speculative Theology

It will be clear from the preceding section that speculative theology is not a suprastructure of positive theology, but that it attempts to establish the meaning and content of the data supplied by positive theology. In its positive function, theology is seen to be speculative, and in its speculative function it is seen to be at the same time positive. I have already indicated the possibility of reflection about the faith, and shall now deal with this in greater detail.

1. *The meaning of the speculative "intelligentia fidei" according to the First Vatican Council.* The First Vatican Council opened up a few discreet perspectives on the speculative function of theology:

> When reason illuminated by faith searches with diligence, piety, and prudence, it attains—through the gift of God—a certain understanding of the mysteries [of faith], and an abundantly fruitful understanding at that: both from the analogy with what it knows by natural mysteries and from the interconnection of these very mysteries with each other and with the final purpose of man.[53]

I have included this quotation here in my examination of the functions of speculative theology because it was the intention of the *Acta* of this council, assuming the positive function of theology, to define the speculative function of theology more precisely.[54] The council was compelled by the situation

[53] DS 3016 (= DR 1796): "Ratio quidem, fide illustrata, cum sedulo, pie et sobrie quaerit, aliquam Deo dante mysteriorum intelligentiam eamque fructuosissimam assequitur tum ex eorum, quae naturaliter cognoscit, analogia, tum e mysteriorum ipsorum nexu inter se et cum fine hominis ultimo; . . ."

[54] See the *adnotatio* to the preliminary draft of the definition of the dogma (*CLC* VII, 526): "fide nimirum supposita inquiritur quomodo veritates in revelatione sint propositae, quae est theologia positiva (ut dici solet); atque inde assumptis etiam veritatibus et principiis naturalibus aliqua analogica intelligentia rerum per revelationem cognitarum deducitur, quid sint in se ipsis:

prevailing at the time to define dogmatically in a positive and subtle manner the function of the human intellect in theology. On the one hand, the church was confronted with German semi-rationalism (Günther especially, but also Hermes and Frohschammer), in which the function of the intellect in the *intelligentia fidei* was exaggerated and faith was rationalised; on the other hand, it was confronted with French fideism (Bautain, Bonald, and de Lammenais), which underestimated the function of the intellect with regard to faith. This situation obliged the council not to limit itself to mere anti-heretical formulations, but constructively and positively to clarify the faith in this question. Bishop Pie of Poitiers officially explained this positive meaning in his *relatio* ("motion"): "in the second paragraph is set out what is and what is not *the part of reason* in the clarification of supernatural truth,"[55] although it must be recognised that, despite its positive content, the definition was in the first place a reaction against the excessive rationalisation of theology (as, for instance, by Günther[56]):

In order to check the indiscretion of certain men of our own time, who have wished to be wise to a degree that prudence forbids us to be wise, . . . we solemnly teach and declare . . .[57]

'fides quaerit intellectum'; haecque est theologia speculativa" ("faith already being presupposed, it is asked how the various truths are propounded in revelation, and this is the so-called 'positive' theology; then, these truths in their turn being assumed, and with them the principles of natural knowledge and nature, an analogical understanding of the things known through revelation, of what they are in themselves, is deduced: 'faith seeks understanding'; and this is speculative theology").

It was from this text that the definitive dogmatic formulation was elaborated in stages.

55 "In secunda paragrapho exponitur, quales sint et quales non sint *partes rationis* in excolenda veritate supernaturali" (*CLC* VII, 200).

56 *CLC* VII, 87–8.

57 "Ad temeritatem quorundam hominum nostrae aetatis cohibendam, qui voluerunt plus sapere quam oportet sapere ad sobrietatem . . . docemus et declaramus . . ." (*CLC* VII, 509).

In the first place, the council pointed out that the subject of theological insight was the *human intellect*—but the intellect in association with faith, *ratio fide illustrata*. A stand was made against Günther with this expression *illustratio fidei*, which corresponds with the *fide supposita* ("faith being presupposed") and the *fide praelucente* ("with faith as a light shining ahead") of the commentaries.[58] This is an implicit recognition that theology is not an act of faith, but a human mode of thought, an intellectual activity, made in the light of and in the closest association with faith. Consequently the addition *Deo dante* ("by the gift of God"), which is not further explained in the *Acta*, should not be formally understood in the sense of a charism, in other words, that theology is a true charismatic activity. Although such charismatic utterances cannot, *per se*, be excluded, this addition does not allude to a special grace, but to the providential function of theology as reflection on the faith. The work of theology should also be undertaken as a serious scientific work (*sedulo*). Since, however, it is a science of *faith*, the qualifications *pie et sobrie* were inserted, in opposition to the rationalism of Günther. This was also apparently an allusion to Rom 12:3.[59] The scientific work of theology should therefore be carried out in an atmosphere of religious "awe" for the mystery, in humility towards the transcendence of the mystery of faith. It should be performed *sobrie*, that is, without audacity, as though it were possible to understand the meaning of faith in the same way as it is possible to comprehend the object of purely human thought. For this reason, the following sentence was also included in the definition of the dogma:

However [reason] is never rendered capable of perceiving these

[58] *CLC* VII, 526.

[59] *CLC* VII, 509: "oportet sapere ad sobrietatem" ("it is well to know and understand with prudence").

[mysteries of faith] in the same way as it perceives the truths which constitute its proper object.[60]

The task of understanding the meaning and content of revelation is therefore quite different from that of philosophy.

The result of this humble reflection on the faith is that the content of faith is *understood* (*aliqua intelligentia*) in a very special way, and that this understanding of the faith must be regarded as particularly fruitful (*fructuosissima*) for the life of faith itself. The council summarised the ways in which speculative theology is able to throw some intelligible light on the content of faith under three headings. In the first place, it is able to do this by appealing to natural, human insights—to man's experimental knowledge as made explicit in philosophy. It is clear from the *Acta* that this refers to the *usus philosophiae,* that is, to the use of philosophy in theology.[61] It is typical of the spirit of the theology of those days that only this speculative function was mentioned in the *adnotatio* to the preliminary draft of the dogma,[62] without any allusion whatever to the two other functions of speculative theology! These two other functions were not even mentioned in the first proposed *schema* of the dogma.[63] It was only in the eighth session of the commission that Bishop Gasser of Brixen[64] suggested the inclusion of the two other functions:

. . . from the inner coherence by which the truths of revelation

[60] DS 3016 (= DR 1796): "nunquam tamen idonea redditur ad ea perspicienda instar veritatum quae proprium ipsius obiectum constituunt."

[61] See the *adnotatio* to the preliminary draft of the definition (*CLC* VII, 526): "humana ratio et philosophia in religionis rebus non dominari sed ancillari omnino debent" ("in matters of religion, human reason and philosophy should assume, not a dominating, but an ancillary, function").

[62] *CLC* VII, 226.

[63] *CLC* VII, 1630.

[64] Mansi 53, V, 191.

are connected with each other, and from the marvellous congruity which connects them with our final destiny.[65]

This important addition, which was accepted, with a few alterations in style, into the definitive dogmatic definition,[66] was a fortunate correction to the one-sided theology of Franzelin and Kleutgen who, together with Bishop Conrad Martin of Paderborn and Bishop Deschamps of Malines, had a lion's share in the composition of the dogmatic formula.[67] The second and third, and otherwise closely connected, functions of speculative theology are therefore the intelligible synthesis of the data of faith on the basis of their mutual relationship and at the same time of their religious saving value in the context of the ultimate meaning of human existence.

Before I proceed, on the basis of this solemn definition of faith, to a deeper analysis of the central functions of speculative theology, as a function of the one theological reflection which includes positive theology, I must attempt to analyse more precisely why speculative theology is possible and legitimate—in other words, I must examine the so-called "analogy."

2. *The basis of the possibility of a speculative theology.* The natural and the supernatural form only one order of salvation under the providential guidance of the God of salvation, who created us in order to deify us in the manner of redemption. Nature and, as a result, the whole activity of the human mind are thus included in a supernatural Christian order. By the exercise of its own distinctive function, the human mind in activity is already participating in the realisation of man's supernatural destiny. But, because

65 *CLC* VII, 1657: "ex contextu, quo veritates revelatae inter se, et ex mirabili congruentia, qua cum fine nostro ultimo connectuntur."

66 *CLC* VII, 253.

67 *CLC* VII, 1646–7.

of the unity of the natural and the supernatural, in which human thought is included, the human mind must also play a part *in* the life of faith itself. It must reflect about faith. On the other hand this "nature," and thus the human mind, is included in the mystery of the "supernatural," with the result that the whole of this mental activity within the life of faith fades into mystery and, as it were, disappears behind a cloud, where the intellectual result is deprived of the control of the human eye. In this way, the whole of speculative theology is subject to the constant correction of the divine mystery of salvation.

It will also be clear from this that speculative thought should be steeped in *positive* theology, and can therefore only make progress when it is in constant contact with scripture and with the whole tradition of faith. To regard the datum of faith simply as a point of departure for self-sufficient speculation is an essential betrayal of the basic law of reflection about the faith. As P. Kreling insisted again and again throughout the whole of his academic career,[68] the most sensitive point of all speculation about the faith is our *sense for the mystery*. I, too, must stress this fundamental law of all thought within the mystery here—in the first place, it is the basic law of all thought about God in general, and subsequently of all thought about the God of salvation.

a. *The mystery in our natural thought about God* (analogy). There are no real concepts about God in our natural knowledge of God. We may try to come into contact with something of the divine reality by means of our own creaturely concepts, but their content will always be of a creaturely kind, and as such cannot be ascribed to God.[69] We

68 See his inaugural address: *De aard der heilige godgeleerdheid,* Nijmegen and Utrecht 1928; and his valedictory Lecture: "Beschouwingen rond de theologie," *NKS* 54 (1958), 1–9.

69 See also J. Pieper, "L'élément négatif dans la philosophie de S. Thomas d'Aquin," *DV* 20 (1951), 35–49.

possess no idea of God or of any of his attributes that is both positive and capable of being properly predicated of him. Knowing, I can grasp something of the reality of God, but I cannot conceive it in its divine content, in its reality of God himself. My concept has, as it were, an inner dynamism. It refers, beyond its content, to the divine, which must be in the direction indicated by this concept; but the content of my concept can tell me nothing at all about the specifically divine reality that I do grasp by knowing.[70] I am not saying here that our natural knowledge of God is merely a blind shot in the dark, aimed at a completely unknown reality. God is really situated within the perspective indicated by the intelligible content of the so-called *transcendentalia,* that is, of the reality constituted by *being,* which is our own reality and which does objectively refer us to God. But he cannot be grasped conceptually. It is true that our concepts do objectively refer us noetically (and thus not pragmatically) to God, but it is impossible to situate God more accurately within this perspective—our gaze fades in the cloud of the mystery. The specifically divine manner of being escapes us utterly. It is revelation that makes us know what surprises the specifically divine manner of being, of being good and so on, has in store for our human thought. Revelation enables us to know that God is one and not many, and as believers we are bound to maintain this strict monotheism. But the specifically divine manner of being one eludes our natural thought, and so revelation surprises us with the fact that this specifically divine manner of being one is nothing less than Trinity!

Again, we also have a natural knowledge of the omnipotence of God, but have no conception whatever of the specifically divine manner of this omnipotence. One way in which this was revealed to us was in the impotence of the cross! We also know that God cannot be changeable, but we

70 See *ST* I, *q*. 13, a. 4.

can only to some extent sense the specifically divine manner of this non-contigency from our experience of the answered prayer of supplication. God's non-contingency remains perfect and undiminished, but the divine manner of its realisation surprises us in so many ways that it cannot and may not be identified with the static unchangeableness of a terrestrial model. The most sensitive point of our real knowledge of God is that we *know* that God is quite different from the reality of which we have knowledge. In this sense, what is specifically God's we know only in conscious unknowing. But this conscious unknowing or negative knowledge of God is nonetheless a true *knowledge* because it is implicit in a positive knowledge, the conscious content of which also objectively applies to God, the one who is totally different, even though we can neither know nor express *the way in which* this applies to God. All this prompts us to exercise great caution in speaking of God and in using philosophical insights in theology, although the use of philosophy in theology is legitimate because of the absolute nucleus contained by human knowledge.

b. *The mystery in our supernatural knowledge of faith.* We experience this aspect of mystery even more powerfully in the concepts of faith, although the *analogia entis* ("analogy of being") still remains the basis of the *analogia fidei* ("analogy of faith"). If our natural knowledge of God in its concepts contains a *natural* openness for the transcendent, this openness is brought about in the concepts of faith by positive revelation. In this case, it is no longer the natural intellect that discloses in the content the objective perspective towards God. God, who reveals himself in a human dimension, gives to our human contents a new dimension which they do not possess of their own accord. Revelation opens up in our conceptual and figurative human knowledge a new objective perspective. This content orientates us, by virtue of revelation, objectively towards the specifically divine manner of being as this reveals itself. In this way, for example, the fatherhood and sonship of God, as an affirmation of faith of the first and the second persons of the Trinity, is really an extension of our human experiential intelligibility, "father" and "son." We cannot, however, grasp conceptually the realisation of this fatherhood and this sonship.

The concepts of faith are therefore not purely negative, nor are they purely metaphors, similes, or non-contradictions (as A. Farrer believed). They really are authentic knowledge, not merely pragmatic or symbolic knowledge. The concepts of faith really have something to do with intelligibility, an intelligibility which, by virtue of revelation, is open to the mystery. The typical, noetic value of our concepts of faith (as an element of our knowledge of faith) is, as it were, to be found in a projective act of the mind in which we reach out for God, without actually grasping him conceptually, in the firm conviction that God really is in the direction towards which we are reaching, e.g., the direction which, thanks to revelation, is objectively indicated by the humanly intelligible content of "father" and "son." The fact that Christ, *totus in suis, totus in nostris* ("whole and entire in his own sphere and in ours") expresses the divine reality of salvation in humanly intelligible terms as "father" and "son" guarantees for us the objective and absolute value of the statement: God *is* Father and Son. The *expression* of this objective divine reality is therefore as an expression also unmistakably closely linked to a human content. By virtue of revelation, however, this precisely defined human content has a real and referential value with regard to what God really is in himself, even though it does not lay hold of this by a concept. The act of the knowledge of faith is thus objective in the manner of an intending act—we do not really apply the purely conceptual content of "father" and "son" to God but, *in the direct line of this and of no other conceptual content* (used by revelation), we truly intend the divine reality.

God is therefore really Father and Son. This statement has no merely pragmatic value, as though we conceived God only by analogy with the manner in which a father acts towards his son. This would be modernism. On the other hand, however, when we say in faith: "God is Father, God is Son," this knowledge is not a conceptual grasp of the distinctive manner in which this fatherhood and this sonship is realised in God. This human content is, by virtue of revelation, only an *objectively* noetic reference to the specifically divine manner of being which in any case continues to escape us. It is clear, then, that the classic view of M. Pénido completely by-passes the heart of the matter in reducing the analogous knowledge of faith to the level of "God bears the same relationship towards his Son as a father bears towards his son."[71] This does not take us any farther forward. If the analogy is conceived as a concept that is proportionately one and equally applicable to both human and divine fatherhood, then the characteristic intelligibility of the content of faith is ultimately cancelled out, and is reduced simply to a comparison between two knowns and two unknowns. There is also the question as to whether we can so strip a human intelligibility of its creaturely manner of realisation that any "content" will still remain that is equally applicable to both God and man!

What is more, this is completely at variance with the most profound inspiration of Thomism, which absolutely refuses to apply (*attribuere*) the conceptual content itself to God and prefers to speak of "intending God" (*intendere Deum*) through the objectively referential value of our conceptual contents.

To conclude, then, the entire objective, true, and speculative value of our concepts of faith resides in their *objective*

[71] M. Pénido, *Le rôle de l'analogie en théologie dogmatique,* Paris 1931, 258ff.

projection[72] in the direct line or the direction (and in no other line or direction) which is indicated by the content itself of these concepts (which are accessible to us), with the restriction, however, that we have no suitable conception of the specifically divine manner of realisation of this content. The entire argument is based on the view that knowledge implies more than merely "explicit, conceptual" knowledge.[73] The mystery is preserved, but we have an objective view of it. Both the mystery and the speculative intelligibility are thus guaranteed, in accordance with the constant demand both of the whole of the tradition of faith and of the church's teaching office. On this basis, both positive and speculative theology are possible. Not only does this establish the possibility of a speculative theology—it also points out the direction in which it must proceed.

3. *Theocentric (trinitarian) theology with a christological method.* It will at once be apparent from the foregoing that speculative theology is essentially christological with regard to its method, but theocentric with regard to its subject.[74] Revelation, which is the object of theological reflection, is concerned with an *oikonomia,* an economy of salvation, as the revelation of *theologia.* This basic idea can be summarised in the words of Augustine: "the history of the temporal dispensation of divine providence."[75] The essential datum of revelation is a *mystērion,* that is, a temporal plan of salvation as the appearance of the eternal, trinitarian mystery of God revealed for the salvation of mankind. To confine theology to

72 By this word *objective* I completely dissociate myself from the "intellectual dynamism" of Maréchal.

73 D. de Petter's articles on human knowledge are also valuable for the study of theology. See *TP* 1 (1939), 84–105; 2 (1940), 515–50; 11 (1949), 3–26; and 17 (1955), 199–254.

74 See *ST* I, q. 1, a. 7.

75 "Historia dispensationis temporalis divinae providentiae" (*De vera religione* 7 [*PL* 34, 128]).

the study of the history of salvation is to neglect the aspect of the mystery that is revealed in the history of salvation. On the other hand, to study pure *theologia* is also to neglect the fact that the *theos* only reveals himself to us as God in an *oikonomia.* If we accept, correctly, with Aquinas that the true subject of theology is the living God, the *Deus salutaris* or the *Deus sub ratione Deitatis*—that is, the saving God, God as seen under the aspect of his godhead—(for it is precisely as such that he is our salvation), then it is clear that we shall only be able to reach this living God where he revealed himself as such—in Christ Jesus, who is the public manifestation of God. This at the same time shows that theology which is orientated towards the history of salvation is not opposed to theology which accepts the *ratio Deitatis* ("aspect of godhead") as the principle of theological study and that a theology which, on the other hand, is directed towards the *ratio Deitatis* in everything cannot neglect the history of salvation, in which God manifests himself precisely as God.

Just as philosophy cannot reflect about God if it does not take God's creatures as its point of departure and continuously concern itself with these creatures, in which the mystery of God is recognised, so too can theology say nothing about the God of salvation unless it proceeds from and stays close to the history of salvation, in which God affirms himself as God. Yet the philosopher recognises God as a supraterrestrial and suprahistorical transcendent being who is not a function of the world, but a being on whom the world is dependent. Similarly, theology regards God as transcending the history of salvation and as leading an intertrinitarian, independent life. Theology can, however, only obtain a view of this life through the plan of salvation, and must therefore constantly rely on the economy of salvation. The more thoroughly theology explores this economy, the more deeply it will penetrate the *ratio Deitatis,* God as God. On the other hand, however, theology should not be identified with knowledge of the temporal order of salvation, for God transcends the history of salvation.

This is something that is often forgotten nowadays. There are deviations here both to the right and to the left, and the central truth is forgotten—*either* that the living God, who is reached by the light of faith, has only expressed what is capable of being positively known about his being at the level of the historically situated economy of salvation, *or* that the mystery of the history of salvation is only the revelation of a supratemporal mystery of God himself. In the first case, the christological method is neglected. In the second case, what is forgotten is that theology cannot be identified with christology, and that God is greater not only than the human heart, but also than the history of salvation. Is it therefore not typical that, in a recent theological *summa,* which is otherwise, in many respects, very striking,[76] there is no genuinely *theological* treatise on God or the Trinity, although it contains all the other normal theological treatises? Theology is undoubtedly concerned with the intelligibility of the living God, and the history of salvation is the only way towards this understanding.[77]

This is why I can hardly accept Y. Congar's solution here, which is to make a distinction between theocentric and christocentric theology, that is, between theology and the Christian life itself.[78] According to Congar, theology as a science should consider everything in relation to God and should therefore be theocentric, whereas the Christian life should consider everything in relation to Christ and thus be christocentric. This cannot be a true view. It must, on the contrary, be the structure of revelation itself and the life of

76 *Fragen der Theologie heute,* Einsiedeln 1957.

77 See *ST* I, q. 2, Prol.: "Christus qui secundum quod homo, via est nobis tendendi in Deum" ("Inasmuch as Christ is man, he is for us the way by which we strive after God").

78 See "Théologie," *DTC* 15–1 (1946), col. 458.

faith that determine whether theology and the Christian life should be theocentric or christocentric. This division between theology and the Christian life is all the more disastrous in view of the fact that theology itself acts as a (human) critical authority in respect of the true orientation of the Christian life. It is theology that must determine—although itself subject to the supreme critical authority of the teaching office of the church—whether in the life of the spirit the orientation should be christocentric or theocentric.

If the life of the spirit is christocentric, then so is theology: the norm of both is the content of revelation itself! And it is clear from what has gone before that it must be formulated as follows: both the life of the spirit and theology are at once theocentric and (to avoid using the term *christocentric*) christological. The all-important fact is the *manifestatio Dei in Christo,* the revelation of God in Christ—hence a theology based on the history of salvation, and thus on christology. Historically, anyway, it is clear that the basic insights into the trinitarian dogma were gained along the paths of the history of salvation. Belief in the consubstantiality of the Son with the Father was clarified by the patristic consideration of the saving mission of Christ—if Christ is not really God, consubstantial with the Father, we are not redeemed and deified.[79] And when I go on to speak about the symbolum of faith,[80] it will be clear that, in scripture, the christological attitude has always been based on the all-embracing orientation towards the mystery of God.

This is of the utmost importance for the conceptual structure of theology. Just as the creaturely enters our natural knowledge of the divine, so also does the christological enter our knowledge of the living God: "in the [sacred] discipline we use his accomplishment, whether in nature or by *grace,*

79 See, for example, Athanasius, *De synodis* 51 (*PG* 26, 783).

80 See Part II, Chapter 8: "The Creed and Theology," on pp. 203–217 below.

in place of a definition [of God]."[81] This christological aspect in our theological concepts is the properly theological index of the analogy of our theological knowledge of the faith. If in general analogy is our knowledge of the one through the other, in theology it is our knowledge of God through Christ. If, for example, we wish to gain a deeper insight into God's perfections—his goodness, his justice, and so on—then we must, theologically speaking, not in the first place appeal to what philosophy can tell us about God's goodness from a philosophical analysis of the created world, but rather study the history of salvation, about which the bible can tell us and in which God's specifically divine goodness is revealed to us. Philosophical insights may certainly be important in this connection, but they undergo a metamorphosis, since the goodness of God's creation would appear to be also bound up with the theologal existential relationship of man towards God, with whom I enter into personal relationship. *He* is the creator, and the world of creation, as the expression of God's goodness, thus acquires a deeper meaning—it becomes the subject of conversation in the personal communion between God and man. Seen from the point of view of man, it is an answer to human questions put to the living God; seen from the point of view of God, it is a task given to man as an extension of his intimacy in grace with God.

It would therefore be wrong to contrast theology on the basis of the history of salvation with so-called "abstract metaphysical theology." It would be quite wrong to think that, after having taken the *ratio Deitatis in tribus personis* ("the principle of God in three persons") as a dogmatic datum from Denzinger, we can better understand this fact by making a direct appeal to philosophical ideas, as though philosophy could simply be transferred to this reality which is completely new to philosophy at least in its explicit form and

81 *ST* I, q. 1, a. 7, ad 1: "utimur in doctrina . . . eius effectu vel naturae vel gratiae, loco definitionis."

which transcends it. It is only when, after a lengthy study of the history of revelation and the tradition of the church, an initial synthesis is, as it were, objectively forced upon us, that philosophy can provide us with insights that will bring the doctrine of the Trinity into harmony with monotheism in our thought. Metaphysics can, of course, help us in this, since this science of reality in general regards God as being, *sub ratione entis* ("under the aspect of being"), and the *ratio Deitatis* ("the aspect of godhead," of God as God) which is considered by theology is nothing other than God's proper being. No division can therefore exist between the two, as though the *Deitas* were a kind of super-mystery in relation to the mystery of God with which philosophy is concerned. Theology which is based on the history of salvation also contains naturally metaphysical elements.

With this in mind, we can now look more closely at certain functions of speculative theology, as outlined by the First Vatican Council.

4. *Some of the main functions of speculative theology:*

a. A deeper knowledge of faith through the search for the mutual connection between the mysteries of faith (*ex nexu mysteriorum inter se*)

The provision of a scientific synthesis of what is offered by a broadly based positive theology is regarded as the most important function of speculative theology. Although the entire temporal order of salvation is grounded in the free initiative of God's grace, in which natural determinism plays no part, this should not prevent the theologian from seeking an intelligible connection between the mysteries of faith. Although God's free will has no cause, he has nonetheless established an organic and structural connection in all that he has freely brought about.[82] The history of salvation and the content of revelation form a single whole, in which the one fact of salvation or the one truth of faith is based on another datum, with the result that the mutual connection of these mysteries of salvation and their synthesis provide us with a deeper insight into revelation. Originally, it was precisely this function of theology which led to the question of the theological conclusion.

(i) *A historical outline of the problem of the theological conclusion.* It is clear from the history of the church that this problem was seen in a different light in the patristic and the earlier scholastic periods from that in which it was seen in the later scholastic period. Although neither the church fathers nor Aquinas used the technical term *conclusio theologica,* they were certainly familiar with the idea, if in a somewhat different sense from that which it had in the later scholastic period. The *conclusiones fidei* (a term which was used by Aquinas) were for them first and foremost the *truths of faith* into which a deeper insight had been gained because of their connection with other truths of faith. The task of demonstrating the mutual connection between various truths of faith came within the scope of what Aquinas called the *modus argumentativus.*[83] This was the discursive function of theology, and the example that Aquinas always used in this context was that of our resurrection as illustrated by the resurrection of Christ himself.

This discursive function of Aquinas was not, however, a pure deduction. He was very well aware of the fact that, when various data of faith are mysteries, their mutual connection also merges into the mystery. Since, however, the mystery

82 See *ST* 1, q. 19, a. 5: "non propter hoc Deus vult hoc, sed vult hoc esse propter hoc" ("it is not that because of one thing God wills another, but rather that he wills one thing to be because of another").

83 See especially *ST* 1, q. 1, a. 8; *Quodl.* 4, q. 9, a. 3.

is not "nonsense," but intelligible in faith, it is possible to indicate certain intelligible connections and thus to achieve a speculative synthesis. The central point of this connection does, however, merge again and again into the mystery, so that purely logical arguments are not decisive in this case. It was because of this mystery aspect that Aquinas preferred to speak of arguments of convenience. It was only when it was a question of the *praeambula fidei* that there was a clearer and more decisive insight into the intelligible connection. The argument of congruence, on the other hand, points both to the presence of intelligible connections and to the mystery that surrounds these connections. The whole of the *conclusio theologica* in the sense which Aquinas gave to it is connected with his doctrine of the *articulus fidei:*

> The objects of faith in the Christian faith are said to be distinguished into articles (*articulos*), inasmuch as parts are divided off which have a certain *mutual harmony and coherence.*[84]

According to Aquinas, the object of faith is not in the first place a number of truths, but the *Veritas prima* [*salutaris*]—the single, saving Truth par excellence. But this *Veritas prima,* as it is known to us in faith (and, it should be added, as it is manifested in the history of salvation), is, as it were, made plural in various judgements of faith.[85] These, however, form a single organic whole, in which some cardinal points act as joints by means of which the whole functions as a harmoniously connected entity. In this way, the content of revelation formed, in Aquinas's view, a single whole of mutually connected truths of faith, the synthesis of which reflects, at the human level, the single truth of salvation as this exists

84 *ST* II–II, q. 1, a. 6: "credibilia fidei christianae dicuntur per articulos distingui, in quantum ut partes dividuntur, habentes aliquam coaptationem ad invicem."

85 See *Verit.,* q. 14, a. 12: "Plurificatur per diversa enuntiabilia" ("it is made plural in the various objects of proclamation").

in the "knowledge of God and of the saints." Aquinas called the search for the objective implication of the one mystery of faith in the other one of the most fruitful tasks of theological thought. Because of the structure of the Aristotelian concept of *scientia* (the scientific nature of which consists in the establishing of intelligible connections), he also called theology in this respect a *scientia,* at least insofar as this discursive thought takes place in close association with faith.[86] The truth of faith which throws light on another truth was in this context known as a *principium,* and the truth of faith that was clarified in this way was called a *conclusio.* If we do not wish to place too much emphasis on the technical Aristotelian manner in which this central theological activity is carried out, it must be said that the essence of theology as practised by the great fathers of the church is to be found here—the search for the inner connection between the mysteries of faith.

It can, however, happen that other connections are brought to light by this intelligible interpretation which turn out to be pure *theologoumena.* These are the insights which were later given the name of "strictly theological conclusions." Aquinas did not deny the possibility, and even the factual existence, of these conclusions. Several can be found, in his christology especially. But an analysis of the articles in which he systematically explains the theological method shows that such conclusions are, in his view, peripheral rather than central to theological reflection. This is also clear from the part played in this matter by Aquinas's doctrine of the *articulus fidei.*[87] A suggestive text is, for example:

86 This is the full import of *ST* I, q. 1, a. 2, in which the *scientia* aspect of theology is based on its subordination (*subordinatio*) to faith.

87 A good study of the "article of faith" in Aquinas can be found in: J. Parent, *La notion du dogme au XIIIe siècle,* Ottawa 1932; see also A. Lang, "Die Gliederung und Reichweite des Glaubens nach Thomas von Aquin und den Thomisten," *DTF* 20 (1942), 207–36, 335–46; 21 (1943), 79–97.

Faith is clarificatory of something else insofar as one article [of faith] clarifies another, as the resurrection of Christ does the future resurrection.[88]

In the first place, however, the famous text in the *Summa* should be read in this context. In this text Aquinas quotes the same example:

This discipline does not adduce proof to demonstrate its foundations which are the articles of faith; but it proceeds from them to demonstrate something else.[89]

Not all the truths of faith, it should be noted in passing, are "articles of faith" for Aquinas, but only the essential truths of faith. And the "something else" to be demonstrated is not primarily the strictly theological conclusion, but rather another truth of faith on which an article of faith throws light:

As the apostle argues from the resurrection of Christ to demonstrate the resurrection of the faithful.[90]

Aquinas is not here raising the question of the so-called "virtually revealed," although the possibility is not denied that one is thus taken outside the sphere of faith. Summing up, he says:

Faith is clarificatory of something else, *either* insofar as one article (of faith) clarifies another (article), as the resurrection . . . ,

88 *3 Sent.* d. 23, q. 2, a. 1, ad 4: "fides est manifestativa alterius . . . in quantum unus articulus manifestat alium, sicut resurrectio Christi resurrectionem futuram."

89 *ST* 1, q. 1, a. 8: "haec doctrina non argumentatur ad sua principia probanda quae sunt articuli fidei; sed ex eis procedit ad aliquid aliud ostendendum."

90 *ST* 1, q, 1, a. 8: "sicut apostolus ex resurrectione Christi argumentatur ad resurrectionem communem probandam."

or insofar as other particular conclusions are derived theologically from the articles themselves.[91]

And even these "other particular conclusions" are not in themselves strictly theological conclusions, since there are also, in Aquinas's view, truths of faith which are not articles of faith. It is only on the periphery of Aquinas's theological activity that the so-called "strictly theological conclusions" appear.

When, therefore, he calls theology a *habitus conclusionum ex principiis,*[92] a drawing of conclusions from premisses, it is important to bear two things in mind. First, Aquinas aimed to define theology only according to one function. And secondly, he saw this discursive function as an illumination of the mutual connection between the truths of faith. It was only in the fourteenth century that the *conclusio theologica* properly so called made its appearance, establishing a sharp distinction between, on the one hand, a conclusion drawn from two premisses of faith, and, on the other, the strict "theological conclusion" drawn from a premiss of faith and a premiss of natural reason. At this same period discursive thought was seen as the basic and central method of theology, and we know from Guillaume Durand (d. 1334) that this was already considered the current opinion in his day:

In the third place theology is generally, though I do not know whether truly, understood as the drawing of these [conclusions], and *at the present time* this sense is in general use in conversation.[93]

91 *3 Sent.* d. 23, q. 2, a. 1, ad 4: "fides est manifestativa alterius sive in quantum unus articulus manifestat alium [articulum], sicut resurrectio . . ., sive in quantum ex ipsis articulis quaedam alia in theologia syllogizantur."

92 *3 Sent.* d. 25, q. 2, a. 1, ad 4; *ST* II–II, q. 1, a. 5, ad 2. See also *ST* I, q. 1, a. 2.

93 ". . . tertio acciptur theologia communius, nescio si verius, pro habitu, eorum et hic modus *nunc* vertitur communiter in ore loquentium."

Later the strictly theological conclusion was raised to the level of the real object of theology, and this development was completed in the seventeenth century. Suarez and John of St. Thomas initiated this breach with patristic and earlier scholastic thought. The older view of speculative theology, which had as its main task the scientific formulation of the synthesis of faith, was thrust completely into the background. Theology became centrifugal in respect of faith, placing itself in its manner of thought outside faith instead of within it, instead of thinking the faith itself. This divergence on the part of later scholasticism contributed a great deal to the depreciation of speculative theology. What had been no more than peripheral to patristic and earlier scholastic theology was raised to the level of the essential activity of theological science.

(ii) *The discursive function in theology.* This brief outline has already provided us with a certain insight into the discursive function of theology. This function must now be considered rather more closely, in view of the opinion expressed by some theologians that, according to Aquinas, there is no place for human thought in theology: "la raison est une étrangère en doctrine sacrée."[94] In the book mentioned earlier in this chapter (see note 44 above), L. Charlier threw doubt on the value of the theological conclusion, and thus on the legitimacy of establishing intelligible connections between the mysteries of faith, basing his opinion on the fact that a theological syllogism always employs four terms. The

---

See A. Lang, "Die conclusio theologica in der Problemstellung der Spätscholastik", *DTF* 22 (1944). See also A. Lang, "Das Problem der theologischen Konklusion bei M. Cano und D. Bañez," *DTF* 21 (1943), 87–9; V. Heynck, "Die Beurteilung der Conclusio theologica bei den Franziskaner Theologen des Trienter Konzils." *FS* 34 (1952), 146–205 (with bibliography on p. 147 *n.* 3 and p. 107 *n.* 54).

94 "Reason is an alien in sacred theology" (J. Bonnefoy, *La nature de la theologie selon saint Thomas d'Aquin,* Paris and Bruges 1939, 57).

so-called middle term functions as a term of faith in one of the premisses and as an intellectual term in the intellectual premiss. On the one hand, the mystery undoubtedly possesses an aspect of intelligibility—which is precisely what is accepted into the syllogism—but, on the other hand, this aspect of intelligibility in the premiss of faith is only an *aspect,* which is lost in the mystery. We can therefore never know a priori whether the theological conclusion—even though it may be quite legitimately drawn according to the laws of the syllogism—is really in accordance with reality.

This, then, is Charlier's thesis. Most authors seem, in their criticisms of this thesis, to be rather impressed by this reasoning. Even if the legitimacy of the theological conclusion is accepted, it is still necessary, they think, to introduce certain shades of meaning. First, the intellectual premiss must be verified against the whole tradition of faith. Secondly, the theological conclusion can only be regarded as valid if it is confronted with the whole tradition of faith. Only then can we have absolute certainty.

All this points to the fact that we have to do here with a deeper problem of a fundamental and general nature. This problem is above all concerned with the value and meaning of the syllogism itself—in other words, with the epistemological meaning of reasoning. Pure logical deductive thought is only applicable to formal sciences, such as mathematics, the initial data of which man himself clearly and exhaustively defines, with the result that no surprises are able to occur in the logical and consistent reasoning that follows. This is, however, not applicable to the "real sciences"—that is, to those sciences which are concerned with the mystery of reality. This reality, both at the natural and at the supernatural level, cannot be completely understood in terms of conceptualism. Any study of the value of discursive thought in theology must therefore be preceded by a study of the discursive aspect of human knowledge itself. If this is done, it becomes immediately apparent how easily reasoning as a *psychological* activity of the mind is confused with the structure of *logical* relationships in a syllogism. The syllogism itself is, in other words, raised to the level of a psychological activity, when in fact it only acts as a logical check on reasoning as a psychological activity. Human knowledge comes into contact with reality only in and through a knowledge in which experience and conceptuality form a unity. If the concept is isolated from experience, then one is excluded by the fact itself from reality.

From the psychological point of view, reasoning is the evolutive element in man's experiential knowledge, but only as controlled by the *object* (and not by subjective factors). In this sense, the so-called *simplex apprehensio* (lit. "simple apprehension") and the *iudicium* (lit. "judgement") are only logical aspects of a single psychological event which we call "evolving experiential knowledge," a knowledge which is always to some extent expressed in concepts. Concept and experience therefore belong essentially to each other—the concept is experience itself in its explicit aspect.

Newman correctly called this growing experience an "implicit reasoning"—a gradual development towards the expression of what had been present from the very beginning in experience, although implicit and unnoticed. Explicit reasoning reviews the noetic structures that are contained in implicit reasoning or in evolving experiential knowledge (which is also never completely without concepts). It is precisely these structures that are accepted into the syllogism. The confusion, however, arises from the belief that the exclusive point of departure of the real reasoning is the concept as such, as this is, for example, accepted into the major premiss. But the point of departure is, on the contrary, experience *in unity with* an initial conceptual expression. The syllogism itself has no psychological value. It only acts as a check on the explicit aspect of the various stages of evolving experiential knowledge. It is simply a logical proof of the correctness of the theory—we are not able to find anything from it for the first time, but only to check logically what has already been found. This accounts for the difficulty experienced, for example, by students who have to put something that they have not really understood themselves "in a syllogism"! The syllogism is, so to speak, a logical precipitation from experiential knowledge. The conceptual aspect is therefore of its very nature an aspect of a much richer whole. If we were to confine ourselves purely to logical reasoning about a reality from its conceptual content, we should never be able to tell where we stood, however logically the argument was constructed—in such a case, all contact with the reality would have been lost beforehand. How, then, can the conclusion tell us anything at all about that reality? It is clear, therefore, that the real value of reasoning can only be found in experiential knowledge together with its conceptual expression, and not in the concepts on their own, divorced from human experience.

If this is borne in mind, theological reasoning can be seen in a totally different and a more real light—as an essential factor in the renewal and advancement of theology. The theological syllogism itself is only the logical control of the growth of genuine theological reasoning from an earlier implicit stage of faith. Psychologically, there is a unity here between the life of faith and man's experiential knowledge (in which both faith and intellect play a part), a process of growth that is controlled by the mystery of salvation. This growing experience and the reflection on it throw light on aspects which were previously only implicitly present in this experience. A logically intelligible connection between the expression of this experience in its first stage and its expression in its last stage can in many cases be seen intellectually, but that this connection is ultimately convincing must be attributed to the experience that underlies the concepts. If this experience is ignored and we only consider two explicit concepts, then we can never be sure where the comparison will lead us—or, to put it more precisely, we cannot know whether the logical connection that we see tells us anything real about the *reality!*

Once more we find that speculative theology must at the same time be positive theology, if it aims to pronounce judgements that are concerned with reality. In some cases, the theological syllogism (this is really a contradiction—we can only properly speak of a *logical* syllogism!) is, as Newman said, only a later schematic arrangement in conceptual terms of the growth of the consciousness of faith. (In such cases, we are confronted with the fact that "theological conclusions" are defined as dogmas, although not because they are conclusions to syllogisms.) In other cases, the theological syllogism is a projected schematic arrangement, a provisional theme that serves as a working hypothesis which, as history shows, frequently plays an essential part in the development of dogma, but in other cases turns out to be unfruitful and wrong. To put this more precisely, the already formulated theological conclusion is, in some cases, the expression of a still tentative stage of an experience of faith which is striving to express itself more fully. We do not know whether the conclusion is in accordance with reality, and we are, in this sense, ahead of experience! This "working hypothesis" is valuable on the one hand in that, and insofar as, it is suggested by a real aspect of the content of revelation, and on the other hand in that it focuses vital attention on the data of the sources and of the tradition of faith. This further study, especially of the implicit tendencies of the tradition of faith in the bible, the patristic period, and later stages, can increase our certainty of the correctness of the conclusion until the conclusion can eventually express the experience of faith. This is the enormous part which theological thought plays in the development of dogma. It is only by studying in concrete the development of a particular dogma that a clear understanding can be gained of the full scope of what has been outlined above, and there is ample material for such a study.

(iii) *The theological system and theological systems.* Scientific study implies unity and synthesis. In the science of theology, the many different partial insights develop into a single all-embracing fundamental view from which the whole content of revelation can be surveyed. The search for the mutual connection between the mysteries of faith eventually gives rise to a theological system. It is clear, then, that the value of a theological system should not be measured, at least primarily, by the excellence of the philosophy used in it, but by the fact that the theological synthesis succeeds or does not succeed in giving a place to all the traditional data that are investigated. On the other hand, however, it is also clear that every theological system will remain incomplete and capable of perfection because revelation is inexhaustible. Although supernatural truth, like every truth, is absolute and unchangeable, it still shares, insofar as it is known by us in faith, in human imperfection and thus in the evolutive character of every human possession of truth. Even though every such possession of truth is adequately true (that is, it is not simultaneously true and not-true), this adequately true possession is not exhaustive. Every insight is therefore capable of growth and amplification. Light can be thrown on the same datum from many different sides and it can be approached from various directions, with the result that different and complementary, but correct, views of the same question are always possible.

Typical examples of this are the synoptic, the Johannine, and the Pauline views of the figure of Christ that I have already mentioned, the later Alexandrian and Antiochian christologies, and finally the Thomist and the Scotist views.

The difference in value between the biblical and the theological views is, of course, that all the elements of the various biblical christologies are correct, whereas this cannot be claimed a priori in the case of the various theological views of the figure of Christ. Leaving aside what is really mistaken, it is nonetheless clear that there is in the Antiochian and the Scotist school of thought an authentic christological datum which is not expressed in so many words in the Alexandrian and the Thomist school of thought. Every theological system is therefore essentially imperfect, incomplete, capable of further inner growth, and in need of amplification from other systems. This does not, however, mean that all theological systems are equal in value. What it does mean is that the excellence of one system as against another is also dependent on whether in its own inspiration, methods, and basic principles it is especially *open* to inner growth and amplification.

The capacity of a given theological system to assimilate, to absorb new insights, not in an eclectic, but in a truly harmonious, manner, and thus to live and grow itself, is undoubtedly the best proof of its superiority. To claim that all systems are equal in value would be tantamount to affirming a pure relativism of human knowledge. However excellent a system may be, it should never be forgotten that a system is not concerned with the system itself, but with *reality*. The system, as a system, is always the defective expression of this reality. In itself the system has no value: to affirm that it did would be tantamount to making the system, to making theology itself, the object of theology, instead of the mystery of salvation. To practise theology through, for example, Aquinas—that is, to allow oneself to be initiated into the mystery of salvation in and through the Thomist system—naturally presupposes a historically faithful exegesis of Aquinas's works. This is, however, not theology, but only textual exegesis of the work of a theologian, however eminent he may be. The practice of theology through Aquinas, however, means a *syntheologein* (lit. "to practise theology along with"), a struggle for the reality of revelation itself conducted together with Aquinas. This is precisely why all authentic positive theology is at the same time also speculative theology.

It is from the inner growth of a theological system and of theology itself that the differences between various schools of thought can be gradually brought together, through the openness of a given system, to form a higher view. At the same time, opinions will again differ on certain points, and new schools of thought and systems may result from this. This is an inherent characteristic of the imperfection of all human knowledge at any period of human consciousness.

b. "Ex eorum, quae naturaliter cognoscit, analogia" ("by analogy from the things which reason knows by natural means"): a deeper insight into the intelligibility of the separate truths of faith

The search for the mutual connection between the truths of faith necessarily includes another theological function, that of the *determinatio fidei*—the more precise definition of the intelligibility or the content of a particular datum of faith. I have already stated the principles of this function in the section dealing with the analogy of faith. It is obvious, for example, that, by appealing to the anthropological structure of man, who is in the world as a spirit through his own corporeality, theology can throw light on the sacraments. It will also be clear that philosophical anthropology, guided by faith, can play an important part in illuminating not only the sacraments but also eschatology. A correct philosophical insight into the unity—and, in a certain sense, also the duality—of the human spirit and body must clearly be of inestimable value in throwing intelligible light on the content and meaning of hell, purgatory, heaven, resurrection, and so on, in the context of man's ultimate end and the definitive redemption of his soul and body. The same applies to the clarification of the mystery of Christ, the fact of God's personal appearance among us as man.

Such insights, the result of human experience and made explicit in philosophy, are indispensable to the task of throwing a sure and safe light on this mystery, especially if we are, in our expression of the mystery, to avoid a tendency towards a kind of monophysitism or Nestorianism—deviations which not only affect the orthodoxy or the correctness of the speculative expression of the mystery of Christ, but also unconsciously harm and distort our personal contact with Christ. This function also includes (but should not be identified with) the task of demonstrating that the content of faith does not contradict intellectual insights. Thus, speculative theology may, for example, not only demonstrate that the dogma of transubstantiation is not contradictory to philosophical insights into the nature of the physical, but also place the essence of this dogmatic fact in the proper perspective with the aid of philosophical insights.

This activity of speculative theology finally also leads to a renewal of a growth in our manner of representing the concepts of faith. This does not mean that the concepts themselves are changed in this process, which would imply a false appreciation of the objectivity of human knowledge, an acceptance of pure relativism. It is not truth which changes and not even the conceptual aspect of our knowledge of the truth, but the perspective from which man views reality through concepts in the course of history. Our possession of the truth and our concepts thus *grow* from within. Older concepts continue, therefore, to be true, so long as they were previously correct, even though they may have been inadequate. Inwardly enriched, they survive in the newer concepts of faith. If this were not so, our conceptual knowledge (as an aspect of the whole of knowledge) would have only a pragmatic, relative value, which would a priori deprive also our modern concepts of faith of their serious meaning. The truth contained in the older concepts of faith and theology will therefore find a place among the many shades of meaning contained in the newer concepts of faith and theology.

The church certainly prefers to adhere to the concepts of faith that have already emerged in the church and have even been sanctioned by centuries of use within the church, and it has good reasons for doing so. In the Middle Ages, for example, on the occasion of the rise of progressism, which appealed to Aristotelian and Arabian philosophy in order to explain the faith, Pope Gregory IX (1228) expressed his concern as to whether reason was not thereby given too great a place in theology.[95] In different circumstances, but with the same concern for the soundness of the faith, Pius XII reacted in *Humani Generis* against the tendency to minimise the value of human thought in theology. Human reasoning, which was in the first case, because of its newness, the cause of unrest in the church, became in the second the element which the teaching authority of the church attempted to safeguard. There is no question of ambiguity or opportunism here. The inhibiting influence of the church's teaching authority is not prompted by the conviction that the traditional concepts are in themselves the best, but by considerations of safety, or, in certain cases, by the justifiable belief that the theologians in question are going too far and thus endangering the purity of the faith. To handle dogma in a dilettantish fashion is not only "extreme imprudence" and unworthy of theology—it also means that it becomes "no more than a reed shaken by the wind."[96] Aquinas too wrote in the same spirit:

95 See *De terminologia et traditione theologica servanda* (DS 824 = DR 442).

96 "Ipsum dogma facit quasi arundinem vento agitatam" (*Humani Generis*, DR 3015 [omitted in DS]).

Concerning divine matters a man should not readily speak otherwise than holy scripture speaks.[97]

The church therefore shows great prudence in preferring to adhere to concepts that have gained a firm meaning through centuries of use within the church and in being chary of as yet untried modern, existential ideas, since the fashionable attitude of being modern is a human psychological characteristic which has no place in the serious study of the faith.

On the other hand, it would be equally unjust to interpret this somewhat inhibiting influence of the church as a damper in theological progress. Pope Pius XII expressed his surprise in a speech that certain theologians had interpreted *Humani Generis* in this sense. The encyclical itself pointed to the possibility of and the need for a perfecting and refining of the traditional concepts,[98] and added that theologians had nothing to fear if they simply attempted to adapt the church's teaching and methods to present-day conditions and needs[99]:

Let them make a very exhaustive investigation into the questions which contemporary culture and the spirit of the times have brought into the open, though with that prudence and caution which is fitting.[100]

This is in any case objectively demanded of every science, and a fortiori when that science is concerned with the word of

[97] *CEG* 1: "de divinis non de facili debet homo aliter loqui quam S. Scriptura loquitur."

[98] *Humani Generis,* DS 3883 (= DR 3011): "vocabula . . . ab ipsius Ecclesiae Magisterio adhibita, perfici et perpoliri posse" ("the designations used by the magisterium of the church itself are open to a process of perfecting and refining").

[99] *Humani Generis,* DS 3880–81 (= DR 3008–09).

[100] *Humani Generis,* AAS 42 (1950), 578 (from the conclusion, omitted by both DS and DR): "in quaestiones novas, quas hodierna cultura ac progrediens aetas in medium protulerunt, diligentissimam suam conferant pervestigationem, sed ea qua par est prudentia et cautela."

revelation of the living God. Such tactless handling of the data of faith is all the more embarrassing, in that it brings genuine attempts at renewal into disrepute, and constant renewal is an inner demand of the life of faith itself.

As I have already said, the true illuminating principle, the *lumen quo,* of theology is to be found in the unity of the light of faith and that of the human mind. To express this in concrete terms, it is to be found in the effective contact between the mind of faith and the spirit of the age. As a *believer* in the content of revelation as kept alive in the tradition of the church, the theologian is essentially tied to this tradition. As a believing *man,* however, he is aware of the spirit of the age in which he is living, and he must be thoroughly familiar with this spirit, not only so as to be able to recognise the symptoms of disease that are present in it, but also so as to see "that an element of truth sometimes lurks hidden in the lies and falsehoods themselves."[101] In addition to this, God's salvation is addressed to all men, including those who are living today, even though it comes to them via the medium of the history of Israel's salvation and the man Jesus. This divine address must again and again be related to the contemporary situation in which man here and now hears the word of God and in which he has to embody this word into his life and thought.

It is precisely this constantly renewed assimilation of faith, prepared by a growth in theology, that causes faith to grow and dogma to develop. Any neglect of the growth and renewal of theology is therefore ipso facto an offence against the life of faith itself. If theology is not subject to continuous renewal in this way, the intellectual believer especially tends to feel that the life of faith, with its consequently undeveloped concepts, is not in accordance with his own views of life. As a result, it

101 *Humani Generis,* DS 3879 (= DR 3008): "quia nonnumquam in falsis ipsis commentis aliquid veritatis latet."

often happens that even a deeply Christian intellectual unconsciously accepts the doctrine of "double truth." Such Christians, because of their evolved and contemporary consciousness, no longer feel at home with a synthesis of faith which is presented in a conceptual framework which is alien to them and which bears traces of a past civilisation. Some even give up their faith because of this. As soon as attempts are made, however, to renew theology with prudence and with scientific precision, and the results of these attempts begin to emerge, the church herself at once becomes more open in her appraisal. Thus, the same pope, Gregory IX, who issued a grave warning to the magisters of Paris in 1228 was already much milder in 1231 in his judgement of the "Aristotelian modernism" of the time.

Theologians have therefore to be the "antennae" with which the church feels modern thought, so as to assimilate those elements of it that can be used and to reject what cannot.[102] The theologian is called to stand at a dangerous crossing of the roads—at the point where faith comes into contact with modern thought and the whole of the new philosophical situation, but where no synthesis has as yet been achieved. It is he who is expected to provide this synthesis. Living theology is therefore always a step ahead of the official theology of the church and ventures along paths where it is still unprotected by the church's teaching authority. (Three-quarters of Aquinas's teaching on the sacraments was, for example, pre-dogmatic, and his theology on this point formed the preparatory work for the later sacramental dogmas.) In this sense, theologians are by definition the progressive factors in the life of faith and the thought of the church. They are the catalysts, since, as Aquinas himself has said, nothing is so paralysing as habitual thought which makes us adhere

102 *Humani Generis,* DR 3021 (omitted in DS): "ne adeptam veritatem amittat, vel corrumpat") ("lest he ([i.e., the Christian theologian or philosopher] lose the truth already arrived at, or corrupt it").

firmly to traditional views that, on critical analysis, frequently turn out to be false views.[103]

This is particularly true of thought based purely on a system. A condition of the development of personal insight is a living contact with tradition, not in order to undergo it passively, but to re-create it and to verify it against the present-day experience of life and personal reflection on it. As Husserl has correctly observed, acquired traditions as such are "dead"; they are deposited as a sediment, and come to life only when that to which they originally bore witness and which brought about the existence of a particular science is reactivated.[104] In other words, personal insight is something inherited, but meant to *make* itself tradition by giving a living and continuously progressive meaning to the reality with which it is confronted. Within the sphere of thought about the faith, this is equally true of theology. It is because many theologians are apprehensive about the particular risks inherent in this active task that they tend to withdraw into a purely "positive" theology and thereby escape these risks —and with them, the theologian's special responsibility! In this way, they restrict themselves to repeating in their reflection what others have thought about previously, and thus fail in the task of thinking about the faith themselves, to the profit of the life of faith today and in the future. It is only when theologians living in the present themselves think about the faith and thus really practise theology—always on the basis of a positive study—that theology can ever be an

103 SCG 1, 11: "Consuetudo autem, et praecipue quae est a puero, vim naturae obtinet; ex quo contingit ut ea quibus a pueritia animus imbuitur, ita firmiter teneat ac si essent naturaliter et per se nota" ("But habit, and especially habit acquired in childhood, has all the force of nature. For this reason, what the mind is steeped in from childhood it holds on to as firmly as if it were something known naturally and self-evidently").

104 "This entire continuity is a unity of the making of a tradition up to the present time, which is itself making tradition" (E. Husserl, "Die Frage nach dem Ursprung der Geometrie als intentional–historisches Problem," *RIP* 1 [1939], 220).

important religious and social factor in human life today and in the future.

The answers given by theology and inspired by revelation are at the same time conditioned by the mental and social situation of mankind. Secular, economic, social, and political structural reforms, scientific, biological, and psychological advances, and progress in depth psychology and medicine, together with new philosophical insights—all these have presented the life of faith with new problems and have frequently caused theology to arrive at different solutions from those arrived at in the past. (Think, for example, in the light of the fundamentally different economic structures of today, of Aquinas's views on charging interest on loans—a practice which, at the time of Aquinas, was regarded as sinful usury.) Sometimes it can even happen that this human progress results in theology accepting the view that those principles which previously inspired the solution to a problem themselves presupposed a human situation that had survived from the past and is no longer valid. In this way, the developed human situation can lead to a purer statement of these principles.

This shows clearly enough that an intense presence-in-the-world is a necessary condition for theology, if it is to avoid becoming a discipline that is practised in an enclave and has no effect whatever on the religious life and on the lives of men. If theology loses sight of all these factors, it will almost inevitably sink to the level of bewildering theological presumption, which in turn can easily develop into genuine theological pride. When this happens, what is relative is regarded as absolute, and the theologian behaves as though he possessed supreme power over truth. In these circumstances, he often falls prey to a certain supernaturalism and becomes inclined to simplification. He tends to overlook the structure of secondary causes and will, for example, deal in a purely "theological" manner with the problems and difficulties of prayer, yet fail to appreciate the psychological factors, in which the crux of the problem is frequently to be found. What is absolute in the faith can sometimes deteriorate into a personal absolutism. This almost automatically leads to heresy-hunting, in which the theologian who humbly listens to the word of God wherever it is to be found is bound to suffer. For the same reason, such "absolute" theologians are often only half acquainted with the teaching of other schools of theology and have frequently gained this half-knowledge only from works of secondary importance. This teaching is then presented by them in such a way that no one can understand how it was possible for any serious person to propagate such theories. Or they talk, for example, about hell, heaven, and purgatory, and even about numerous "limbos," as if they had in fact visited them, and are thus able to describe them in all their memorable detail. Every scientist is exposed to the danger of falling a victim to these vices, but the theologian is especially prone to it, because his science, theology, in its aspect of wisdom, has as the object of its study the ultimate meaning of human life, God himself.

It follows, then, that speculative theology may not be identified with scholastic theology, which is only one historical form in which speculative thought about the faith has appeared. Not infrequently manuals are published with the title *Theologia speculativa seu scholastica* ("Speculative, or scholastic, theology"), which is of course clearly incorrect. From this it would seem that Athanasius was not a speculative theologian! One tragic result of this confusion of speculative and scholastic theology is also that, if scholastic philosophy, rightly or wrongly, does not appeal very much to an intending theologian, he must ipso facto turn his back on speculative theology and practise only positive theology. As a consequence, he will only study the glories of the past, and have no concern for what is to make the faith glorious in the future.

On the other hand, however, the church has testified, at least as far as education in schools is concerned, to her preference for the scholastic speculative synthesis as expressed especially in the works of Aquinas. The reason for this is that it is precisely here that faith and thought were synthesised—though only in accordance with the possibilities of that particular period of history—with remarkable harmony within the delicate fabric of the mystery of faith.[105]

What the canonical obligation to Thomism (according to *CIC* 1360, § 2) precisely implies was explained in an authentic and clear manner by Pope Pius XII in his address delivered on the occasion of the fourth centenary of the Gregorian University.[106] According to this official explanation, no more should be inferred from this canon than the church intended it to say, namely, the acceptance of the *praeambula fidei* (neither more nor less) as these have been accepted by the church from the very beginning and as it has been brilliantly synthesised by Aquinas. For the rest, the church allows theologians and philosophers complete freedom.

c. "Ex mysteriorum nexu . . . cum fine hominis ultimo" ("from the connection of the mysteries with the ultimate destiny of man"): theological intelligibility from the saving value of the content of revelation

God revealed himself, not as a being existing somewhere far away, but as the God of salvation—as *my* and *our* God, who is personally concerned with my and our life. Theology has to do with the God of the covenant, "Deus qui sub ratione Deitatis est salus nostra" ("God who under the aspect of his

105 For the true, not subjectively interpreted, meaning of the papal recommendations of the "Thomism of Thomas," see the outstanding critical work of F. G. Martinez, *De l'authenticité d'une philosophie à l'intérieur de la pensée chrétienne,* Madrid 1955.

106 *AAS* 45 (1953), 682–90.

godhead is our salvation"). This saving aspect of God forms an essential part of the content of faith. Something possesses this saving significance through the fact that it was revealed.[107] Every revealed truth is therefore a religious truth. This clearly shows how incongruous was the position of so-called "kerygmatic" theology, which claimed to deal in theology only with those truths of faith that have a saving value, as though there were other truths that do not have this saving significance—truths that ought preferably to be confined to the periphery of our theology and preaching.

It is, of course, a fact that the theologians of the later scholastic period, unlike those of the patristic and the earlier scholastic periods (see, in this connection, the medieval meaning of the *articulus fidei*—the saving value of the datum of faith functioning here as the principle according to which the articles were ordered), directed their attention exclusively to the *determinatio fidei*—that is, to the delimiting of the faith—and in the long run lost sight of the religious aspect of the truths of faith. It was to a great extent in reaction to this that kerygmatic theology arose, studying primarily the saving value of revelation, but on the other hand neglecting its intelligibility. Both of these one-sided approaches forget that being itself, reality, is a value for man. We cannot, however, arrive at the saving value of a dogma unless we reach —as far as it lies within our ability—the intelligibility of faith itself, by making ourselves aware of the content of faith itself. And it is simply impossible, because of the very structure of human knowledge, to make ourselves aware in this way of the content of faith without also implicating concepts. The objective *being* of the content of faith, and thus its in-

107 Aquinas, *3 Sent.* d. 24, q. 3, a. 1, ad. 3: "Non omnia quae in divina sapientia supra rationem sunt, ad fidem pertinent, sed solum *cognitio finis supernaturalis* et eorum quibus in finem illum supernaturaliter ordinamur" ("not everything which is above human reason in the divine wisdom pertains to faith, but only the *recognition of our supernatural end* and of those things which supernaturally direct us to that end").

telligibility, is its saving value—the saving value is not simply added to the content of faith. To dissociate the value of the content of faith from the *determinatio fidei* is to run the risk of slipping into a vague mysticism, since only the sense of the content of revelation, which is understood in faith, is the emanating principle of the ethical and religious activity of living Christianity. Scientific theology, practised according to the objective demands of the content of faith, is consequently also the best kerygmatic theology. The saving value must emerge, not from pious corollaries that are added, but from scientific theological speculation about faith itself.

In this function, it is obvious that theology also provides a philosophical analysis and expression of the whole problem of human life and existence. For, although the mystery of salvation and theology transcends the plane of philosophy, the philosophical problem nonetheless raises questions to which only faith can provide a perhaps unsuspected and transcendental, but a certainly ultimate and essential, answer. The whole of this philosophical consideration is brought within the context of faith, and within theology it develops into what is called a "Christian philosophy."

d. The *praeambula fidei:* a deeper knowledge of faith through the theological study of the natural basis of faith

Life led in the light of revelation is a life led in personal communion with the living God, man's encounter in faith with his God. Such an encounter presupposes a natural basis —the existence of two persons, God and man, who meet each other, with all the natural implications of what is implied in the human state of being a person. If man does not make definite contact with God at one point that is not grace (in the theological sense of the word), then the God who reveals himself cannot address man meaningfully. Hence the solemn declaration by the church that the existence of God can in principle be naturally known[108] and that the human soul is immortal.[109] These and other natural truths are called the *praeambula fidei,* and form the vital basis on which faith is made meaningful to man. Man's reaching out for God and the life after death must in some way be clear to him from his secular, human situation, if God's covenant activity with man is to be meaningful for him and assimilated by him.

Thus, the secular problem of the state of being man must, for example, to some extent raise the eschatological problem, if the Christian revelation of the *eschata* or last things is to be meaningful to man. Faith is, after all, not a belief in nonsense or in contradictions. The problem of the human experience of life, as made explicit in philosophy, forms a natural basis for the life of faith. Although it has to be reinterpreted in a Catholic sense, Bultmann's thesis concerning the need for an "anterior understanding" (*Vorverständnis*) is a thoroughly Christian thesis which the church always accepts in her constant struggle against fideist tendencies. Theology, as speculation about the faith, has therefore the task of throwing light on the *praeambula fidei.* In a precritical stage of human consciousness, it was sufficient to be pre-critically, spontaneously, and naturally convinced of these *praeambula.* The first Christians had, for example, no need to prove the existence of God as a basis for faith—the generally accepted idea of God's existence was sufficient as a natural basis for faith. In a critical stage of human consciousness, however, such as our own time, faith itself demands that the *praeambulum fidei* be worked out critically and scientifically. At this level, theology clearly has great need of philosophy. With the help of philosophy, the theologian can explore the human basis of faith (for example, the immortality of the soul as an attribute or implication of

108 DS 3004, 3026 (= DR 1785, 1806).
109 DS 1440 (= DR 738).

human personality). This at the same time ensures the authentic presentation of the distinctive character of the life of faith itself (man's immortality, for example, as an implication of his intimacy in grace with the living God). Both views of man's immortality are quite different, but they nonetheless have a common point of contact.

The theologian makes use of philosophy here with the ultimate aim of serving a theological purpose. This does not, however, mean that, since he already accepts, for example, the existence of God in faith, he can afford to be careless about the so-called "proof" of the existence of God, as though he could provide a proof overnight when philosophers have spent their whole lives wrestling with the problem. Apart from the fact that this betrays a real lack of seriousness, it also means that the theologian in this case completely loses sight of the value of the *praeambulum!* The explication of the existence of God must therefore take place in as critical a manner as it does in philosophy. But it is also true that the theological context within which the theologian clarifies the *praeambulum fidei* gives his thought an orientation towards those aspects of the human reality that can lead him to a satisfactory solution. The search for truth presupposes good will and openness of mind, qualities which are a priori present in the sphere of faith itself.

There is more. In the fundamental problems of human life—problems that are concerned with man's destiny and the ultimate meaning of his life—man is readily influenced by affective prejudices. Whenever God is considered, even only as a hypothesis, man can never remain neutral. He knows in advance that the result is bound to contain consequences concerning his attitude to life. This seriously interferes with his insight into the anthropological basis of faith, all the more so because he and all mankind live in a situation tainted by sin. Tradition also refers to a moral necessity of revelation to be able to understand these *praeambula* in the proper way.

Actually faith and religion have in general been the deepest source of inspiration for these philosophical truths. Even Plato was aware that he should establish the *religious* conviction of the immortality of the soul, as expressed in the Greek religions in the sixth and the fifth centuries, on a *rational* basis. This is a case of pagan religious life providing the inspiration for philosophy. The need to explore these *praeambula* theologically is so compelling that, if there is no existing philosophy, the life of faith itself will create one of its own, in order to be able to reflect meaningfully about faith. This occurred in the case of the patristic thinking about the resurrection of the body. None of the known philosophies—neither the Aristotelian nor the Platonic method—was capable of providing the elements required for the elucidation of this belief without contradictions. The church fathers therefore created, from faith itself, a Christian anthropology, by means of which the attempt was made to assess the correct relationship between the soul and the body. Athenagoras thus arrived at a new conception of man: "If there is no resurrection, human nature is no longer genuinely *human.*"[110] Examination of the *praeambula fidei* is therefore one of the authentic functions of speculative theology, as a science of the intelligibility of faith.

I must in this connection also mention the apologetic function of theology—the *theologia fundamentalis,* which is also to some extent concerned with the natural basis of faith. This does not imply that we should base faith on natural insights. The guarantee of faith, which is of a supernatural kind, is to be found in faith itself, the act of believing. Faith is not a conclusion drawn from an examination of history from which it should appear that God has really addressed man. It is in and through the affective attraction of grace (the *lumen fidei* which reaches the intellect via the will, according to the definition given by the Thomist tradition) that

110 *De resurrectione mortuorum* 13 (*PG* 6, 999).

we come into contact, in the act of faith, with God's testimony.

God's invitation to believe, to which I come in the act of faith, is what motivates my consent in faith. I believe because I rely on, and place my trust in, the grace of the God who invites me to believe. Grace itself draws me and establishes in me the disposition and the willingness to accept what the church proposes that I should believe. Faith is, however, not simply an act of grace—it is also an act, in grace, of *man*. This poses the problem: how can I find a moral justification for the fact that I give my consent to something, the inner evidence of which I do not see, but in connection with which I confidently rely on the word of God? I must therefore have moral guarantees.

With my natural intellect I can approach the fact of God's revelation through the converging interplay of various signs, all of which point to the fact that a special intervention on the part of God is active in Christianity. Everything converges on the same point—everything that happened in the Old Testament and in Christ, and that is happening now in living members of Christ's church today, points with strong moral certainty in the direction of the fact that all this is in a very special sense the work of God, and cannot be explained without reference to this divine intervention. On this basis, I have sufficient humanly based guarantees that I am not being morally foolish in bestowing my intellect in faith on what is not evident in itself. The act of faith itself is infallible and absolutely certain by virtue of the grace of faith, and the reasonable human justification of my act is morally certain. It is not that this reasonable justification gives me faith—it only explains the moral basis of my act when I reflect critically about it.

It is therefore necessary to make a distinction between the natural value of faith as a datum of spontaneous human life and the natural value of faith in theological reflection and scientific study. Believing Christians in the concrete may be unable to express the human grounds for their faith in words, but nonetheless really possess a justification of it. Present-day apologists therefore have a great responsibility in an age such as our own, when the life of faith is so lacking in homogeneity. They must above all take the typology of the life of faith into account—a child's "reasonable" justification of his faith is not the same as that of a woman, and a woman's justification is again different from that of an adult man. Apologetics must be very sensitive to the contemporary situation, then, since the moral justification of an act, although it is always tied to objective norms, is nonetheless very personal and something that can differ from person to person.[111]

Conclusion. It will be clear from the foregoing discussion of the functions of speculative theology that it is in no sense a superstructure to faith, or something that begins where positive theology ends. In all its functions, theology is both positive and speculative. It is impossible to be a good dogmatic theologian unless one also devotes oneself to the study of holy scripture, patristics, later theology, and so on, as well as contemporary philosophy. Aquinas himself provides us with an example of this. We can scarcely demand that the dogmatic or moral theologian should be a specialist in all these spheres, but the results of his theological thought will certainly to a very great extent depend on the measure in which he is adequately abreast of all this. Without scientific research, no living and developing theology is possible, and however "up to date" one may aim to be, one's theology will inevitably become silted up into a flimsy actualist activity that will collapse like a house of cards at the first serious

111 *Theologia fundamentalis* includes not only apologetics but also that part of theology which seeks to explain the essence itself of theology and its method. This is attempted, for example, in the different sections and chapters of this book.

criticism. It is hardly possible to think of renewing theology with the help of a few insights into the bible and a few modern existential ideas, the deeper implications of which are barely understood because the works of Heidegger, Sartre, or Merleau-Ponty themselves have frequently not even been read. In such cases, what should be an intelligible clarification of the word of salvation becomes no more than idle chatter.

THE TENSION BETWEEN THEOLOGICAL INCARNATION AND DISINCARNATION

Theology is always a "stammering" in the face of the transcendent mystery of faith: "balbutiendo ut possumus excelsa Dei resonamus" ("by stuttering out the great truths of God as best we can we echo them"). It is in theology a matter of good form constantly to acknowledge this humility, which is not merely a question of words, but also something that must be apparent in the manner in which theology is practised. The attention of theology must always be directed to the mystery of salvation that is announced and not to the human means which help us to approach it. In this way, theology must always maintain a middle position. In the content of faith there is both a tendency towards incarnation in human thought and a fundamental resistance to rationalisation. On the one hand, theology should not sink into so-called "evangelism," which is only aware of the mystery and the "folly of faith," nor should it tend towards an uncontrolled incarnation, which is only conscious of the meaningful intelligibility of faith.

We know from the history of the church that "pure evangelism" which refuses to become incarnate in doctrine and institution results in the ultimate suicide of the genuine evangelical attitude, as, for example, in the case of the *fraticelli.*[112] But on the other hand, we also know from church history that, whenever faith becomes too incarnate, as though it could be completely absorbed by human thought, there is always an imminent danger of naturalism and rationalism. Sound theology can only develop if it progresses diffidently between this Scylla and that Charybdis. It must actively maintain a constant tension between incarnation and disincarnation, between transcendence and humanising. In this sense, theology is, at the level of thought, a problem of what is called "Christian humanism," of the natural and the supernatural. And, just as the harmonious relationship between the natural and the supernatural is, at the moral level of human life, not a "datum," but a task full of conflicts and risks, so too does the harmonious relationship between the impulse towards incarnation and disincarnation, at the level of theological thought, only come about dramatically in conflicts and polemics, between stern excommunications and splendid syntheses. Throughout history, therefore, theology is always passing through a crisis of growth, as a result of which its true face is always appearing in a purer form "until we all attain to the unity of the faith" (Eph 4:13).

THEOLOGY AS THE LIVING ORGAN OF THE CHURCH

Theology is a science of the content of faith, of which the immediate norm is the church. The content of revelation is a communal possession of the church, the fundamental value of the church's life. The authority of the church is itself governed by the norm of the content of constitutive revelation and thus at the same time by scripture. Theology studies this deposit as it has been explicitly laid down in the bible and as it is present in the living church, and is therefore responsible for preparing the way for the doctrine and the

112 See DS 910–16 (= DR 484–90).

kerygma of the church's teaching authority. In this sense, the teaching authority, itself determined by the objective content of revelation, must learn from theologians, despite the fact that it is always the norm and the judge of all theological statements about the bible, tradition, and so on, and that it does not rely in its apostolic teaching office on theological advice but on the charisma of the teaching function. As Congar correctly observed (in connection with positive theology),

> What the teaching church requires of the positive theologian is that he should exercise a kind of biblical and patristic function within and close to the teaching church, to present tradition to the church in the monuments and testimonies of this tradition.[113]

This function of serving the church applies equally to modern speculative theology, which helps the church's doctrinal and pastoral authority in its guidance of the moral and religious life of faith in the church and the world. Theologians must therefore be the living organs (besides other, nonscientific, properly religious organs) through which the church reflects about her deposit of faith and consciously appropriates it.

Theology is, then, in the service of the church as the *human* (and thus fallible) critical authority of the life of the church—of its preaching, its spiritual life, and so on—whereas the church's teaching office is the official critical authority (and thus, in certain circumstances, infallible) for the whole of the life of the church and for theology itself. This function of serving the church implies, within the limits defined by the teaching office, a certain freedom for the theologian and for theological thought (in accordance with the demands of the content of revelation)—theology would not be able to exercise this function of service to the church if

113 Y. Congar, *Vraie et fause réforme,* Paris 1950, 529–30.

there was no opportunity for *serious* new attempts to be expressed.

The *ecclesial* character of theology means that the task of teaching in a faculty of the church is a specifically *ecclesiastical* one with a "canonical mission." The doctrinal *kerygma* is the exclusive task of the apostolic office, and therefore of the hierarchy of the church (or of whoever is delegated to this task by the hierarchy). Scientific theology, on the other hand, is in principle the task of every believer, whoever he may be, so long as he wishes to put himself at the service of the life of the church in this capacity. The official and ecclesiastical *teaching* of theology, however, requires a canonical mission, since it is the scientific extension of the apostolic *kerygma*. Theology is finally protected by its ecclesial nature from personal preferences for, and personal emphases placed on, certain data of faith.

Theology is attentive to the emphases of the content itself of the mystery of salvation, and even needs to maintain a certain distance from purely contemporary problems, in order to present the totality of faith as purely as possible and to avoid the danger of furnishing a one-sided theological synthesis of faith. As Christians, we do not live from one truth of the faith, but from the totality of dogma, even though this may still be implicit in many respects. The explication of an aspect of faith that has perhaps continued to remain implicit because of the contemporary situation always means that the life of faith is broadened and deepened. Although modern theology has above all the function of serving the present generation and that of the immediate future, it can only exercise this function purely when it puts this generation in touch with the integral synthesis of faith as suggested by positive theology and elaborated by speculative theology.

In the long run, a speculation of this kind will certainly be the most up to date, and able to provide a sound answer to contemporary problems. Otherwise, we are confronted with the verifiable contemporary fact that very many problems—problems not always of central, but undeniably of immediate, importance to us today—give rise to fine new theological treatises or even to new disciplines, while we are still obliged to look for the essence of revelation in the classic but out-of-date treatises about (for instance) "the one-in-three God, Christ, the sacraments, and the last things." The essence of theology is not itself reflected on, as if this were not of current importance. This is ultimately bound to distort the concrete life of faith into unauthentic experiences and to truncate the integral meaning of faith, and theology will thus be committing an offence against its responsibility and task in respect of the soundness of the Christian life of faith. A properly orientated theology must constantly act as a counterbalance against this subjective tendency towards one-sidedness and misplaced emphasis. Such a theology is moreover also the best constructive criticism of earlier tendencies towards one-sidedness, which are otherwise only combated by one-sided arguments in the opposite direction.

THE STRUCTURAL DIVISIONS OF THEOLOGY

I have already referred—in the introduction to this chapter (see pp. 87ff. above)—to the fact that theology gradually became divided into branches. I do not propose to go into the genesis of these divisions here. For the most part, they came about because of the defects of the existing scientific theology, but at the same time also because of a certain need to specialise, since it became impossible for one theologian to deal with the whole of theology. Specialisation of this kind is the inevitable consequence of a living and growing science, and it need not be a disadvantage so long as the whole science continues to be reflected in each individual branch, and moral theology (for example) is not divorced from its breeding ground, dogmatic theology.

The correct place for a particular branch in a particular "treatise," to make a harmonious development, can also be disputed. This is all to a certain extent relative, however. I cannot discuss the problem fully here,[114] but can only draw attention to its most important aspect. This is that the fundamental vision of Christianity—the historic plan of redemption in Christ as the revelation of the trinitarian mystery of God and thus the salvation of man—must be gradually illuminated in the whole science of theology; and that this fundamental vision, suggested to us by revelation itself, is thoroughly elucidated in each individual branch of theology, including moral theology, since God's invitation to salvation in Christ and his church demands an active, living response from man in the world.[115]

[114] See, for example, K. Rahner, "The Prospects for Dogmatic Theology" and "A Scheme for a Treatise of Dogmatic Theology," Chapters 1 and 2 of *Theological Investigations* I, New York, Taplinger, 1961.

[115] In addition to those mentioned in the footnotes, the following works have been consulted in connection with this article:

a. Concerning the term *theology:* P. Battifol, "Theologia, Theologi," *ETL* 5 (1928), 205–21; Y. Congar, "Theologie," *DTC* xv–1 (1946), 341–6; J. de Ghellinck, "Pagina et S. Pagina: Histoire d'un mot et transformation de l'objet primitif désigné," *Misc. Pelzer,* 23–59; G. Paré, A. Brunet, and P. Tremblay, *La renaissance du XIIe siècle,* Paris and Ottawa 1933, 102f. and 307–12; R. Roques, "Notes sur la notion de theologia chez le ps.–Denis Aréopagite," *RAM* 25 (1949), 200–12: J. Stilmayr, "Mannigfaltige Bedeutung von Theologie und Theologe," *TG* 11 (1919), 296–309.

b. Concerning the essence and methods of theology: J. Beumer, *Theologie als Glaubensverständnis,* Würzburg 1953; J. Beumer, "Konklusionstheologie?" *ZKT* 63 (1939), 360–5; H. Birault, "La foi et la pensée d'après Heidegger," *Philosophies chrétiennes: Recherches et débats* 10, Paris 1955, 108–32; C. Boyer, "Qu'est-ce que la théologie?" *Greg* 21 (1940), 255–66; M. Chenu, *Une école de théologie,* Kain and Etiolles 1937; M. Chenu, "Position de la théologie," *RSPT* 24 (1935), 232–57; Y. Congar, "Théologie," *DTC* xv–1 (1946), 341–502; Y. Congar, "Comptes rendus," *BT* 15 (1938–9), 490–505 and 528f.;T. Deman, "Composantes de la théologie,"*RSPT* 28 (1939), 286–344; H. Duméry, "Critique et religion," *RMM* 4 (1954), 435–53; K. Eschweiler, *Die zwei Wegen, der neueren Theologie,* Augsburg 1926; A. Gardeil, *Le donné révélé et la théologie,* Jusivy 1908 and 1932[2]; R. Guelluy, "La place des théologiens, dans l'Eglise et la société mediévales," *MM* 1, 571–89;

M. Labourdette, "La théologie, intelligence de la foi," *RT* 46 (1964), 5–44; A. Lang, "Die ersten Aufsätze zu systematischer, Glaubensbegründung," *DTF* 26 (1948), 361–95; J. Leclercq, "L'idéal du théologien au moyen âge," *RSR* 21 (1947), 121–48; B. Poschmann, *Der Wissenschaftscharakter der katholischen Theologie,* Breslau 1932; G. Rabeau, *Introduction à la théologie,* Paris 1926; G. Söhngen, *Philosophische Einübung in die Theologie,* Freiburg and Munich 1955; G. van Ackeren, *Sacra Doctrina: the Subject of the First Question of the Summa Theologiae of St. Thomas Aquinas,* Rome 1952; H. Urs von Balthasar, "Was soll Theologie? Ihr Ort und ihre Gestalt im Leben der Kirche," *WW* 9 (1953), 325–32; P. Wyser, *Theologie als Wissenschaft,* Salzburg and Leipzig 1938.

c. Concerning the history of theology: R. Aubert, *La théologie catholique au milieu du XXe siècle,* Paris 1954; J. Beumer, *Theologie als Glaubensverständnis,* Würzburg 1953; M. Chenu, *La théologie au XIIe siècle,* Paris 1957; M. Chenu, *La théologie comme science au XIIIe siècle,* Paris 1957[3]; J. de Ghellinck, *Le mouvement théologique du XIIe siècle,* Bruges 1948[2]; J. de Ghellinck, *L'essor de la littérature latine au XIIe siècle,* two parts, Paris and Brussels 1946; M. Grabmann, *Geschichte der scholastischen Methode,* two parts, Freiburg 1909–11; M. Grabmann, *Die theologische Erkenntnis- und Einleitungslehre des hl. Thomas von Aquin,* Freiburg 1948; E. Hocédez, *Histoire de la théologie au XIXe siècle,* three parts, Brussels 1947–52; A. Landgraf, *Einführung in die Geschichte der Theologischen Literatur der Frühscholastik,* Regensburg 1948; G. Paré, A. Brunet, and P. Tremblay, *La renaissance de XIIe siécle,* Paris and Ottawa 1933; D. van den Eynde, *Les normes de l'enseignement chrétien dans la littérature patristique,* Louvain 1933.

6 The Bible and Theology

GOD'S ADDRESS AND MAN'S RESPONSE: SCRIPTURE AND THE CHURCH

Revealed religion is by definition a dialogue, an *encounter* on the part of man with the living God. This is, I know, a modern existential catch-word, a fashionable word that is used in season and out of season. It sometimes takes considerable courage to use it yet again. Nonetheless, it is truly only another, more modern word for a reality that has always been recognised in the life of religion—the reality of man's personal relationship with God by virtue of grace and God's personal address. If we take the phrases "encounter with God" and "experience of God" in their strict meaning, then we must accept that they define the heavenly vision of God and not the life of grace on earth. In the case of our religious life on earth, we can only refer to an experience of faith and love, in which an interpersonal relationship with God in faith is made possible by a subjective mediation, a knowledge that we are addressed in grace by God. But it is also a datum of faith that there is no *objective mediation* in this communion of grace with God. By definition, this means that the communion of grace is a real interpersonal relationship between God and man, a partnership in which God personally addresses man, and man personally replies to him in faith. This is an encounter with God in faith. The dogma of grace is thus correctly and soundly expressed in modern terms.

Faith is man's response to the living God's disclosure of himself. The approach to the inward aspect of a being depends upon the nature of that being and takes place in various ways. Every being is in principle open to other beings, but the mode of this openness is different in the case of material things, of spiritual beings, of man, and finally of God.

Material things have no inward, personal aspect. They are given up to the searching and dominant spirit of man. For this reason, we never refer in this context to "encounters" with things, plants, and animals: man freely lays his hands on them.

It is quite different in the case of spiritual beings. They are, by virtue of their freedom, the source of what they really are—they have, or rather they are, an inward, personal secret. It is not possible freely to lay hands on this secret from outside. They are accessible to others in their inward aspect only insofar as they reveal and disclose themselves in freedom. A spiritual being *makes* itself known. The more a spiritual being disposes of itself as a free person, the more the openness towards the other will be a personal act of freely giving love, of intimate self-communication. The other really *encounters* the fellow person. This encounter is only possible if there is a willingness to meet on both sides—on the one hand, an intimate self-disclosure, and on the other, an attentive, receptive surrender.

It is even more complicated when human beings are involved. Every human relationship with another takes place via corporeality. The human person is outwardly open through his corporeality. This also points to the limited nature of man's free, personal possession. The body reveals, but at the same time conceals, the secret of the human person. Whether he wants it or not, man is partly open and accessible to his fellow men—his corporeality betrays his inward aspect. Partly, however; he only reveals himself in freedom, because his physical expressions to a certain extent originate with a free act. A personal encounter between men does not come about through pure mastery of the other's physical, unintentional expressions. That would reduce man to an object. A truly human encounter takes place only when the human person voluntarily reveals himself to the other, who opens himself to this revelation. Every forced approach to a fellow human being is an elimination, a disregarding, of the human person, and can therefore never be a "personal encounter." In such a case, all that is reached in the fellow human being is what is for him not typically personal. The secret of his life is concealed from us. That is why, in every case of true human encounter between men, *revelation* and *faith* are present. It is only in an environment of love that this revelation and this faith acquire their full significance.

God is the absolute source of his inner secret and a person in the absolute sense of the word. (Precisely for this reason, although it is beyond our comprehension, he is *per se* one being in the unity of three persons.) He can be approached in the secret of his personal life only when he allows himself to be encountered. It is only in this case that revelation and faith, as the constitutive factors of the true encounter, gain their full significance. There is therefore, in the idea of the "encounter with God," a reference to our own natural existential experience. Without this secular, human significance, the theological concept of "encounter with God" and the concepts "revelation" and "faith" would have no meaning for us.

Although we can to a certain extent view the absolute reality of God as a mystery from creation, in which God reveals himself so to speak indirectly, the real form of this mystery was fully revealed to us only in the history of salvation, which reached its climax in the *epiphaneia,* the epiphany, or appearance, of the Son of God as a man among us. Man's response in faith to the God of revelation is essentially correlative to this objective revelation or self-disclosure on God's part. Nothing, therefore, can be said about the structure of the act of faith that is not essentially related to the content of revelation itself. Both the act and the content of faith are based on grace which, as it were, holds this essential correlation between believing and the content of faith together in us through the spiritual affinity, given to us by God in the light of faith, with the saving reality that comes to us from history and above all from the historical reality of Christ. This intensive unity of the inward and outward aspects also has an anthropological basis. Every human activity is characterised by the human condition—the material world, our being-in-the-world, is our only access to explicit consciousness of any sphere of knowledge. We know only in the physical state. We only know the non-physical insofar as this is connected with the physical—the "I" and the "others" insofar as they are in the world, and ultimately God too, insofar as he is the creator of all this, or insofar as he manifests himself in grace in this world, that is, in the history of salvation.

Consequently every human activity is characterised by an *outward orientation* and by an *inward spiritual aspect,* an inward appeal that inspires our human acts in and towards the world. Although it is only brought about in grace, believing is nonetheless a real human act, characterised by our human condition. That is why the act of faith is also characterised by its orientation "outward" towards the world of men and things in which Christ appeared at a definite moment of time and founded his church. At the same time, this act of faith is also characterised by an inward aspect, by an accompanying conversion, a "turning inward," in which (in a constant outward orientation) an inward spiritual appeal in grace is also experienced, a divine invitation which calls upon us and inspires us to take the personal initiative to surrender in faith to what comes to meet us from public revelation. In the grace of faith, God gives us a spiritual affinity with precisely that reality that we encounter in our being in, and experience of, the history of salvation.

We must keep these two aspects of faith constantly in mind if we want to consider the problem of the (to some extent) different standpoints of the exegetical or biblical view and the dogmatic view of faith. Believing includes an aspect of conscious knowledge which, for the Christian, is not simply any knowledge, but a knowledge through being addressed. This address evokes a listening. Revelation and faith together bring about a dialogue between the living God and man. This structure is to be found not only in faith in constitutive, or completed, revelation, but also in faith in the revelation that is still taking place and is still open. For this open revelation came about dialogically—that is, in dialogue, God gradually unfolded his saving plan in and through the dialogic relationship of the Jewish people, in faithfulness or in opposition, with Yahweh.

Revelation was brought about by God himself, not only as the creator who sustains human history, but also—and formally—as the God of salvation, acting in respect of the very human freedom that makes history. It was in human history that God brought about what he planned to do in his concern for man and his salvation, and he did this in such a way that his action to save man became visible in a veiled manner in history as an act of God. This saving activity itself was revelation—it was revealed by becoming history, and it became history by being revealed. In this way, revelation was a growing process which was given its definitive form in Christ and in the early apostolic church. The Old Testament has, as an expression of religious faith, a certain independent value of its own, but this Old Testament revelation must ultimately be seen principally as the prehistory of the Christian revelation, as a growth towards the mystery of Christ, which is the centre and the *telos,* the end and goal, of the whole of revelation. The entire salvation history of the Old Testament was directed towards this final stage of revelation, and the first word of revelation can only be fully understood when it is considered in the perspective of this definitive revelation in Christ.

Revelation, then, is to be found primarily in God's saving activity. Nevertheless, it is only *as understood by* the people of God that this saving history acquires the full significance of revelation. This history had, in other words, to be understood in grace. From its consciousness of salvation, of being the people of God, Israel understood its history and interpreted it as an act made by God in respect of his people. God's saving activity was not only a divine act, but also a divine interpretation of this act, in and through the prophetic word, which threw light on the presence and meaning of God's saving activity. God did not simply say something *about* our salvation—he caused it to come about in history, the meaning of which he himself had to interpret in and through the prophetic word:

> You must understand this, that no prophecy of scripture is a matter of one's own interpretation, because no prophecy ever came by the impulse of man. (2 Pet 1:20f; see also Amos 3:8; Is 42:9.)

Revelation-in-reality and revelation-in-word are thus the pillars supporting the religion of revelation. But this is not all. It is clear from the comparative history of religion that a community which is historically founded and maintains itself in history almost of necessity realises this by means of its "book," its own "scripture."[1] This anthropological structure is introduced by God as an essential element into the revealed religion. It was by way of Israel's oral traditions, which

[1] K. Rahner, *Inspiration in the Bible,* New York, Herder, 1966. See also his article "On the Inspiration of the Bible" in *The Bible in a New Age,* London 1965, 1–15.

themselves were the expression of Israel's own awareness of its salvation and of its religious reflection about its history, sifted and tested by the prophets, that the bible came into being. In scripture the people of God became explicitly conscious of its election by God and of the way in which this came about, and in its association with scripture and its attentiveness to the prophetic word it understood and constituted itself as the people of God. God brought about the constitutive elements of his people, including holy scripture, in the same way as he brought about Israel itself. Rahner even sees in this the foundation of the inspiration of the bible.[2] The history of salvation, the word, and holy scripture together form one single continuous activity of grace, which appears to us in a historical and tangible form.

The following structure can be distinguished in this process. God's saving activity was primarily realised in the history of Israel, as a living and visible communion with God. The religious dimension of this history was expressed in the community's growing consciousness of salvation, by reflection about and understanding in grace of historical events which were apparently purely natural. This gradual growth in the community's awareness of its supernatural essence took place only in the tradition, which represented the work of God in the community in a more and more splendid perspective and made the people responsible for its own supernatural realisation. Yahweh expressed himself in this tradition as the word of God. Finally, God set his seal on this tradition in holy scripture, with the guarantee (of divine inspiration) that this expression was the true reflection of his saving decision as he wanted to see this realised in his people.[3] This structure (of

2 *Inspiration in the Bible* and "On the Inspiration of the Bible."

3 See also H. Suasso, "Heilige Schrift en Traditie in het Oude Testament," *Bijd* 15 (1954), 1–23. See also L. Cerfaux, "La parole de Dieu," *Etudes de Pastorale 5: La Bible et le prêtre,* Louvain 1951, 29–30: "The truth is that inspiration, in the technical theological sense, which

tradition, word and becoming scripture) is also the same in the case of the New Testament revelation, although this process was accomplished in a shorter space of time.

Although we should not regard the holy scriptures as the totality of the revealed Christian religion, we must concede that they form an essential, fundamental, constitutive, and irreplaceable element of it. Together with the apostolic office, living Christian preaching and the sacraments, they form part of the church's constitution, as instituted by Christ. They therefore form part of the fundamental structure of the apostolic church, of the deposit of faith which acts as a constant norm to the post-apostolic church. In this respect, the church, and consequently the church's teaching office, have to consider holy scripture as *normative*. This is not contradicted by the affirmation that the church's teaching authority is the ultimate judge of all scriptural interpretation. Because of its apostolic charisma the church is the guarantee of correct exegesis. Its teaching authority is the direct norm of *our* faith, but this authority is itself determined by the early apostolic church, and thus also by scripture, as its norm. Drawing nourishment and life from the bible and the reality of salvation, the church is the norm of our faith, our exegesis, and our theological speculation or dogmatics.

THE QUESTION PROPER TO DOGMATICS: THE CONTEMPORARY CONTEXT OF GOD'S WORD

This means that dogmatic theology is not possible without exegesis of biblical theology. It is not that the dogmatic theologian looks in the bible for references in support of his own theses. The proper relationship is precisely the other way

---

this idea assumes when we apply it to the bible, is not an entirely new intervention which has its meaning in itself. It continues and completes a movement, and the reason for its existence is to be found in the origin of this movement."

around—Christian exegesis and biblical theology have a critical task with regard to the contemporary propositions of dogmatic theology. Of course, scripture is not the only source of dogmatics, but, as the original archives of the mind of the church, it is the constant and inviolable norm for every theological activity, even though it must be read *in* and *with* the church whose scripture it is. In this respect, dogmatic theology implies Christian exegesis and biblical theology. The dogmatic theologian, then, is at the same time also an exegete and a biblical theologian.

On the other hand, however, dogmatic theology is more than biblical exegesis or theology. The content of faith is the content of God's address to man. God's word is directed through the medium of salvation history and the church's scriptural teaching authority to the whole of mankind, including men who are alive today. God's word must again and again be related to the contemporary spiritual situation of the men who listen to it here and now. This listening to the one word of God here and now—the bible itself testifies to this contemporary reception of the word—is so intimately connected with revelation that it to some extent coincides with revelation itself. Despite the newness of its formulation in comparison with a scriptural affirmation, the definition of a dogma is a reflection of the original word of revelation.

When, for example, the Council of Chalcedon expressed the saving reality which is Christ in the affirmation: "two natures, one person,"[4] the community of the faithful at that time heard the same thing in these words as the apostles had heard from the reality of Christ, but their manner of appropriating this same word of God was different. This appropriation nonetheless forms part of the dogma—it is the dogma itself. A dogma is a correct, although never exhaustive, listening to a reality or a word of revelation. The *man-*

[4] See DS 301–02 (= DR 148).

ner in which revelation and scripture are heard again and again by man, *who makes history,* is precisely what is called "tradition." Tradition is simply the constant and always contemporary listening in grace to the reality or word of revelation which found its constitutive expression in the apostolic church with its scripture. It is therefore possible to claim, along with other exegetes, that scripture has, as it were, a double context. The first is the biblical context proper, which is established by exegesis and biblical theology. The second is the context of each period of the church's history—in other words, the contemporary context. This is the context which is investigated by the dogmatic theologian and which is connected with what is known as the "development of dogma."

It is important to note that there is no question of trying to find the later dogma *as such* in holy scripture. An exegesis of this kind would in fact be "ento-egesis." But the word of God, proclaimed in scripture, was not simply addressed to the Jews and to the early apostolic church—it is addressed to men of all times. The exegete attempts to establish precisely how this word was spoken to and heard by the Jewish people and the early church. The dogmatic theologian, on the other hand, attempts to establish how this same word, heard by Israel and the apostolic church but nonetheless addressed to us as well, should be heard in a pure form by us in the twentieth century. A study of this kind must be preceded by the establishment of precisely how God spoke to Israel and the apostolic church, and how these understood and experienced his word. That is why there can be no dogmatic theology without exegesis and biblical theology. The Old Testament and apostolic listening to the word of God belongs to the constitutive phase of revelation. It is therefore *ephapax,* once-for-all—a unique, unrepeatable event, acting as a constant norm to the obedient listening of the post-apostolic church. Exegesis has consequently a position of honour in all theological speculation.

On the other hand, however, although public revelation is closed, God's address to man is still a *present* reality. His revelation in Christ is a personal giving of himself by the living God. In it, he gives himself in a personal gesture to be intimately known and experienced by us. He comes forward in this gesture to meet man, inviting him to share a living communion with himself. That is why the saving reality of revelation, as directed towards us, includes not only God's historically datable saving acts with their prophetic interpretation (the so-called "public revelation"), but also an inward address by God in and through the grace or "light" of faith, by means of which we can also personally perceive and assent to God's gracious offer of salvation with our hearts.

As de la Potterie has so painstakingly pointed out, the bible has itself expressed this in the phrase *to chrisma tou hagiou*—"the chrism (unction) of the Holy One (Holy Spirit)."[5] This *chrisma* is the word of Christ himself, the *fides ex auditu* ("faith as listened to and heard"), as called to mind by the Holy Spirit, the *locutio interna* ("inner voice"). The inward *chrisma* is intrinsically linked with the *fides ex auditu.* The church's listening to the word of God has, expressed figuratively, a horizontal and a vertical dimension. There is an inner confrontation with God who proclaims himself here and now as well as proclaiming himself an *anamnesis,* a memorial and commemoration, of that to which scripture and tradition testify concerning God's speaking to man.[6]

5 See 1 Jn 2:20, 27; and I. de la Potterie, "L'onction du chrétien par la foi," *Bbl* 40 (1959), 12–69. This article provides an outline of the scriptural basis of the Thomist doctrine of the *lumen fidei.* In my opinion, certain adjustments need to be made to de la Potterie's exegesis: see J. Ysebaert, *Greek Baptismal Terminology: Its Origins and Early Development,* Nijmegen 1962, 263ff.

6 For the *anamnesis* character of Christianity, see Nils A. Dahl, "Anamnesis: Mémoire et commemoration dans le christianisme primitif." *StTh* 1 (1948), 69–95.

In connection with the scriptural doctrine of the "unction of the Holy Spirit," the great medieval theologians, such as Aquinas, for example, imitating the fathers of the church, also refer to an "inward, divine instinct that invites us to believe."[7] An early council of the church, the Council of Orange, also mentions an inner impulse and illumination.[8] God's intervention in history, culminating in the person and the life of the God-man, is intelligible to us men in and through the public word of the divinely inspired prophets and ultimately of Christ himself. Scripture provides us with an inspired account of this, and finally the heart of every believing Christian is opened to the divine content and meaning of this revelation by the grace of faith. One of the fathers of the Council of Trent alluded to this reality of grace when he said:

> Because he was not always to remain among us physically the Son of God sent the Holy Spirit who will reveal God's secrets in the hearts of the faithful and will instruct the church *every day* until the end of time, and will settle any doubts that may arise in the minds of men.[9]

Divorced from public revelation, the inward grace of faith or the "inward speaking of God to man" would be in no way explicit, and the word of God would thus not be heard. On the other hand, however, listening to outward, public revelation without this inward light of faith could not bring about a true surrender in faith to the word of God, as in that case it would not be heard according to its divine content.

It is clear, then, that faith in the church is determined by the historical event in Israel and in the man Jesus, as proclaimed in scripture. It will also be clear that this faith is

[7] See, for example, *EJ* c. 6, lect. 5; *ST* II–II, q. 2, a. 9, ad 3.

[8] See DS 377 (= DR 180), quoted in the *Constitution on the Catholic faith* of the First Vatican Council (DS 3010 = DR 1791).

[9] *Conc. Trid.*, ed. Goerres, V, 11; see also XII, 508.

the result too of the *present* self-revelation here and now of the heavenly Christ *through* his Spirit in the church.

This also means that dogmatic theology, if it wishes to hear the pure word of God, must study first scripture and then past tradition. But, because this same word is also spoken to us, the dogmatic theologian will have to ask different questions of scripture and tradition from those asked by the exegete or the historian. Among the questions asked by the exegete and the biblical theologian are, for example: What did Israel, inspired by God, think about itself as the people of God and about Yahweh as the God of Israel? What did Christ think about himself and about man? What did the early church, confronted with the risen Christ, think about itself and about Christ? Assuming all this, the dogmatic theologian goes further. It is not that he aims to extend the results of Christian exegesis in human, philosophical ideas and build a superstructure onto what the exegete, guided by the church, has heard of this divine speaking. But, governed by the norm of what Israel and the apostolic church have heard of the word of God, the dogmatic theologian (in other words, the present-day believer who listens in holy obedience to the word of God from the vantage-point of his own, contemporary situation and meditates on it in holy reflection) has, as it were, the task of listening to the same word of God in all its inner associations in a new way and of formulating it for his own time. It is really nothing new that he does, but it is something quite different.

It is precisely this which indicates the difference in perspective between Christian exegesis and dogmatics, and at the same time establishes the connection between the results of the two studies. This is because it is precisely this listening in grace to the word of God—that is, faith—which is the guarantee of the identity that exists between scripture and dogma, between scripture and tradition, and between scripture and a theology that is subject to the norm of the church and does not aim to be a superstructure built onto the heard word of God but a reflection about it.

The difference between the point of view of Christian exegesis and that of dogmatic theology should therefore not be seen as though the exegete were *outside* the faith of the church and studied biblical texts in the manner of a specialist studying secular literature. There is of course a radical difference between the point of view of pure biblical criticism or philological and literary exegesis and that of Christian exegesis proper, although the latter does make use of the critical method. The difference, however, is that, like the dogmatic theologian, the Christian exegete listens to the word of scripture in his research as a believer and, like the dogmatic theologian, tries to understand this word with his intellect illumined by faith. In scholastic terms, it is possible to say that the *lumen quo* of Christian exegesis is the same as that of theology or of dogmatics. Both exegesis and dogmatics are critical sciences and both are also sciences of faith which employ critical thought. What is more, the object that is studied in this light is also materially the same in the case of both of these sciences of faith—it is the revealed word of God, as it is heard and accepted in the reaction of the believer.

This, however, is the formal distinction between the Christian exegesis and dogmatics. The manner in which the exegete hears and examines this revealed word of God in faith, systematises it, and synthesises it, differs from the manner in which the dogmatic theologian studies this same word of revelation in faith and attempts to synthesise it in accordance with its inner structural divisions. The Christian exegete and the biblical theologian examine God's word as it was given to and heard by the Old Testament people of God and the early apostolic church in its precise biblical context. The manner in which the exegete appeals to human reason is therefore also different from that of the dogmatic theologian. He seeks first and foremost to understand a given type of thinking about the faith, such as that of Paul, and is not concerned with speculative reasoning. The dogmatic theologian, on the other hand, examines the same word of God, but rather as it is addressed to all men at all times and as it should be heard by them here and now. We may indeed say, in the concrete, as it is addressed to *us,* the people of today.

This topical note—"as it is addressed to us, the people of today"—is not added because of a subjective feeling for contemporary needs, but in the knowledge that God does not simply address man, mankind in the abstract, but speaks to men who are making history, men in the concrete—man in biblical and in patristic times, medieval man, modern man and man today. This does not in any way place a relative value on the word of God. In faith, man in the concrete—man as he is at every period of history—is always in search of the objective content of God's revealed word. But, however absolute and unchangeable supernatural truth, like every truth, may be, it nonetheless shares, as a truth known by us in faith, in the characteristics of everything that is human—in the imperfection, the relative value, and the evolutive or historical aspect of every human possession of truth. The same meaningful datum can be approached and illuminated from various sides, with the result that different, but correct and complementary, views of the same reality are possible.

This vision of truth from different perspectives is an essential factor in all human knowledge. It can be found in scripture itself. We rightly speak of a synoptic, a Johannine, or a Pauline view of Christ, and recognise the difference between the eschatological vision of the Johannine writings and that of the Pauline epistles, and so on. Listening to scripture and tradition, deciphering the many studies made in the history of the church of the word of revelation, and devoting his attention to the proclamation of the faith by the church of today and to the various tendencies in the modern church, the dogmatic theologian is always trying to hear this same word of God in its totality and to synthesise it in accordance with its inner structural divisions—and to do this, moreover, ever more adequately, even though his work is essentially relative, in that he always leaves much for future generations to accomplish. He does all this so that God's word may speak to the present and the next generation concretely in present-day and future preaching. That is why his use of human reason and understanding is rather more an appeal to speculative reasoning, whereas that of the exegete is more an appeal to critical positive reasoning.

This term should not, however, be wrongly understood, as sometimes happens. Speculative reasoning is not an ability to "build something up" onto a datum, but an ability to grasp the data of faith as meaningful according to their inner intelligibility and their interrelationship, as, for example, Paul himself attempted to do. What was done by Paul, who had the guarantee of the charisma of inspiration and was within the constitutive phase of revelation which had, at his time, not closed, is also done by the dogmatic theologian, who works in a purely scientific and thus fallible way—he tries to penetrate more deeply into the meaning of the given realities of salvation, by tracing their mutual relationship and their saving significance for human life and by attempting to throw light on their meaning by human analogies.

It is possible to object to some of the contributions made by exegetes and biblical theologians on the score that, although they do accurately reproduce the original conviction and ideas of the biblical authors, they (perhaps unconsciously) allow this description to pass as a normative description and neglect to use the critical element essential to dogmatic theology. The biblical theologian can, of course, only make use of this critical element when he functions not only as a biblical theologian, but also as (simply) a theologian—in other words, when he does not only listen to the bible (although he will do this first and foremost), but when he also listens to the church's life and thought in the light of the bible throughout the whole history of the church. No study of the dogmatics of the angels is, for example, complete when the New Testament teaching on the angels has been accurately set out, and similarly no study of revealed mariology is complete simply by providing a full-length outline of the image of Mary in the gospels.

But, on the other hand, the objection can be raised that certain dogmatic theologians are not acting as speculative theologians if they look for biblical evidence for already established theological arguments. It is precisely because of the identity that exists, within Christian development, between the word of God as testified by scripture, and the word of God as dogmatically defined, that there must be in scripture itself an objective dynamic force which can be established only by Christian exegesis and dogmatic theology and not by the philological and literary method. This does not mean that we make Paul or John say what the church now states explicitly to be true. It means that we point out the "limits" of Pauline or Johannine thought in scripture as seen from the vantage-point of later dogmas. These limits are, as Lévie has rightly said,[10] not purely negative—they indicate an imperfect state, a beginning, a tendency or, as Auzou expressed it, they are "des réalités en marche."[11]

[10] See "L'Ecriture Sainte, parole de Dieu, parole d'homme," *NRT* 78 (1956), 561–92, 706–29; "Les limites de la preuve d'Ecriture Sainte en théologie," NRT 71 (1949), 1009–29; "Exégèse critique et interpretation théologique," RSR 39 (1951) *Mélanges Lebreton 1*), 237–52.

[11] G. Auzou, *La parole de Dieu*, Paris 1956, 92.

THE "SENSUS PLENIOR" OF SCRIPTURE

It is on this reality in depth of holy scripture that the so-called *sensus plenior*[12] of the Old Testament (i.e., its Christian significance) and the *sensus plenior* of the New Testament must be based. Although it is not identical with the later explicit content of faith, this second plenary sense is nonetheless intimately connected with the development of dogma. The light of faith brings us into direct contact with the *reality* of Christ and with the whole reality of the mystery of salvation, and not simply with a biblical account *about* these realities. The truth never exists formally in a book or in a word. It is to be found in the writing and speaking and in the listening and living spirit. Divine revelation, which is presented to us in scripture and tradition, can only be perceived by us in our hearts when God himself discloses its meaning to us in our hearts by the light of faith. If the inspirer of the dogma—that is, the Spirit of Christ in and through the church's formulation—is also the author of scripture, albeit in the mode of the human, historically conditioned word, then it is clear that the first (that is, the biblical) pronouncement of the Holy Spirit concerning a definite reality of salvation will be inwardly related to the later word

12 There is an immense bibliography relating to this subject, from which I can only select a few typical works: J. Coppens, *Les harmonies des deux Testaments,* Paris and Tournai 1949; J. Coppens, "Le problème du sens plénier," *ETL* 34 (1958), 5–20; L. Cerfaux, "Simples réflexions sur l'exégèse apostolique," *ETL* 25 (1949), 565–76; J. Gribomont, "Sens plénier, sens typique et sens littéral," *ETL* 25 (1949), 577–87; R. E. Brown, *The Sensus Plenior of Sacred Scripture,* Baltimore 1955; R. E. Brown, "The History and Development of the Theory of a Plenior Sensus," *CBQ* 15 (1963), 141–62; E. F. Sutcliffe, "The Plenary Sense as a Principle of Interpretation," *Bbl* 34 (1953), 333–43; C. Courtade, "Les Ecritures ont-elles un sens plénier?" *RSR* 37 (1950), 481–99 (the author answers this question in the negative); see J. Coppens' reaction to this, *ETL* 27 (1951), 148–50; J. Michl, "Dogmatischer Schriftbeweis und Exegese," *BZ* 2 (1958), 1–15; R. M. Grant, *The Letter and the Spirit,* London 1957; I. de la Potterie, "Le sens de la parole de Dieu," *Lumen Vitae* 10 (1955), 15–30; J. Schmid, "Die alttestamentlichen Zitate bei Paulus und die Theorie vom sensus plenior," *BZ* 3 (1959), 161–73.

concerning the same reality of salvation that the Holy Spirit causes to be expressed in the dogma.

It is because this divine word became a human book that it calls, like every other text, for the historical, philological, and literary method. (The encyclical *Divino Afflante Spiritu* insisted on this.) But it is the divinity of this word that eludes this method. This divine element can only be heard when the critical method is taken up into the light of faith that is "in sympathy with" this saving reality. The intention of the Holy Spirit who "has spoken through the prophets" transcends what the sacred writers were able, in their limitation, to express of it. But, despite their limitation, they nonetheless succeeded in expressing something, however vaguely, of what the Holy Spirit meant and of what was made clearly explicit in the later teaching. It is true that it is also the task of the Christian exegete to warn the dogmatic theologian again and again against "ento-getical" practice. The Christian exegete has above all to establish, as far as he is able, the precise quality of, for example, Paul's thought, marking off the limits of Pauline thought from what other sacred writers, later theologians, and even dogma itself have said about the same religious theme. On the other hand, however, revelation is a totality which transcends the individual synthesis of each sacred writer. Even the totality of all the sacred writers together (a totality which forms the real object of what is known as "biblical theology" as against exegesis) is transcended by the divinity of the word, which even in scripture is expressed only in a human way and therefore always has a prophetic openness, the meaning of which can only gradually be approached through the life of the history of the church.

Although it was spoken only as a human word, the divinity of this word forms the basis of the *sensus plenior* of the scriptural *sensus literalis,* or rather, it is identical with it. This explains why it is necessary in every case to see the *sensus plenior* as a direct extension of the *sensus literalis* of the philological and literary exegetical method. If there is any division between these two *sensus,* then what we have is no longer a *sensus plenior,* but possibly a typological *sensus* (in the broadest meaning) or even a *sensus accommodatius,* an adaptation of a biblical word. This is a necessary consequence of the very structure of this word, which is divine, but presented to us in the mode of a human word. Just as Christ is God even in his humanity, and is consequently God in a human manner, so too is the word of scripture theandric, and the human meaning of scripture which can be recognised by the exegete is human precisely in its divinity.

This human word contains something extra, an objective dynamism. We can only with great difficulty become aware of the meaning of this in the church. It is only through the light of faith that we have any spiritual affinity with the divinity of this word. On the basis of this living contact with the reality itself of faith and not simply with the biblical word about this saving reality, we can, for example, read a deeper meaning, which is probably not exegetical in the Christian sense, into Mary's presence at the crucifixion and in the cenacle. It is in this way possible to find evidence in the scriptural texts that, although the writers of the New Testament were themselves ignorant of the later dogmas in the explicit form given to them by the church, there is a certain objective dynamism in their writings that points in an obscure manner to what later on was heard clearly and explicitly by the church as the word of God.

To keep to the same example, when we see in holy scripture how clearly Mary is viewed as a figure of the church in the Book of Revelation and in the fourth gospel, to such an extent that even what is primarily intended—namely, "Lady Church"—merges into one single image with "Lady Mary"; when we go on to establish that even in the gospel of the infancy the Old Testament themes of the indwelling of God in the people of God, in the church of the Old Testament, form the prism through which the reality of "Mary, the mother of Jesus" was seen, then it becomes clear to the Christian exegete and the dogmatic theologian that the distance between the church's dogmas on Mary and the gospel image of her is certainly not so great as had hitherto been believed. The very fact alone that the central idea of God's eschatological indwelling in the "daughter of Zion" and in the holy city of Jerusalem was taken over by the New Testament and applied to Mary, often in a confused and allusory way, makes these scriptural affirmations, which at first sight seem very simple, point to deeper meanings that only became clearly conscious in the mind of the church with the passage of time.

It should also be clear from the same example that this objective dynamism of the scriptural sense—the so-called *sensus plenior*—is really a scriptural sense and not a *sensus consequens,* or conclusion drawn from scriptural meanings. The fact that certain characteristics of the "daughter of Zion" were taken over and applied to Mary and that others were not—that the church was, in other words, selective—shows that the church was determined in this very selective process by the objective dynamism really present in scripture as the expression of the divinity of the scriptural human word. The dogmas of the church are formally not theological conclusions drawn from New Testament data—they are not a *sensus consequens* (which *as such* cannot be called a sense of scripture). They have rather an intimate connection with the *sensus plenior* of scripture—they are explicitations of something that was already vaguely present in the apostolic consciousness (of which scripture is the written expression).

Within the church's life of faith and protected by her teaching authority, theological thought has an irreplaceable function to fulfil in connection with this explicitation. This gives rise to the impression that the church's dogmas should belong to the *sensus consequens.* This, however, is the result of a misunderstanding of the psychological structure of human reasoning. Psychologically speaking, discursive thought is simply the totality of experiential knowledge, in other words, constantly growing experience, but as controlled by the total object which is also implicitly present in the consciousness from the very beginning. In explicit reasoning, the original datum is seen in the light of the implications discovered by experiential knowledge and by reflection. These implications then emerge as conclusions, but they were nonetheless present in the consciousness from the very beginning, although unobserved. This also applies to the knowledge of faith, although this is a knowledge through being addressed. If this were not so, then the fact that the so-called "new truth," that is, the dogma, has really been formally revealed by God and is therefore to be accepted on his authority would not be recognised. A *locutio attestans,* a divine testimony, is of its very nature also a call to man to react actively, to listen to the definite content of what God communicates to him, a summons to obedience in faith. What was formally revealed must already have been heard, in one way or another, in apostolic times. The appeal that is present as such in the divine testimony can never be an invitation to draw conclusions. It is rather an *invitatio ad credendum,* a call to faith.[13]

It necessarily follows from the closing of the deposit of faith that the true developments of faith, the later dogmas, must from the beginning have been present in God's speaking testimony which invites us to believe. The Christian *kerygma* was after all not only addressed to men in apostolic times. It is also addressed to men of all times, and in such

[13] See E. Dhanis, "Révélation explicite et implicite," *Greg.* 34 (1953), 187–237; see also Part I, Chapter 4: "The Development of the Apostolic Faith into the Dogma of the Church," on pp. 57–83 above.

a way that this originally heard *kerygma* has to be translated again and again into statements that will relate what is heard to the constantly changing spiritual situation of man. In view of this, it is a priori to be expected that revelation will testify to certain aspects formally, but only by means of suggestions, with the result that the church will only become aware of these as formally attested by God when a new problem arises.

An inadequate example drawn from the secular sphere may help to make this clear. In an examination, if the teacher wants to lead the student to the answer that the student simply cannot find, he suggests the answer without directly communicating it, although he formally intends to communicate what he has suggested. What is explicitly communicated—in which the real intention of the teacher is only suggested—is the means by which the student may remember the truths intended. The case is quite different when the student establishes, by his own reasoning from a truth formally intended by the teacher, a different truth—one that was not in any way intended by the teacher, but that is consistently related to the truth intended by him. There is an element of discursive thought in both cases, but they are quite different from each other.

Something similar occurs in the case of revelation. Theological reasoning may well play a part in it and may even be necessary, but only reaction in faith of the whole community to this truth disclosed by conclusion can determine whether it was really revealed by God, and ultimately only the teaching authority of the church is competent infallibly to guarantee the authenticity of this reaction on the part of the believing community. In this way, later dogmas, occasioned by many different causes which direct and stimulate, perhaps over the course of centuries, the attention of the reaction in faith of the community, really come from the deposit of faith to which scripture testifies.[14] When God let the sacred writers see Mary, for example, via the unheard-of characteristics of the ideal "daughter of Zion" (an ideal that was never fulfilled in Israel), then he formally *suggested* the later Marian dogmas in these essential characteristics, of which the apostolic church was aware, and thus revealed them *formally* and not simply virtually.

The same principle that the word of scripture is divine in the mode of the human, historically-conditioned word enables us also to throw light on the *sensus plenior* of Old Testament texts. These texts have no immediate "Christian" meaning. Their strict meaning is for the Jewish people itself. When, however, we situate these texts within the whole context of the plan of salvation that was fulfilled in Christ, and consequently realise that the first word of the Old Testament acquires its full and definitive meaning from what was accomplished in Christ and what the New Testament had to tell us about this, then it becomes evident that the Old Testament *sensus literalis* is at the same time borne up by an "objective dynamism" which points, via the strictly Jewish meaning, to the Christ who was to come. Christ himself said:

[14] It therefore seems to me to be theologically impossible to support the opinion of those who, faced with the imminent definition of the dogma of the Immaculate Conception, asserted that there was no need for this dogma to be either explicitly or implicitly present in scripture, and even that there was no need for it to be present in any way in tradition. In connection with these tendencies, see V. Sardi, "Breve esposizione degli Atti della commissione speziale," *La solenne definizione del dogma dell'Immacolata Concepimento di Maria Santissima: Atti e Documenti,* Rome 1904–5, part 1, 792. This proposition is indisputably true in that we are apologetically in no way able to point to the dogmas of the church through tradition, from scripture down to the present time. This is quite impossible. But it is certainly necessary to be able to demonstrate in one way or another, because no new revelations are made to the church, that the later dogmas come from the closed *depositum fidei* and are not added to it. The explicit continuity cannot be demonstrated, but there is more in human psychology than simple "explicit knowledge."

Everything written about me in the law of Moses and the prophets and the pslams must be fulfilled. [Lk 24:44.]

Scripture refers to an "opening of the mind" to understand the writings of the Old Testament (Lk 24:45). What was written in the Old Testament is, without prejudice to its independent, strictly Old Testament meaning, ultimately written for us Christians, as the first letter of Peter says (1 Pet 1:10–12). We, Christians, with unveiled face behold in the Old Testament the glory of the Lord (2 Cor 3:14ff.).

It is true, throughout the history of the church, Christians have looked far less for the *sensus plenior* than, with a patristic and medieval exuberance worthy of a Claudel, for typological meanings in all kinds of Old Testament events. But the fact of abuse does not prevent proper use, and scripture has continued to be a living book for all believers. After the exile, it was read and re-read in the light of new events of constantly growing expectations of the Messiah, so that, for example, psalms that were probably written at an earlier period became more messianically explicit by being used as prayers and hymns in the synagogue. The Septuagint translation frequently bears witness to a deeper understanding and interpretation of scripture because of the developed consciousness of faith of Judaism and is therefore a help in tracing the *sensus plenior*—to such an extent that voices have been raised in recent years in defence of the inspired character of this translation. At a later stage, the same scripture was read by the primitive apostolic church in the light of Christ's incarnation and resurrection from the dead. Finally, we too read the same scripture in the light of the history of salvation of the church which is guided by the same Spirit.

There is of course no point in seeking, with medieval artlessness, to find every truth, because it is borne up by the Spirit who is also the Spirit of scripture, in holy scripture: "omne verum dictum est sensus Sacrae Scripturae" ("every true statement is of the sense of holy scripture").[15] It is only when the christological (or mariological) meaning is a direct extension of the real literal sense of scripture, of a kind that can be established by exegesis, that we may speak of a *sensus plenior* or of a christological (or mariological) meaning of an Old Testament text.

BIBLICAL THEOLOGY: THE POINT OF DEPARTURE FOR DOGMATIC THEOLOGY

It will be clear from the foregoing that it is a constant duty for the dogmatic theologian, as it was for the apostolic church, to re-read scripture retrospectively, assuming the results of Christian exegesis. As Aquinas correctly observed, "Even the true prophets did not perceive everything that the Holy Spirit intended in their visions, words, and actions."[16] The divinity of this inspired human word can only be made fully and explicitly conscious in and through the life of the church under the guidance and protection of the church's teaching authority that acts as the instrument of the Holy Spirit who spoke through the prophets.

According to the New Testament, and especially the gospels of John and Luke, the Holy Spirit was sent partly in order to give the church a Christian understanding of scripture. The Acts testify to this deeper insight in the case of Peter, Stephen, Philip, and Paul after Pentecost, when they "spoke," full of the Holy Spirit (Acts 4:8; see also Acts 6:5; 7:55; etc.). For the dogmatic theologian, scripture is not just one of the many documents that he has to study. It has for

[15] See C. Spicq, *Esquisse d'une histoire de l'exégèse au Moyen-Age,* Paris 1944; H. de Lubac, *Exégèse médiévale: Les quatre sens de l'Ecriture,* Paris 1959 (parts 1 and 2) and 1961 (part 3).

[16] *ST* II–II, q. 173, a. 4.

him as well a unique, primary and irreducible meaning. It is true that Christians receive the word of God from the church, but in so doing they receive the word of God to which scripture testifies. Biblical and dogmatic theology cannot be set against each other, even though each has a different way of viewing things directly. The church, tradition, subject to the guidance of the Spirit, can only suggest to us what Christ himself has said and done and what he was when he was still on earth. And this is an event to which the apostolic *kerygma,* as this comes directly to us in holy scripture, bears immediate witness. Just as the post-apostolic church is built on the authority of the apostles, the sacraments, and the proclamation of the faith, so too is it built on holy scripture, which stands on the altar next to the chalice in the form of a missal.

At one time, anti-Protestant tendencies in the church made it seem as though the vital significance of the Christian reading of scripture was pernicious. That time is, however, past, and as a consequence of this dogmatic theology has in recent years acquired a fresher and more authentic character. Because it is a testimony about the origin of the reality which we call in theology "tradition," scripture is really the *caput divinae traditionis* ("source of divine tradition"). The church does not derive its dogmas from theological conclusions drawn from scripture, but it recognises its own living dogma in scripture. Congar was therefore right when he said:

> I respect and I never cease to study the science of the exegetes, but I challenge their supreme authority.[17]

Christian exegesis does not have the last word to say on the subject of revelation. Although this comes to us through

[17] Y. Congar, *Vraie et fausse réforme dans l'Eglise,* Paris 1950, 498–9.

the medium of the history of salvation of the Old and the New Testaments and the inspired testimony about this, it is after all directed to all men at all times. What believing humanity, guided by the Spirit working in the church, personally makes its own of this revelation can differ, at the explicit level, from what holy scripture has explicitly made its own. But the scriptural expressions continue to be expressions of the same faith that the church now confesses. There is therefore, at the explicit level, an acquisition, in the course of the history of the church, in comparison with scripture, viewed in its explicit character. In this acquisition and progresss, dogmatic theology plays a subordinate part which cannot and may not be left exclusively to Christian exegesis and biblical theology.

On the other hand, however, the exegete has, as I have already said, a critical function with regard to dogmatic theology, because it is he who studies the origin and beginning guaranteed by God and the tendency first set in motion by God which, because of its original direction, is bound always to have an authoritative critical function with regard to the further course of the movement. In this sense, we may with Rahner call scripture the "*hegemonikon*" (i.e., critical ruling principle) of dogmatic theology.[18]

Let me conclude by saying, in the light of this brief argument, that dogmatic theologians frequently draw both too much and too little from scripture, for the simple reason that they only consult it in order to find evidence for really or supposedly established theological theses. They ought instead, proceeding from the starting-point of faith, to follow and to experience themselves at close quarters the movement from the Old to the New Testament. They ought also to follow personally the searching tendency of the early apostolic church which approached the Christian mystery of

[18] K. Rahner, "Biblische Theologie," *Lexikon für Theologie und Kirche*, part 2, Freiburg 1958[2], cols. 449–51.

salvation from the Old Testament themes in the light of the incarnation, and at the same time let itself be absorbed in this tendency of *fides quaerens intellectum,* of faith searching for understanding, for which the New Testament itself so clearly provides us with the example.

7 The Place of the Church Fathers in Theology

Already by the time of the rabbinical writings there was constant reference to the "tradition of the fathers." This meant that the law, interpreted and expounded by different generations of teachers, was handed down to the living generation. The idea of the "elders" was echoed in the word "fathers." In the ancient world, a teacher was usually called "father" and his pupil or disciple "son."[1] The Christian teachers were also automatically called "fathers" in the patristic period. To begin with, this title had no special meaning. In the fourth century, however, this typically Christian concept of "father" developed until it had a clearly defined meaning, and this growth went together with the development of the idea of the "tradition of the church."

It was in this century that a very clear distinction was made between scripture or the apostolic *kerygma* and the "tradition of the fathers." In its content, tradition is the same as the apostolic teaching. This was called "tradition" insofar as it had not come directly to the generation living at the time in holy scripture, but had been passed on "from hand to hand" by previous generations—with their own elucidations but nonetheless with the original inheritance faithfully preserved—to the subsequent generations. Thus the *traditio*

[1] See, for example, 1 Cor 4:5; 1 Pet 5:13; and Irenaeus, *Adv. Haer.* IV, 41, 2.

patrum was the "tradition of the older generations." The teaching of the church was, however, vested in the college of bishops. Tradition was therefore even earlier—for Irenaeus, for example—the apostolic *kerygma* itself, insofar as this was preserved and passed on (in a mature, but at the same time in an essentially unchanged, form) to the living generation of men via the links in the chain of succcessive bishops.

The technical term *church father* appeared for the first time in the fourth century as a result of this view. Christians were by this time already removed by a distance of several centuries from the immediate witness of the apostles. From the time of Athanasius onwards, it was therefore becoming less common to refer directly to scripture and more common to refer directly to the "authority of the fathers." There was a firm conviction of the responsibility of the episcopate in each generation for the "received doctrine" which, after having been clarified in the light of contemporary problems, was handed down to the next generation. The fathers, that is, the teaching bishops of previous generations, formed the link between the apostolic faith and the later generations.

This was, then, the patristic idea of "father of the church." The "fathers" were in this case quite concretely defined. As far as the local churches were concerned, they were the founders of those churches.[2] As far as each individual Christian was concerned, the father was the "baptising bishop" by whom he was initiated into the mysteries of salvation.[3] Thus two streams of faith came about—"inspired scripture" and the "tradition of the fathers."[4] Together with scripture, the fathers formed the norm of faith.[5] The legitimacy and truth of a proposed new doctrine was tested against its con-

2 Basil, *Epist.* 210, 3 (*PG* 32, 772).

3 Basil, *Epist.* 204, 2 (*PG* 32, 746).

4 *Epist.* 5, 3 (ed. Pasquali, p. 90).

5 Cyril, *De recta fide ad reg.* 2 (*PG* 76, 1204); *Epist.* 39 (*PG* 77, 177).

formity with the doctrine of the earlier fathers. The very fact that these fathers held a different opinion was sufficient (at least at the time of Athanasius) for the proposed new doctrine to be condemned.[6] The authority of the fathers was decisive.[7]

The bishops of the local churches who enabled Christians to live from the apostolic faith by their teaching, especially in connection with the Christian initiation, but also on other occasions, were therefore regarded in the fourth century as fathers of the church whose teaching was, with scripture, normative for the Christian faith. The normative principle that already held good in the fourth century and was a guiding thought in the great councils of the fifth century (the idea that what was "patristic" was apostolic) shows that in those days the concept *father of the church* was really an ancient formulation of what we now call the "living tradition of the church," at least insofar as this is formally vested in the college of bishops. This explains why one of the essential elements in the modern concept *father of the church* is "approval by the church."

Nonetheless, the idea of "father of the church" was enlarged even in the patristic period, especially in the west (Augustine, Jerome, Vincent of Lérins), to include all ecclesiastical writers, even if they were not bishops. All Christian writers therefore came to be regarded as fathers of the church insofar as they were representative of the church's tradition of faith.

In his *Commonitorium* (Chapter 41), Vincent of Lérins formulated this in the following way:

> Whenever a new question arises to which no answer has yet been given, reference must be made to the views of the holy fathers, to

[6] Athanasius, *Contra Apoll.* I, 20 (*PG* 26, 1128); *Ad Serap.* I, 28 (*PG* 26, 593–4); *Contra Arian.* I, 8 (*PG* 26, 28); I, 3 (*PG* 26, 17).

[7] See also Basil, *Hom. c. Sab.* 4, 5 (*PG* 31, 609, 642); *De Spiritu Sancto* x, 25 (*PG* 32, 112).

those who, each in his own time and place and in the unity of faith and the community, were tried and tested teachers [*magistri probabiles*]. And everything that they have held, one in spirit and in consent, must without any doubt or scruple be regarded as the true and Catholic teaching of the church.

As time passes, the links between the early apostolic *kerygma* and the living generations in the church become more numerous. The concept *father of the church* is thus bound to include more generations than those of the time before the fourth century. In itself, then, the "fatherhood" of the church could be as long in duration as the apostolic succession, which originally meant more or less the same as the concept *church father*. In later centuries, however, a limit was set to the extent in time of the idea of father of the church, and the name *church father* was reserved for those who were closest in time to the apostolic church. *Antiquitas*, or the fact that they were active in the period of *Christian* antiquity, thus became one of the essential characteristics of the church fathers.

The patristic period was regarded, more or less correctly, to have ended with John Damascene (749) in the east and with Isidore of Seville (636) in the west. Aquinas called these fathers the *sancti;* their works had an "authentic" value, whereas the later *theologians* were only called *magistri,* and their works had no decisive authority (*robur auctoritatis*).[8] This change is, in my opinion, partly connected with the historical fact that theology came, with the passage of time, to be less and less directly the concern of the bishops themselves, because of their increasing administrative activities. This gave rise to the so-called "theological argument," dissociated from the teaching function of the hierarchical church, and this argument ipso facto acquired a value which was different from the *patristic* "theological arguments." It was perhaps

8 See M. D. Chenu. "Authentica et magistralia," *DTP* 38 (1925) 3–51.

this change which determined the somewhat arbitrary limit set to the period of the church fathers.

In the technical language of the church, then, the word *church father* acquired a classic, clearly defined, and permanent meaning, which may be recognised by four essential characteristics.

1. *Christian antiquity*. The fathers of the church are representatives of Christian antiquity—they formed the first link between the apostolic period and later periods, and they are for this reason accorded a position of special privilege. This qualification might in itself seem arbitrary, like the limits that mark off the patristic period, but a very profound idea is in fact contained in it. The fathers were the first Christian writers to attempt, after the closing of revelation, to solve the problems brought about by the confrontation between the apostolic *kerygma* and the post-apostolic age by means of theological reflection. They were, in other words, the initiators of the church's theology, of conscious thought about faith within the church—it was they who laid the foundations of the theological "faith-in-search-of-understanding" for later generations of Christians. They have a special value, then, in that they laid the foundations of theology. As bishops teaching within the church, they cannot be regarded as in any way superior, for example, to the church's hierarchy today.

2. *Orthodoxy in doctrine*. To say that they were orthodox does not mean that individual fathers did not commit error in doctrine. The orthodoxy of the patristic doctrine should rather be seen in their collective testimony of the church's doctrine—the *consensus patrum*. Aquinas called their testimony "arguments from the proper sources of theology, but with only probable evidence."[9] The value which is ascribed

[9] *ST* 1, q. 1, a. 8, ad 2: "argumenta ex propriis sed probabiliter."

to them is theirs not as private theologians, but as active witnesses of the living tradition of the church. This brings us to a third characteristic of the fathers.

3. *Explicit or implicit ecclesiastical approval.* "The authority of the teaching of the Catholic teachers is derived from the church. We are therefore bound to place more trust in the church's authority than in that of Augustine, Jerome, or any teacher."[10] The church fathers drew their doctrine from the church and were witnesses of the apostolic *kerygma* only as representatives of this living tradition. This inner communion with the church is implied in their works, but it is only the church's teaching authority that can give official recognition to this. In fact, this official recognition was also accorded to many individual church fathers by the church's appointment of some of them as doctors of the church (*doctores ecclesiae*). The terms *father of the church* and *doctor of the church* thus coincide only partially. Not all the fathers have been made doctors of the church, and there are also medieval and modern doctors who could be called "fathers of the church" were it not for the fact that they lack the attribute of "Christian antiquity." But this characteristic is in fact one of the essential attributes of the concept *father of the church.* The patristic doctors of the church are the leading figures among the fathers. The church's universal and implicit regard for the fathers was only given concrete *expression* by the church's raising them to the rank of doctors of the church.

Basil the Great, Gregory Nazianzen, and John Chrysostom have been the eastern doctors of the church from the very earliest times, and later Athanasius was also accorded this distinction especially by the western church. Since the eighth century Ambrose, Jerome, Augustine, and Gregory the Great have been regarded as the four great patristic doc-

[10] *ST* II–II, q. 10, a. 12.

tors of the western church, and later other fathers have been created doctors of the church. The only factual difference between the fathers of the church and the patristic doctors of the church is that some of the fathers are regarded, because of the clearly universal orthodoxy and the influence of their doctrine in the church, by an "explicit declaration of the church" (by the pope or the Congregation of Rites) as authentic teachers of the church's life of faith.

4. *Holiness of life.* Only those patristic writers who have from the earliest times been venerated as saints (even if they have not been "canonised") are regarded as fathers of the church. This is less a question of their personal holiness than of the holiness of their testimony.

Like the church fathers themselves, these characteristics must be seen as a whole. It is not a question of eminent individual figures, but of a single great community, scattered in time, but equally inspired, of greater and lesser personalities, whose voices echo each other so that the whole sounds like one great choir singing in unison. This ensemble alone guarantees the Catholic and apostolic nature of their teaching.

For all these reasons, modern theological speculation, in addition to making a fundamental study of scripture, cannot neglect the compelling need to study patristics, as this will always have an authoritative critical function with regard to the solutions that the theologian attempts to provide to contemporary problems.

8 The Creed and Theology

In the ancient world, it was the custom to break some object, such as a coin, in half for the purpose of identifying, for example, two partners. Each of the partners would then keep one piece (*tessera*). When these two pieces were placed together (*symballein;* hence *symbolon*) at a later date, the partnership could be recognised or proved by this. Thus *symbolum* came to mean a sign of recognition and distinction, and at the same time a sign of unity. In this way, the formulated confession of *Christian* faith came, in the *latinitas africa* (that is, the north-African part of the Latin-speaking world), to be called *symbolum*—a *symbolum* of faith, in other words, a sign of recognition for the members of the same community of faith, and at the same time a sign distinguishing Christians from those who did not profess the true faith. This background meaning of the name *symbolum* of faith has been lost today. The *symbolum* is more or less the charter of the Catholic confession of faith—a charter that, although it has been accepted almost literally by the non-Catholic confessions, has nonetheless been given a different content and meaning by the Reformation.

In these official and ecclesiastical *symbola,* creeds, or confessions of faith, two groups can above all be distinguished—the *symbolum apostolicum,* or Apostles' Creed, and the more elaborate conciliar *symbola.*

HISTORICAL SURVEY

The Apostles' Creed

From the fourth century[1] until the fifteenth and even the sixteenth century, the view was generally held in the Latin church that the twelve articles of faith had been drawn up personally by the apostles themselves, and called "apostolic" for that reason. In the course of time, the name of each of the apostles was even attached to one of the twelve articles.[2] It was the eastern church that gave the first impetus to reflection about this. Mark of Ephesus observed at the Council of Ferrara and Florence that the eastern church had no idea of any possible apostles' creed.[3] The humanists, and especially Erasmus, stated the problem of the origin of the *symbolum apostolicum* more precisely, although it was only in the last century that really serious research was undertaken into the subject, and that this research grew into a separate scientific study.

In the meantime, the first and altogether too vociferous result of this research, which denied that this *symbolum* had any connection at all with the apostolic age, has already been superseded. It was possible to go back as far as the third century or thereabouts. Before that, everything was in obscurity, but it was realised that the Apostles' Creed, although it was of a much later date than the apostolic period itself, nonetheless went back to stereotyped confessions of faith which can be found scattered about in scripture. In its content and form, the *symbolum apostolicum* is certainly apostolic, since it is an expression of the apostolic tradition of faith, a great deal of the prehistory of which can be traced until we end up with the known formulae of faith of holy scripture.

1 See, for example, Ambrose, *Ep.* 42, 5 (*PL* 16, 1125).

2 An echo of this tradition can be heard in Aquinas, *In 3 Sent.* d. 25, q. 1, a. 2; in *ST*, however, he is silent about this legend.

3 Harduinus, *Conciliorum collectio* IX, 842–3.

1. If we read the Acts of the Apostles listening to the echoes of Peter's[4] and Paul's[5] sermons—echoes which may be regarded as classical patterns for missionary preaching in the apostolic age—we are bound to observe how stereotyped formulae of faith recur again and again in these sermons, concerning the death, resurrection, and ascension of Christ. We are also certain to be struck by the way in which this central saving fact of Easter is surrounded by similarly stereotyped proclamations of the mysteries that prepared for and were subsequent to the paschal fact. At his baptism, Christ was proclaimed as the Messiah.[6] His public life in signs and miracles,[7] his appearance after the resurrection,[8] and the descent of the Holy Spirit[9] were also proclaimed. The whole of the redemptive mystery of Christ, expressed always in more or less stereotyped terms which are reminiscent of the later twelve articles of the creed, can be found scattered about in Acts. It is possible to sense the apostolic kerygma and early Christian catechetics in these affirmations of Christ's human, Davidic, messianic descent,[10] his suffering[11] as one rejected,[12] his resurrection,[13] his sitting on the right hand of God,[14] the resurrection as the beginning of the messianic age of the *Pneuma* (Spirit),[15] and thus of salvation,[16] with the prospect of the Lord's second coming.[17] All this requires on our part repentance and baptism.[18] This unmistakably brings us face to face with the constant bases of the apostolic preaching and confession of faith.

The epistles corroborate this. Similar formulae are to be found throughout them, and these are frequently introduced

4 Acts 2:14–39; 3:12–26; 4:9–12; 10:34–43.

5 Acts 13:16–41.

6 Acts 10:37–8; 13:23–5.

7 Acts 2:22; 10:38–9.

8 Acts 2:32; 3:15; 5:32; 10:39–42; 13:41.

9 Acts 2:23; 5:32.

10 Acts 2:30; 13:33–4.

11 Acts 3:18.

12 Acts 4:11.

13 Acts 2:25–31; 13:34–7.

14 Acts 2:34–5.

15 Acts 2:17–21.

16 Acts 2:39; 4:12.

17 Acts 3:20–1.

18 Acts 2:38.

by a reference to tradition, *paradosis*—"we have received it in this way and we pass it on to you in this way."[19] What is involved is a *regula fidei,* a standard or norm of faith,[20] a *depositum,* a venerable inheritance that must be faithfully guarded,[21] a confession of faith.[22] The principal formulae of the later *symbolum,* such as "who died for us,"[23] "who died and rose again,"[24] "who is at the right hand of God,"[25] and "the Lord of the dead and of the living,"[26] are also already to be found here, scattered about in the epistles.

In addition to these already constant kerygmatic formulae, the New Testament also contains confessions of faith of a more official character, as used in preparation for baptism or in liturgical gatherings. The necessary confession of Christ as preparation for baptism especially[27] was given a fairly constant form.[28] Furthermore, standard confessions of faith are to be found in the case of exorcisms, miraculous cures and so on. Characteristic, too, is the confession of faith in times of persecution,[29] and generally in liturgical gatherings.[30]

The standard New Testament confessions of faith are without doubt mainly christological. There are, however, also bipartite confessions in which the Father is mentioned together with the Son, Jesus Christ.[31] It is possible that these bipartite confessions of faith arose because of the preaching of the gospel to the non-Jews, who had to be instructed in

19 See 1 Cor 15:1ff.

20 Rom 6:17

21 Tim 6:20; 2 Tim 1:14.

22 Heb 4:14.

23 1 Thess 5:10; Gal 1:4; 2:20; 2 Cor 5:14; Rom 4:25; etc.

24 1 Thess 4:14; Rom 4:25; 8:34; 14:9; etc.

25 Rom 8:34; Eph 1:20; Heb 1:3–13; 8:1; 10:12; 12:2; 1 Pet 3:22.

26 Rom 14:9.

27 See Acts 22:16; 8:37.

28 Acts 2:38; 8:16; 10:48; 19:5; 1 Cor 1:13–15; Mt 19.

29 1 Cor 12:3; Rom 10:9.

30 1 Cor 16:22; Col 3:6; Phil 2:6–11; 4:5; 4:20; 1 Tim 3:16; 1:17; Rom 11:36; 16:27.

31 1 Cor 8:6; 2 Cor 1:3; 11:31; Eph 1:3; Acts 4:24–30; Col 3:16–17; 1 Tim 6:13; 2:5; 2 Tim 4:1; 1 Thess 3:11; 2 Thess 2:16; 1 Pet 4:11; Rev 1:2.

monotheism as well as in the mystery of Christ. The New Testament also contains several trinitarian, or at least tripartite, confessions of faith.[32] The addition of the Spirit to the confession of the Father and the Son would seem to have been directly due to the liturgy of baptism. For the purpose of stressing the connection between the event of Easter and the descent of the Holy Spirit (a confession of faith characteristic of the New Testament), an appeal was perhaps made (by Paul ?) to the experience of baptism. It is, in any case, especially in connection with baptism that the tripartite confessions occur in the writings of Paul.[33] We can therefore say that in addition to standard christological confessions of faith there are also trinitarian formulae in holy scripture.

2. As a result of these christological and trinitarian confessions of faith in the bible, two separate, established formulae must gradually have become current—a christological and a trinitarian formula. These two formulae, which arose separately from a different original setting in life, grew in the long run together, again in the baptismal liturgy. It is not absolutely clear exactly when this fusion of the two confessions of faith took place. The first traces of it can be found in the second and third centuries, and there is every indication that the fusion was taking place at this time. The fluctuations in this merging process would seem to suggest this. The two schemes of the *symbola* can be found in Justin—these are sometimes separate[34] and sometimes sketchily joined together.[35] In Irenaeus, the fusion is complete, the christological *symbolum* being included at the

32 Mt 28:19; 2 Cor 13:14; Acts 5:29–32; to which may be added Gal 4:4–6; 1 Cor 6:11; 12:4–6; Eph 1:3–14; 2:18; 1 Pet 1:2–12.

33 1 Cor 6:11; Eph 4:4–6; and especially Tit 3:4–6.

34 *Apol.* 1, 13 (*PG* 6, 345, 348); 1, 61 (*PG* 6, 420, 422).

35 *Apol.* 1, 61 (*PG* 6, 420, 422); 1, 21, 31 (*PG* 6, 360, 376–8).

third confession, that of the Holy Spirit.[36] In Hippolytus' *Traditio apostolica*[37] and in Tertullian[38] we have the first evidence of the definitive fusion, the christological *symbolum* being inserted at the second member of the trinitarian *symbolum*. This merged *symbolum* of faith was in question-and-answer form, as it was also a *symbolum* of baptism. The real form of confession (the "creed") is to be found rather later, in Rufinus for example.[39] This is called the "Roman form"[40] of the apostolic *symbolum*. Since the *Traditio* of Hippolytus is a version of the Roman baptismal liturgy round about the year 215, it is in this *symbolum* of baptism that the oldest preliminary form of the present-day Apostles' Creed is to be found. The scheme itself must be even older, to judge from the allusions to be found in Tertullian, Irenaeus, Justin, and even in Ignatius of Antioch—that is to say, in the first years of the second century. An even older *symbolum* has been found in papyrus from Dêr-Balyzeh in Upper Egypt. This has the same structure in a simpler form as the baptismal *symbolum* of the *Traditio Hyppoliti:*

> I believe in God the almighty father
> and in his only son, our Lord Jesus Christ
> and in the holy spirit
> and in the resurrection of the flesh
> in the holy Catholic church.[41]

We may therefore conclude that the basic form of our Apostles' Creed came about towards the end of the second century, and probably in Rome.

36 *Adv. Haer.* 1, 10, 1 (*PG* 7, 549).

37 Ed. B. Botte, *Sources chrétiennes* 11, Paris 1946, 50–1.

38 See E. Schillebeeckx, *De sacramentele heilseconomie* 1, Antwerp 1952, 240–1.

39 *Expositio in symbolum* (*PL* 21, 335).

40 The *forma Romana*, or R-version, also called the "forma occidentalis antiquior" ("older western form"), is included in DS 12 (= DR 2a).

41 DS 2 (= DR 1b).

3. The present-day text of the *symbolum* of faith that has become classic throughout the whole of the west and that is used in the catechism, at baptism, and at the ordination of priests, can be found for the first time in an *Ordo Romanus* of 950. This formulation is known as the *textus receptus* (i.e., the received text).[42] It does not come from the Roman liturgy, but in all probability from south Gaul. With a few variants, it can be found towards the end of the fourth and in the fifth century. It is substantially present in a *Gelasianum* of the seventh century. It was not until the Carlovingian reform that this text was accepted in Rome. A form occupying an intermediate position between the R and the T versions is the Roman *symbolum* (in Greek), which occurs in a letter written in 340 by Marcellus of Ancyra to Pope Julius.[43]

4. We are less well informed about the *symbola* in the east. In broad outline, they have been constructed in much the same way, but they are more exuberant in form and have more details and more mutual variations. Among the fourth-century baptismal *symbola* that are known to us are those from Caesarea in Palestine,[44] from Jerusalem,[45] from Antioch,[46] and so on.

Conclusion. Although the classic *symbolum* of faith was not formulated by the apostles themselves, it may nonetheless correctly be called "apostolic." It is really a *regula* of the apostolic faith, and faithfully reflects the main themes of the apostolic *kerygma,* the apostolic catechesis of candi-

42 The T-version, or "forma occidentalis recentior" ("later western form"), is included in DS 30 (= DR 6).

43 *PG* 42, 385 and DS 11 (not included in DR). The text is, however, the basis of the rather later *textus receptus* and of all the western *symbola,* and came about in Rome itself.

44 DS 40 (not included in DR).

45 DS 41 (= DR 9).

46 DS 50 (not included in DR).

dates for baptism, and the primitive Christian confession of faith.

The "Twelve Articles of Faith" (the T-version) as such have never been officially and solemnly declared dogma by the extraordinary teaching authority of the church. They have, however, always been regarded as a norm of faith, and are held up *as a norm of faith* by the ordinary and universal teaching authority of the church. The Apostles' Creed is really a dogmatic *symbolum* of faith. It is, after all, essentially a *symbolum* of baptism. And here the *lex orandi lex credendi* is fully valid, here the norm of the church's prayer really is the norm of its faith, for the Catholic creed is firmly rooted in the church's religious life, and especially in its liturgy.

Although the *symbolum* of faith was a baptismal *symbolum* that had to be confessed by the neophyte, initially on baptism itself and at a later stage as a preparation for baptism, it should not be regarded as the quintessential summary of the whole of Christian dogma. It includes only those main truths, a confession of which was required of catechumens. If this in borne in mind, it will be clear why even so essential a reality as the eucharist is not mentioned in it. It contained only the matter of Christian initiation. Not even the whole catechesis of baptism was included in it. Lack of knowledge of history, and above all of the prehistory of the apostolic *symbolum,* led theologians of the Middle Ages to regard the *symbolum* as the all-embracing *articulus* (or "joint") of faith, around which the totality of dogma turned as a necessary assumption or as proceeding essentially from it. It was on the basis of this idea that Aquinas constructed his great synthesis of the *articulus fidei.* Although he was to some extent restricted by the fact itself of the existing *symbolum,* he was nonetheless able to discover, on this basis, a much deeper idea, namely that a revealed truth of faith is an "article" only if it possesses a central saving value by means of which light is thrown on other truths of faith.

The Conciliar Symbola of Faith

Unlike the extremely simple confession of faith of the apostolic *symbolum*, the *symbola* drawn up by the various councils of the church are much more "scholarly." Theological terminology found its way into the confession of faith. These *symbola* were, initially at least, divorced from liturgical experience and were drawn up, on a basis of the apostolic *symbolum*, with anti-heretical intentions in mind. Preeminent among these confessions of faith is the *Fides Nicaena*, the symbolum of faith of the Council of Nicea (325).[47] The basis of this *symbolum* was an eastern form of the Apostles' Creed, that was further elaborated in connection with the heresy which Nicea was combating.

The so-called *Symbolum Nicaeno-Constantinopolitanum*[48] has in fact nothing to do with the Council of Constantinople (381). It is an adaptation in the Nicene style of a current eastern apostolic *symbolum*. From the end of the fourth century onwards, however, this version quickly became generally accepted in the east. It appeared for the first time in the acts of the Council of Chalcedon, where it was called the confession of faith of "the one hundred and fifty fathers who were assembled in (the Council of) Constantinople."[49] There is, however, no mention of it anywhere in the acts of the Council of Constantinople. This *symbolum* can already be found in 374 in Epiphanius,[50] and it was probably also the baptismal *symbolum* of Jerusalem. This is the confession of faith that is used for the creed in the liturgy of the Mass. The practice of including the creed in the Mass is derived from the church of Constantinople—in fact, from a monophysite branch of that church, the Patriarch Timothy (511–17) aim-

47 DS 125–6 (= DR 54).

48 DS 150 (= DR 86).

49 Mansi VI, 957 and VII, 112; see also J. Lebon, "Les anciens symboles dans la définition de Chalcédoine," *RHE* 32 (1936), 809–76.

50 DS 44–5 (= DR 13).

ing, by this introduction, officially to affirm his orthodoxy. This practice was universally accepted in the east, and we find it in 589 also in Spain, and in the ninth century in the Frankish countries, probably having been introduced by Charlemagne.[51] From here, it gradually spread throughout the whole of the north. When the Emperor Henry II went to Rome in 1014, he was astonished to attend a Mass in which there was no creed! Benedict VIII acceded to the emperor's demand,[52] and in this way a *symbolum* of baptism which was originally eastern found its way in the eleventh century into the Roman Mass as well. The same *symbolum* was taken over later by the Council of Trent as a confession of faith,[53] and since this time it has been used, together with the Tridentine additions, as the official confession of faith of the clergy.[54] Because it was taken over by the Councils of Chalcedon and Trent, and because it has a place in eucharistic worship, this *symbolum* has an unmistakably dogmatic value.

There are also the great confessions of Chalcedon, in which the christological dogma is formulated,[55] and a large number of synodal *symbola*, only a few of which are included in Denzinger.[56] The *symbolum* of the Eleventh Council of Toledo,[57] in which the doctrine of the Trinity especially is confessed, is certainly an authentic declaration of the dogma, but it was not confirmed by Innocent III, as was earlier believed.[58] Mention must also be made of the *Symbolum pseudo-Athanasianum*, the so-called *Quicumque*.[59] This was

51 B. Capelle, "L'origine anti-adoptianiste de notre texte du symbole de la Messe," *RTAM* 1 (1929), 7–20.

52 *PL* 142, 1060–1.

53 DS 1500 (= DR 782).

54 DS 1862–70 (= DR 994–1000).

55 DS 300–3 (DR 148 = DS 301–3).

56 For example, the *symbolum* of the First Synod of Toledo, DS 188–90 (= DR 19–20).

57 DS 525–41 (= DR 275–87).

58 See J. Madoz, *Le symbole du XIe concile de Tolede: ses sources, sa date, sa valeur,* Louvain 1938, 161–2.

59 DS 75–6 (= DR 39–40).

originally in Latin and cannot be from Athanasius. Even now, little can be said with certainty about its origin. The liturgical use of this initially individual document is in any case a guarantee of its dogmatic value. It would appear to belong to the same group as the anti-Priscillian *symbola* which originated in Spain.[60] The following may also be mentioned: the *symbolum* of Leo IX,[61] which was included in a longer whole at the Second Council of Lyons;[62] and the confession of faith imposed on Durand de Osca and the Waldenses.[63]

Several additions were made to the *symbolum* of Trent, to which I have already referred (see p. 212 and *n.* 54 above), by the First Vatican Council,[64] and Pius X finally added the anti-modernist oath to it.[65] This oath is not, however, a real *symbolum,* nor is it a confession of faith.

THEOLOGICAL REFLECTION

1. The vision of salvation from which the Apostles' Creed especially was composed is characteristic—in and through salvation history, beginning with creation and culminating in the man Jesus, the Trinity is revealed in its inner life and as salvation for us. Although it may well be true that the christological *symbola* occur most frequently in scripture, it is quite clear that Cullmann's argument,[66] that the transition from the christological to the trinitarian *symbola* implies a post-apostolic shift of emphasis and a mutilation of authentic

60 For example, the so-called "Fides Damasi," DS 71–2 (=15–16); the *Clemens Trinitas,* DS 73–4 (=DR 17–18); and the "Libellus in modum symboli," DS 188–208 (=DR 19–38). Also in K. Künstle, *Anti-priscilliana,* Freiburg 1905, 47, 65–6, and 43–4 respectively.

61 DS 680–6 (=DR 343–9).

62 DS 851–4 (=DR 461–4), where it is found as the first part of the longer "Professio fidei Michaelis Palaeologi imperatoris" (see DS 851–61 =DR 461–6).

63 DS 790–7 (=DR 420–7).

64 DR 1000 *n.* 1 (omitted in DS).

65 DS 3537–50 (=DR 2145–7).

66 O. Cullmann, *The Earliest Christian Confessions,* London, 1949.

Christianity, must be incorrect. What after all emerges clearly in scripture is that the whole mystery of Christ is indissolubly bound up with the theocentric monotheism of the Old Testament faith. The entire saving event is seen in the perspective of the providential guidance of life by God, who holds creation, Old Testament history, and the living mysteries of Christ in his hands.

Beginning with creation, all the saving facts which God accomplished in Abel, Enoch, Abraham, and so on, and in Christ, are mentioned in one breath.[67] The Father, who is the creator, is also the source, the author, and the end of the whole history of salvation, which culminates in Christ—"From him and through him and to him are all things."[68] This theocentric monotheism is seen by the New Testament to be the background to the entire mystery of Christ. "God [that is, the Father] was in Christ reconciling the world to himself."[69] And it was in the power of the Holy Spirit that the Father accomplished all this in Christ—Christ was born of the Spirit of God;[70] he was justified by the Spirit;[71] he was called the beloved Son on the descent of the Spirit during his baptism in the Jordan;[72] he did great works through the Spirit of God,[73] offered himself on the cross through the eternal Spirit,[74] was raised from the dead by the power of the Spirit of God,[75] and was constituted in power by the same Spirit.[76] The God of the covenant, who spoke formerly by the prophets, had now spoken by his Son.[77]

It will be clear from the foregoing that the christological confessions of faith in the New Testament are incomprehensible if considered outside the trinitarian context, and that everything stated explicitly in the Apostles' Creed is what

67 Heb 11:3–40; Acts 4:24–7.
68 Rom 11:36.
69 2 Cor 5:19.
70 Mt 1:20.
71 1 Tim 3:16.
72 Lk 3:22.
73 Acts 10:38.
74 Heb 9:14.
75 Rom 8:11.
76 Acts 3:13–15.
77 Heb 1:1–2.

was the fundamental inspiration of the apostolic *kerygma.* In the apostolic *kerygma,* the primitive catechesis, and the apostolic confessions of faith, the *mystery of Christ* is seen fundamentally in the perspective of the all-embracing *mystery of God.* On the other hand, experience of *pneumatic* activities in the earliest church was closely bound up with the *kerygma* of this mystery of Christ. The earliest catechesis associated the sending of the Holy Spirit with the pre-eminently messianic event—that of Christ's resurrection and constitution as Lord.[78] The fundamental early apostolic theme is therefore unmistakably that the Father, because of the resurrection, gave the fullness of the Spirit to Christ, who consequently poured him out over the entire church. What we have, then, is the work of the Trinity in the history of salvation, culminating in Christ, who reveals the Trinity to us as the *Deus salutaris,* the God of salvation. This whole plan —of the Father's saving initiative, realised in history in his Son who became man and completed by the Spirit of sanctification—can already be found unmistakably in Eph 1:3–14.[79] The trinitarian teaching of the apostles was made more explicit by reflection in faith about the mystery of Christ amid pneumatic experiences in the early church.

The same applies in the case of the apostolic *symbolum.* Christ, the pre-existent Son of the Father, sent by the Father in the flesh, taken up into the glory of the Father by the resurrection, but on the basis of his sacrificial death, manifested in this glory by the sanctifying, revealing power of the Spirit who is active in the church, but who formerly spoke by the prophets—this forms the fundamental dogmatic inspiration of the *symbolum apostolicum.* Creation, redemption, and completion—these are the three phases of salva-

78 Acts 2:33.

79 As a result of recent studies, this passage has come to be regarded as a hymn, or at least as going back to a hymn that was already in use in public worship: see C. Masson, *L'épître de saint Paul aux Ephésiens,* Neuchâtel and Paris 1953, 148–52.

tion, brought about by the triune God or manifested by the work of each of the three persons. Thus the apostolic *symbolum* is also one of the finest examples of the identity existing between the scriptural confession of faith and later development and explication in tradition.[80]

2. A second theological reflection is concerned with the fact that the faith of trust and confidence (the *fides fiducialis*) is in scripture always accompanied by a formulated confession of faith. The personal, existential act of faith, as a fundamental choice, cannot, in other words, be separated from "dogmatic faith," in which the personal attitude is completely dominated by the objective reality of the revelation that presents itself. This is, however, also true in reverse —the dogmatic confession of faith cannot be isolated from the existential act of faith. This is evident from Mt 8:5–13 (the faith of the centurion), Mt 14:22–33 (the faith of Peter who walked on the water to Jesus), and Heb 11:4–38 (the hymn to faith in God's providential guidance of life). The "object" of the *symbolum* is not only concerned with things and events, even though these may be saving events, but with Someone—the living God as God for and with us, as this has been most clearly realised in the man Jesus.

Within the faith of the church as a family, there is in every confession of the twelve articles of the *symbolum apostolicum* a personal act of faith in the living God. Tradition generally and Aquinas in particular have reflected fundamentally about the meaning of the accusative in the "credo in unum Deum."[81] As a "credo" in the living God, the confession of Christ is, against the background of the trinitarian confession, ultimately also bound to be, on the basis of the "for-

80 I cannot analyse here all the various small additions that have been made to the Apostles' Creed throughout the course of time. These have generally occurred in connection with heresies. A good detailed analysis will be found in J. N. D. Kelly, *Early Christian Creeds,* New York, McKay, 1960.

81 See *ST* II–II, q. 2, a. 2. See also T. Camelot, "Credere Deo, credere Deum, credere in Deum," *RSPT* 30 (1941–2), 149–55.

giveness of sins," a "credo in vitam aeternam"—a belief in the resurrection of the flesh and in eternal life. I believe in the God of salvation—the Father, the Son, and the Holy Spirit—who, through the saving activity of Christ and in the power of the work of sanctification of the Holy Spirit, and all this on the initiative of the Father, is eternal life for man both in body and in soul. This is the lasting basis of every *symbolum of faith,* and the inspiration of all theology.[82]

[82] In addition to the works already mentioned, the following have been consulted in connection with this chapter: T. Camelot, "Les récentes recherches sur le symbole des apôtres et leur portée théologique," *RSR* 39 (1951) (*Mélanges Lebreton* 1), 323–38; J. de Ghellinck, *Patristique et moyen-âge,* part 1, Gembloux 1949²; C. H. Dodd, *The Apostolic Preaching and its Developments,* London 1950; C. H. Dodd, "Le symbole des apôtres," *LV* n. 2 (1952); M. Meinertz, *Das apostolische Glaubensbekenntnis und das Neue Testament,* Cologne 1946; A. Michel, "Symboles," *DTC* XIV–2 (1941), cols. 2925–31; P. Schoonenberg, "De apostolische geloofsbelijdenis in de katholieke kerk," *Geloofsinhoud en geloofsbeleving,* Utrecht and Antwerp 1951, 146–93; Y. Trémel, "Remarques sur l'expression de la foi trinitaire dans l'église apostolique," *LV* n. 29 (1956), 41–66.

9 The Liturgy and Theology

The tradition of faith is borne by the entire living church, although the only judge and immediate norm of this tradition is the hierarchical church. The *fides ecclesiae,* the "faith of the church," bears its infallibility within itself. The *sensus fidelium,* the sense of faith of the entire believing community, is, however, borne also by the unanimity of faith of the college of bishops in union with the pope. This singleness of mind may be expressed in many different ways. In addition to the universal councils of the church, liturgical prayer, as the official prayer of the church, is one of the most characteristic expressions in which the unanimity of the church's faith—that is, of the faith of both the believers and the hierarchy—can be made external in a truly authentic manner. What is more, dogmatic values are borne by liturgical prayer insofar as this prayer expresses the faith of the entire community of the church, and in this way the liturgy permits us to penetrate into what really pertains to the faith of revelation. This fact is expressed in the formula *lex orandi lex credendi,* that is, in the idea that the prayer of the church is a norm of faith. This and related formulae were already appearing as early as the fifth century,[1] and the *doctrine* can

[1] See especially Prosper of Aquitaine, *De vocatione omnium gentium* I, 12 (*PL* 51, 664–5); see also *Capitula "de gratia et libero arbitrio,"* DS 246 (=DR 139), which was collected by Prosper, though wrongly attributed to Pope Celestine.

already be found in Augustine.[2] Recent popes have made frequent appeals to this dogmatic value of the liturgy.[3]

Liturgical prayer is lived dogma. Before the church is explicitly conscious of a point of faith, it carries the point implicitly, but actually present, with it in its life, one of the most specific expressions of which is liturgical prayer. The church can become more explicitly aware of its deposit of faith by way of its own distinctive manner of praying. Liturgical prayer is one of the expressions of the "living tradition" of the church insofar as it is the prayer of the church here and now. It also forms part of what is known as the "objectivised tradition" (the remote tradition; sometimes, and incorrectly, also called the "dead" tradition), insofar as these liturgical prayers may perhaps no longer be in use, but nonetheless testify to (are *monumenta* of) the earlier life of the whole church.

In its inmost essence, the liturgy is a sacramental liturgy—according to a patristic and scholastic definition, the sacraments were "public confessions of the Catholic faith." The sacraments are acts of worship in which faith is made external. They are, however, even more than this, for both the hierarchy and the believing community are essentially involved in the sacramental event. However clearly the priestly function in the church is distinguished, according to its own special nature, from the church's teaching function, the sacramental liturgy is nonetheless in principle an act of the church's teaching authority, the exercise of the "ordinary and universal teaching authority" that is implied in the priestly function of the church. We may go even further, for a dogmatic declaration, as an act of the church's "extra-

[2] Augustine, *De dono perseverantiae* XXIII (*PL* 45, 1031–3).

[3] See Pius XI, *Quas primas, AAS* 17 (1925), 598; *Divini cultus,* DR 2200 (omitted in DS); Pius XII, *Divino afflante Spiritu,* DS 3828 (= part of DR 2293); *Mediator Dei, AAS* 39 (1947), 540–1; *Munificentissimus Deus,* DR 3031 (= DS 3900–2), DR 3032 (omitted in DS), and DR 3033 (= DS 3903–4).

ordinary teaching authority," acquires—as was clear, for example, in the definition in 1950 of the dogma of Mary's assumption into heaven—an explicitly cultic and liturgical character. There is no academic instruction of dogma in the liturgical life of faith. The liturgy is the prayerful active experience of the church's universal unanimity of faith, in which the "teaching church" coincides with the entire community of believers practising the faith.[4] The liturgy brings dogma into the hearts of the faithful.[5] It will therefore be clear that the liturgy, as borne by the whole of the church's community of faith—by the sense of faith, that is, both of the teaching and of the believing church, not simply at one definite period, but in continuous confession[6]—is a notable manifestation of the dogmatic faith of the church. The liturgy is dogma itself in its liturgical confession and is therefore a place where theology can find its "material."

All the same, we must be careful to emphasise, in affirming the *lex orandi lex credendi,* the primacy of the objective reality of the dogma which is actively experienced in the liturgy. This is important because the *lex orandi* was, for example, wrongly used by the modernists, who held the view that the liturgy gave rise to dogma.[7] That is why Pius XII stressed, in *Mediator Dei,* the fact that liturgical prayer is only a *manifestation* of dogma. We must also never cease to be aware of the fact that the liturgy, although an important source of this manifestation of faith, is certainly not its only source, and that it is above all a place where sacramental theology and the theology of the Christian life of the spirit

4 The bull *Munificentissimus Deus,* in which the assumption of Mary was declared a dogma, refers in this connection to the *fides pastorum et christifidelium* ("the faith of the hierarchy and of Christian faithful"). See DR 3032 (omitted in DS).

5 See Pius XI, *Quas primas, AAS* 17 (1925), 598.

6 See Pius XII, *Mediator Dei, AAS* 39 (1947), 540.

7 See G. Tyrrell, *Lex orandi, or Prayer and Creed,* London, 1903.

can find their data. In this sense, this traditional liturgical argument coincides with what Aquinas called the *consuetudo ecclesiae* ("practice of the church"), which was, in his opinion, more important in resolving theological questions than the doctrine of theologians or even of the church fathers,[8] because liturgical practice is the most characteristic manifestation within the church of the church's faith, together with the church's explicit and solemn declarations of dogma. It goes, however, without saying that liturgical prayers are not composed with the same degree of precision as a dogmatic or a theological definition of faith and that theological reasoning based on the liturgy must consequently be handled very critically.

I am also bound to mention briefly in passing that dogma and liturgy are constantly acting and reacting on each other and that, as *Mediator Dei* points out,[9] a deeper knowledge of faith does not of itself bring about a development in liturgical rites. This means that we cannot use the much vaguer or even undefined character of ancient liturgical formulae, which were the manifestation of a faith that had still not become perfectly and consciously explicit, to testify against later dogmas which may perhaps have been more precisely defined outside the liturgy. In this connection, the encyclical *Mediator Dei* referred to the incongruity of an "unsound archeologism."[10] Finally, it should be pointed out that the liturgy is a de facto catechesis of faith, and that the most effective catechetical form for modern man, with his distinctive psychological formation, is one that is liturgically inspired. The *lex orandi lex credendi* is manifested in this as an educational method of dogmatic instruction in faith, and

8 See Part II, Chapter 10: "Scholasticism and Theology," on pp. 223–258 below.

9 *AAS* 39 (1947), 542.

10 *AAS* 39 (1947), 542 and 546.

this would also appear to have been very early Christian practice.[11]

[11] In addition to the works already cited, the following have also been consulted: R. Aubert, "Liturgie et magistère ordinaire," *QLP* 33 (1952), 5–16; J. Brinktrine, "Der dogmatische Beweis aus der Liturgie," *Scientia Sacra* (Theologische Festgabe Kard. Schulte), Cologne and Düsseldorf 1935, 231–51; J. Brinktrine, "Die Liturgie als dogmatische Erkenntnisquelle," *EL* 43 (1929), 44–51; K. Federer, *Liturgie und Glaube* (Paradosis IV), Fribourg 1950; H. Schmidt, "Lex orandi lex credendi in recentioribus documentis pontificiis," *Prd* 40 (1951), 5–28.

10 Scholasticism and Theology

The theologically fertile preliminary research of the twelfth century was synthesised and systematised in the thirteenth. I propose to select here two problems from this scholastic synthesis. Firstly, I shall examine the problem of the "sources of theology," a problem that was thoroughly investigated by Aquinas especially. Secondly, I shall go into the question as to whether theology, according to the medieval schoolmen, ought first and foremost to examine the truth of the content of faith, or whether it should above all be concerned to reveal its relevance for the Christian life.

THE SOURCES OF THEOLOGY ACCORDING TO AQUINAS

Introduction:

At present, the problem of the *loci theologi,* or the sources of theology, exactly coincides with that of tradition, but this has not always been the case. In the sixteenth century, Melchior Cano elaborated his classic treatise *De locis theologicis* on a basis of medieval theology. Within this framework, the problem of tradition was treated as a function of speculative, discursive theology. This development was, however, not an extension of the Aristotelian concept of *locus,* as Gardeil mistakenly believed,[1] but, as Lang has pointed out,[2] an ex-

1 A. Gardeil, *La notion du lieu théologique,* Paris 1908.

2 A. Lang, *Die loci theologici des M. Cano und die Methode des dogmatischen Beweises,* Munich 1925.

tension of the humanist concept of *locus,* as elaborated by Rudolph Agricola, who drew his inspiration in this case from Cicero. *Locus* (*topos,* or "place") does not here mean the "premisses of a dialectical syllogism" (Aristotle) which, in later scholasticism, were identified with the "principles" of theology as a *scientia* in the Aristotelian sense, but rather a "place where something is found." In humanism, the *loci* stood in practice for mnemonic key-words, main themes, general schemes, and aids to the collection of material, and were used especially by orators (hence the phrase *locus communis,* a "commonplace").

This soon became fashionable in all the sciences, and *loci* were compiled for each of them, so that the notions and the most important points of view and schemes with which the science in question had to work were already in the possession of whoever had to deal with a specific scientific problem. In this way, various "topics" came about—juridical, medical, historical, and so on. This practice was applied by Melchior Cano to theology, and the so-called "theological topic" came into existence. This topic provided a list and an explanation of the places where theology could look for the arguments it needed in order to throw light on a mystery of faith, to establish theological conclusions, to refute false theories, and so on. The theologian could find in these places the "principles of theology" which had to function in the discursive theology of the scholastic period as the premisses of the theological syllogism. Cano's aim here was above all to examine the theological value of the various places. The theological topic therefore developed into a definite theological treatise dealing with the cogency—and especially with the *auctoritas* —of the data drawn from scripture, the church fathers, theologians, and other sources.[3]

Cano gave to this treatise of the theological topic the ten-

[3] See the more speculative work of E. Marcotte, *La nature de la théologie d'après M. Cano,* Ottawa 1949.

fold division which has since become classic in theology. First of all, he distinguished those *loci* which form an indispensable element in the constitution of revelation: namely, (1) holy scripture, and (2) unwritten tradition. Then he distinguished those *loci theologici* which provide an interpretation of revelation: (3) the universal church, (4) the general councils of the church, (5) the pope, (6) the church fathers, and (7) the *scholastici* (theologians and canonists). Finally, he distinguished the *loci alieni,* which are not really *places* where theology can find this data, so much as ancillary sources which are of use in theological reflection. These are: (8) human reason, (9) philosophical ideas, and (10) the history of mankind.

These ten *loci theologici* provided the traditional theology of the manuals with its classic form of argument—"proof from scripture," "proof from tradition," and "proof from human reason." In this context, "tradition" refers to the *loci theologici* of the second group (that is, numbers 3 to 7). The problem of the *loci theologici* was studied in the whole of this context less for the purpose of ascertaining what was the real norm of faith than for the purpose of establishing what method of argument was appropriate to theology as a science in the Aristotelian sense. This sixteenth-century treatise of Melchior Cano, *De locis theologicis,* was a concrete growth from something that was already present in embryo in Aquinas (*ST* 1, q. 1, a. 8, ad 2), but in a more elastic and less formal way. I shall now analyse this medieval situation.

Thomas discussed the "argument of authority" or *auctoritas* in theology in the *Summa Theologiae* (1, q. 1, a. 8, c. and ad 2).

The word *auctoritas* had various meanings in the Middle Ages.[4] It was used in the first place to denote the quality that entitled a person such as a priest, a writer, a witness, or

4 See M. D. Chenu, "'Authentica' et 'Magistralia,'" *DTP* 28 (1925), 3–31.

a superior, to be taken on trust. By metonymy, therefore, it came to mean the person who was thus qualified, and consequently the writing, the testimony, or some dictum of that person as something trustworthy. Finally, it came to mean the text itself, so that the quotation from a writer was the *auctoritas* or the *dictum auctoritatis*. *Auctoritas* thus coincided in meaning with "quotation."

Thinking from the starting-point of an *auctoritas* is, of course, something that is, as far as theology is concerned, quite self-evident, in view of the fact that theology operates on a basis of revealed data which are in turn founded on the authority of God. The entire technique of thinking that was universally current in the Middle Ages must, however, also be taken into account here. All teaching in the Middle Ages, even instruction in non-theological subjects, was based on a definite text of a certain writer, and this constituted the *auctoritas* in the subject in question. The fundamental subordination to the authority of revelation which characterised the whole of medieval society also had an influence on medieval thought at the secular level—or at least we may say that this Christian attitude affected the general outlook of medieval man to such an extent that, if a new idea or tendency in any sphere was to stand any chance of success, it was automatically promoted under the cover of some *auctoritas*.

This universal reverence for *auctoritas* resulted, in the sphere of theology, in scientific work being regarded primarily as a commentary on holy scripture, an exegesis of the text (*expositio textus*), and eventually as a commentary on this commentary and these glosses on scripture, which continued to function as the basic text. This entire body of work thus became known as "holy scripture," "holy writ," and "sacred doctrine" (*sacra scriptura, sacra pagina, sacra doctrina*), even when an independent theology had eventually developed from the *quaestio* which came about as a result of discrepancies in these *expositiones.* This in the long run led to the question being explicitly asked about the degree of *auctoritas* of the various levels that had been included in this *sacra doctrina* throughout the course of time. Aquinas has appraised these *auctoritates,* at least schematically, in his *Summa.*[5] Because medieval thought was so conditioned by the idea of authority, the *auctoritates* (quotations) naturally tended to play a many-sided role in the theological thought of the Middle Ages. Although even more distinctions can probably be made, it is nonetheless possible to distinguish three fundamental ways in which these *auctoritates* were used in medieval theology: (1) the *auctoritas* as a spontaneous means of expression of thought as conditioned by authority, as a "thinking in biblical quotations"; (2) the *auctoritas-quaestio;* and (3) the *auctoritas-argumentum.*

"*Auctoritas*" *as* "*thinking in biblical quotations*"

Like the fathers of the church, the medieval theologians thought and expressed themselves in biblical language. Bardy and Geenen (see specific titles, pp. 241–242 *n.* 51) called these *auctoritates* "quotations for ornament pure and simple," but they were in fact much more than this. This usage was clearly connected with the medieval view of the meaning of scripture (the *sensus scripturae*):

> Every truth which, with due regard for the context, can be fitted into holy scripture, is a scriptural truth.[6]

It is, of course, true that these *auctoritates* can be left out without any detriment to the line of reasoning, and they were therefore, in this sense, "ornamental." But the problem

[5] *ST* 1, q. 1, a. 8, ad 3.
[6] Aquinas, *Potent.* q. 4, a. 1.

goes deeper than this—the reasoning itself was expressed in biblical quotations. The medieval theologians thought to such an extent in patristic and biblical terms that certain formulae were preserved intact and apparently functioned as implicit quotations, whereas they in fact referred to something very different. Fundamentally, they were really no longer simply quotations, but a characteristic mode of thought in formulae drawn from scripture and the church fathers:

Speaking about God, we should not lightly abandon the language of holy scripture.[7]

"Auctoritas-quaestio"

Differences of opinion among the fathers were so often revealed in the patristic anthologies that a given text or *auctoritas* within the framework of the "yes-or-no" (*sic-et-non*) method could give rise to a problem (*quaestio*). In this context, however, we must bear in mind that as yet no clear distinction was made in medieval theology between holy scripture itself, the fathers' commentaries on it (*expositiones S. Scripturae*), and their writings and statements in general (*dicta sanctorum et doctorum*). Aquinas put the question whether

. . . everything that the *doctores sancti* have said is subject to the impulse of the Holy Spirit.

His answer was that

holy scripture was composed and commented on by the same Spirit, . . . especially in matters of faith.[8]

[7] Aquinas, *CEG* 1: "de divinis non de facili debet homo aliter loqui quam S. Scriptura loquatur."

[8] *Quodl.* 12, q. 17, a. 1.

Precisely because of the differences among the church fathers, there was no unanimity on this point in the twelfth century. One of the first to make a clearer distinction between the *auctoritas S. Scripturae* and the *auctoritas doctorum* was Rupert of Deutz. The idea gradually gained ground that the fathers were not mutually contradictory, but that there was a difference in their points of view—"non sunt adversi, sed diversi." The so-called "equation" of the patristic texts with those of scripture was based on a generally accepted view:

Every truth, no matter who suggests it, has its origin in the Holy Spirit.[9]

What is not opposed to holy scripture is a truth of holy scripture.[10]

Aquinas admitted the possibility of error on the part of the fathers, but only in those truths which did not strictly relate to faith,[11] although he did occasionally admit to possible error on their part even in matters of faith,[12] or at least in those matters of faith that had not yet been defined by the church. This consequently meant that *argumenta necessaria* (that is, *apodictica*) could not per se be drawn from the fathers.

Only holy scripture, and not the patristic exposition of scripture, is a compelling norm of faith for us.[13]

9 "Omne verum a quocumque dicitur, a Spiritu Sancto est"—a statement of Ambrose that was frequently quoted in the thirteenth century.

10 *Potent.* q. 4, a. 1.

11 *Quodl.* 12, q. 17, a. 1; 2 *Sent.* d. 12, q. 1, a. 2; d. 14, q. 1, a. 2; d. 2, q. 1, a. 3.

12 *ST* II–II, q. 11, a. 2, ad 3; less explicitly in *Quodl.* 3, q. 4, a. 2.

13 *Quodl.* 12, q. 17, a. 1: "dicta expositorum necessitatem non inducunt quod necesse sit eis credere, sed solum Scriptura canonica." See also *ST* I, q. 1, ad 8, ad 2.

Their teaching was nonetheless not to be despised; on the contrary, any discrepancies called for a "reverent exposition."[14]

"*Auctoritas-argumentum*"

An *auctoritas-argumentum* is a quotation that is a source of doctrine, the basis of an expounded doctrine. Aquinas divided the different *auctoritates* into theological categories[15]: "the *auctoritates* of canonical scripture provide us with proper and apodeictic arguments (*proprie et ex necessitate argumentando*)"; "the *auctoritates* of the other doctors of the church provide us with undoubtedly proper, though not apodeictic, but 'probable,' arguments (*arguendo ex propriis, sed probabiliter*)"; and, finally, "the *auctoritates* of philosophers are extraneous and only 'probable' arguments (*extranea argumenta et probabilia*)" in theology.

In the first place, it should be noted that the terminology used here is derived from an Aristotelian context. "Argumentari ex propriis vel ex extraneis" ("argument from proper or extraneous principles") alludes to the scientific procedure in *scientia* (i.e. *epistēmē* in the Aristotelian sense), according to which conclusions are drawn from principles by means of discursive reasoning. "Every science proceeds from its own [principles]"[16] as opposed, that is, to extraneous principles. To appeal in one science to the principles of another science could constitute an unlawful transition from the one *genus subiectum*[17] to the other. The object of theology is "God-as-God," whereas in philosophy God is not the

14 *CEG,* Proem.

15 *ST* I, q. 1, a. 8, ad 2.

16 *AAP* I, c. 12, lect. 21 (ed. Leonina, n. 2): "quaelibet scientia ex propriis [principiis] procedit."

17 *AAP* I, c. 7, lect. 15; c. 12, lect. 21 (esp. note 7). By *genus subiectum* is meant the proper object of a science considered according to its formal point of view.

subject, but the *principium subiecti,* the existential ground of what is formally considered by philosophy. The (analogous) definition of the proper subject of theology—that is, God-as-God, *Deus sub ratione Deitatis*—provides the *principia propria* of this science, and an argument which does not proceed from these therefore appeals to *principia extranea.*

Furthermore, the terms *ex necessitate* and *probabilia* are also derived from the same Aristotelian conception of science. Again, the word *principia* must be understood in this concept of "argumentari ex principiis necessariis vel probabilibus" (lit. "argument from necessary or from probable principles"). The "necessary principles" give rise to a *syllogismus demonstrativus,* and the "probable principles" to a *syllogismus dialecticus.* In this context, "probable principles" are those truths which are not evident, and which have not been proved, but which are accepted as true "by all or different or wise persons."

Aquinas saw an analogy here with the theological "arguments of authority" as a source of doctrine. *Probabile* had various meanings in the theology of the Middle Ages[18]: (1) everything that is worthy of our approval— this can therefore be "apodeictic"; (2) everything that can in any way be proved conclusively on the basis of reasoning; and (3) generally speaking, evidence that proceeds not from apodeictic, but from generally accepted, truths, and therefore results in an established opinion—*probabilis* then refers to the good bases of a thesis. Holy scripture, then, because it embraces revelation, provides *argumenta propria et necessaria.* The medieval position is clearly reflected in this article (*ST* I, q. 1, a. 8, ad 2)—in it, Aquinas does not discuss the problem of "tradition," which did not arise in so pronounced and one-sided a form as it was to arise at a later period. It is, however, clear from other texts that Aquinas considered proper and apodeic-

[18] See T. Deman, "Probabilis," *RSPT* 22 (1933), 260–90.

tic arguments of authority to be present elsewhere as well. The following is a summary of his doctrine.

Places where proper and apodeictic arguments of authority are found. Holy scripture:

Our faith is founded on revelation to the apostles and prophets who have written the canonical books.[19]

Scripture embraces the *principia fidei,* or principles of faith,[20] and it would seem that this principle of scripture was meant to be exclusive.[21] All the same, the *sola scriptura*—the principle of "scripture alone"—cannot in any sense be called a medieval view. In the first place, *sacra scriptura* (or *sacra pagina*) was less sharply defined in the Middle Ages than it is now:

By scripture is meant either the canonical bible or the patristic writings.[22]

Furthermore, it is evident from what follows that Aquinas accepted other apodeictic arguments of authority besides scripture.

The apostolic tradition: The *auctoritas* of the apostolic traditions was certainly accepted in the Middle Ages, and especially by Aquinas, even though no conclusive ideas were reached about these traditions at this period. In addition to scripture, Aquinas accepted the authority of the "teaching of the apostles," and he did not restrict this to the apostolic

19 *ST* I, q. 1, a. 8, ad 2.

20 *ST* II–II, q. 1, a. 5, ad 2.

21 *ST* III, q. 1, a. 3.

22 *I Sent.* d. 33, q. 1, a. 5, ob. 3: "aut enim S. Scriptura dicitur canon bibliae, aut dicta sanctorum." This is closely connected with the meaning of *S. Scriptura* and *S. Pagina* in the whole of the first question of the *Summa.*

teaching of scripture alone. Thus, he also accepted the Apostles' Creed in the belief that it had been compiled by the apostles themselves, although we now know that this was historically incorrect. He also made frequent reference, in his sacramental doctrine, to the authority of the *traditio familiaris apostolorum,* the common tradition of the apostles.[23] Despite frequent errors here, due, for example, to the mistaken belief that the Pseudo-Dionysius wrote his work during the apostolic age, what is certainly quite clear is that he attributed a decisive *auctoritas* to traditions which went back to the apostles themselves.

The church:

The formal object of faith is the first truth, insofar as this is made known in scripture and in the teaching of the church.[24]

We find the truth of revelation in holy scripture and in the doctrine of the church. Aquinas usually expressed this in a more medieval and a more precise way: "In holy scripture as the church understands it,"[25] thus affirming scripture as the all-important foundation. Aquinas stressed this ecclesiological principle of *auctoritas* even more emphatically than his contemporaries. He held that the arguments of authority drawn from the "teaching of the church" were manifestly *argumenta propria et necessaria,* basing this view on the infallibility of the church,[26] and further on the fact that the church was indeed the "infallible and divine norm"[27] of the fathers' interpretation of scripture, because the fathers' authority was derived from the church.[28] This ecclesial illumination of

23 *ST* III, q. 64, a. 2, ad 1; *4 Sent.* d. 23, q. 1, a. 4, sol. 1, ad. 1.

24 *ST* II–II, q. 5, a. 3.

25 *ST* II–II, q. 5, a. 3, ad 2; *Carit.* a. 13, ad 6.

26 *ST* II–II, q. 1, a. 9, *s.c;* q. 2, a. 6, ad 3: *Quodl.* 9, q. 8, a. 1; 4 *Sent.* d. 20, q. 1, a. 3.

27 *ST* II–II, q. 5, a. 3.

28 *Quodl.* 2, q. 4, a. 3.

faith (*manifestatio fidei*) of holy scripture was, in Aquinas's view, to be found: (1) in the pope ("more trust should be placed in the decisive interpretation of the pope, whose duty it is to define faith, than in the opinion of any other intelligent exegete"[29]); (2) in the councils of the church;[30] and (3) in the life, the liturgy, and the practice of the whole church. The practice of the church enjoyed, in Aquinas's view, a very high authority indeed—an authority unparalleled by anything else, since its practice was guided by the Holy Spirit.[31] It was especially in his sacramental theology that Aquinas appealed to these practices, with the result that he did not, in principle, distort the facts of salvation history in a speculative, a priori framework, but, on the contrary, based his theory on the facts.[32]

Proper but non-apodeictic places where theological arguments of authority are found. The teaching of the church fathers (*sancti et doctores*)[33]: As I have already said, the teaching of the fathers of the church was not, according to Aquinas, in itself and of its very nature infallible: "the fathers derive their authority from the *auctoritas ecclesiae*."[34] Consequently, "we should place more trust in the authority of the church than in the authority of Augustine, Jerome, or any other

29 *Quodl.* 9, q. 8, a. 1; see *ST* II–II, q. 1, a. 10, and q. 11, a. 2, ad 3.

30 *Quodl.* 9, q. 8, a. 1, s.c. and ad 2; *ST* 1, q. 36, a. 2; II–II, q. 1, a. 9, and a. 10, c. and ad 2; *Potent.* q. 10, a. 4, ad 13, etc.

31 *ST* II–II, q. 10, a. 12; III, q. 66, a. 10, s.c.

32 See, for example, *ST* III, q. 68, a. 8, ob. 2; q. 67, a. 7, ob. 3; q. 71, a. 3, s.c.; q. 70, a. 2, s.c.; q. 72, a. 4, s.c.; q. 72, a. 12, s.c.; q. 73, a. 1, s.c.; q. 78, a. 2, s.c.; q. 78, a. 3, s.c.; q. 78, a. 6, s.c.; q. 79, a. 7, s.c.; q. 80, a. 12, s.c.; q. 82, a. 2, s.c.; q. 83, a. 2; q. 83, a. 6; q. 85, a. 5; q. 87, a. 1; q. 89, a. 6; etc.

33 See M. D. Chenu, "Les 'philosophes' dans la philosophie chrétienne médiévale," *RSPT*, 26 (1937), 27–40. What Aquinas (and the other medieval theologians) meant by *sancti* in this context were the church fathers, as opposed to the *philosophi*, or pagan philosophers (who were outside the sphere of revelation).

34 *ST* II–II, q. 10, a. 12; *Quodl.* 2, q. 4, a. 2.

teacher."[35] These writers were therefore, in Aquinas's opinion, authentic sources of doctrine insofar as they testified to the church's consciousness of faith. As this could not be decided without critical examination, and these writers also frequently spoke on their own authority, their *auctoritates* were not, according to Aquinas, in themselves apodeictic. This was, in his view, so, despite the fact that the respect that they enjoyed in the whole of the church entitled them to a clear presumption in their favour, although their teaching would always have to be concretely examined and checked. At the same time, Aquinas and the other medieval theologians were of the opinion that their doctrines could not simply be dismissed—a correct sense had to be given to what they said by reverent exposition.

The teaching of the theologians (*magistri*): Aquinas made a clear distinction between the *authentica,* or *robur auctoritatis habentia,* that is, sources with an authentic or a normative value for us, and the so-called *magistralia,* that is, the church's post-patristic writers, now called "theologians" or "masters." The latter had no real *auctoritas.* As Chenu has rightly said, "the *dictum authenticum* is compelling, even though we must subject it to reverent exposition, whereas the *dictum magistrale* remains free opinion."[36] Both the patristic and the scholastic writers were called "doctors of the Catholic faith" (*doctores Catholicae fidei*) in the Middle Ages, but a difference was made in their value as authorities.[37]

The masters or theologians undoubtedly had a certain au-

35 *ST* II, q. 10, a. 12.

36 M. D. Chenu, " 'Authentica' et 'Magistralia' " (i.e., the authentic writings and the writings of the masters), *DTP* 28 (1925), 30.

37 See, for example, *ST* II–II, q. 5, a. 1 (according to the critical edition of de Leonina): "quamvis dicta Hugonis a S. Victore magistralia sint et robur auctoritatis *non* habeant" ("although the writings of Hugh of St. Victor are 'magisterial' and do not have the force of authority").

thority, as far as their competence extended,[38] but it was permissible to put forward counter-arguments and even to defend a different thesis without taking them into account. The authority of a theologian who had not been approved by the authority of the church was therefore worth precisely what the proofs that he adduced were worth.

"Extraneous" and non-apodeictic places: These were the *auctoritates philosophorum,* that is, the authority of the pagan philosophers who were outside the sphere of revelation. In the theological context, there could be no question here of a "proper" authority. It should be noted that Thomas was not directly referring here (*ST* 1, q. 1, a. 8, ad 2) to the "reasonable proofs" put forward, for example, by the fathers or by theologians, as has been suggested by certain theologians as an interpretation of this text. He meant simply the "quotations" or *auctoritates* which went back to non-Christian authors and which were to be found either in scripture[39] (as, for example, in Paul, who quoted the *auctoritas* of the pagan Aratus, "we are God's offspring") or in the *Catholici doctores,* or which were employed in theology itself. These *auctoritates* could not, of course, establish the Christian relevance of certain truths, but they did, in Aquinas's view, have some value in connection with the *praeambula fidei* and in speculative theology which, assuming the data of faith, attempts to throw light on their intelligibility. In this case, however, we should be dealing with the "proofs from human reason," and I do not intend to discuss these here, in an exposition of the arguments of authority, especially as Aquinas himself also did not have these directly in mind in

38 In connection with the controversy among medieval masters about the character of a sacrament, Albert said (*In IV Sent.* d. 6, c., a. 4): "neutra habet robur auctoritatis, nisi quantum facit usus magistrorum" ("neither has the force of authority, except insofar as its employment by the masters makes it so").

39 *BT* q. 2, 3, s.c.

ST I, q. 1, a. 8, ad 2. He did not, in other words, consider the apodeictic or only "probable" character of the arguments from reason (*argumenta rationis*) directly and ex professo in a. 8, ad 2. A failure to appreciate the true perspective of this passage has led some authors to draw the wrong conclusion from the *extranea et probabilia:* "reason is extraneous to theology, which knows no arguments other than those of divine authority."[40] There is no direct reference here to philosophical proofs in theology—Aquinas gives an appraisal of these elsewhere.

It is, moreover, quite clear from another work that, in the case of arguments of authority, Aquinas was concerned with the *loci* that compel faith,[41] and from yet another work that the *argumenta auctoritatis ex necessitate vel probabilia*[42] were in fact arguments which did or did not compel the acceptance of faith.[43] Seen in this way, the "proofs from reason" are indeed extraneous to theology and can only be *rationes probabiles vel suasivae,* that is, arguments of convenience,[44] unless they are used in respect of the *praeambula fidei,* which can also be established apodeictically by way of the human intellect.[45] For the real mysteries of faith, only *argumenta rationis probabilia* can be used, and in that case only for the believer (*nisi credenti*)[46]—faith, for example, in the Trinity can be made to appear to some extent plausible on a reasonable basis to whoever believes in this doctrine.

[40] J. F. Bonnefoy, *La nature de la théologie selon saint Thomas d' Aquin,* Paris and Bruges 1939, 57.

[41] *BT* q. 2, a. 1, ad 5: "cogere ad assensum fidei" ("compel us to the assent of faith").

[42] Which Aquinas discussed in *ST* I, q. 1, a. 8, ad 2.

[43] *Quodl.* 12, q. 17, a. 1, c. and ad 1: "Dicta expositorum necessitatem non inducunt quod necesse sit eis credere, sed solum Scriptura canonica quae in Veteri et Novo Testamento est" ("only canonical scripture of the Old and New Testaments, and not the patristic exposition of scripture, is a compelling norm of faith for us").

[44] See, for example, *BT* q. 2, a. 1, ad 5; *SCG* I, 9; *RF* c. 2.

[45] *SCG* I, 9; *3 Sent.* d. 24, q. 2, a. 3, sol. 2 (ed Moos, 769).

[46] *BT* q. 1, a. 4.

In other words, the function of the *ratio* in speculative theology, in which the factuality of the data of faith is already assumed, is not directly involved in the problem answered by *ST* I, q. 1, a. 8, ad 2. All that Aquinas says here is that a truth of faith cannot be intrinsically proved, with the result that, in establishing the *an sit* (the question "whether it is so") of the mystery of faith, the *auctoritas rationis* can only put forward *argumenta extranea et probabilia.* As a so-called *probatio fidei,* or "proof of faith," they are "extraneous" arguments and only recommendatory.

Aquinas's Synthesis

"Argumentari ex auctoritate est maxime proprium sacrae doctrinae" ("the argument of authority is the appropriate method in theology");[47] unlike the purely human sciences, in which the least powerful argument is that of authority, because these sciences rely on ascertainment and insight, theology as a science is based on revelation and thus on the authority of God. In close association with faith, human thought of course performs a co-essential function in throwing intelligible light on the data of God's word. The *ipse dixit* ultimately always refers to the God of revelation, whose word is to be found in the living church. The theological argument of authority must therefore be sought first and foremost in the living tradition of the church, the ultimate judge and norm of which, at least as far as we are concerned, is the church's teaching authority. This living tradition, as the witness of the one revelation, became objective, however, in the following ways.

In the first place, it became objective in the constitutive objectivisations of scripture and the apostolic practices and doctrines that were handed down and which in their turn determine the teaching authority of the church that acts as a

[47] *ST* I, q. 1, a. 8, ad 2.

norm in respect of us. Secondly, it also became objective in the writings of all the church's authors, as witnesses of the tradition that was alive at their time. Among these objectivisations, those of the church's teaching authority—the councils, for example—occupy an exceptional place.[48]

It follows, then, that every argument of authority is, theologically speaking, an argument from tradition in the modern sense of the word—the *paradosis,* that is, God's word living in and practised by the church, is the basis of all theology. Consequently, an argument of authority that relies, for example, on the "unanimity" of the church fathers or of theologians does not derive its cogency from any kind of democratic principle ("fifty-one percent of the votes" or "the absolute majority is right"), but from the fact that this consensus is indicative of the collective reaction of the church's sense of faith, interpreted by and guaranteed as authentic by the church's teaching authority.[49] Directly, or indirectly, every theological argument of authority is therefore an appeal to the infallible authority of God's revelation.

Since the church's consciousness of faith is always identical in its dynamism, we can achieve a better understanding of this consciousness of faith today by appealing to the objectivisations of faith which have taken place in the past and which are the witnesses and the expression of the constantly living tradition of faith. We do not really appeal to the past in this way in order to prove the faith of the church today, but in order to obtain a better grasp of the rich content of the church's present and immortal life of faith. The history of the church is characterised by special emphases and silences —at every period, certain aspects of faith that were previously explicit are kept more in the background, while doctrines

[48] See the article "Overlevering" in *Theologisch Woordenboek,* part 3, Roermond and Masseik 1958, especially cols. 3691–2.

[49] See Part 1, Chapter 4: "The Development of the Apostolic Faith into the Dogma of the Church" on pp. 57–83 above.

that were previously latent are explicitly recognised. The exploration of the entire objective tradition of faith thus provides us with a more intimate understanding of the content of the church's present awareness of faith, which certainly always includes implicit treasures. What must, however, always be ascertained is whether a constant datum of tradition —or at least a datum of tradition that has appeared again and again—was in fact handed down as a datum of faith. And this is not always easy to determine—theology may be able to do this in a scientific, but ultimately fallible manner, but it is only the teaching authority of the church that can do it in an infallible manner.

It is in this perspective that the various arguments of authority acquire their significance, that of pointing out an authentic and biblical doctrine or a constant and patristic view, the *lex orandi lex credendi* or proof from the liturgy, and so on. A great deal of caution is required in the use of all these arguments, as human ideas and terminology that are also conditioned by the prevailing situation play an important part in them. They are, however, such that we can, after examining them critically, derive arguments of authority from tradition in a scientific, even though ultimately fallible, manner. Nonetheless, it will always be the teaching authority of the church that will definitively and infallibly settle the matter in the end.

The argument of authority may, however, have another, human significance (even though it is conducted within the sphere of theology), and here the principle will hold good that this authority is worth precisely what the argument itself is worth. In other words, we accept the argument not because this or that author says it, but because he puts forward conclusive arguments. In this sense, an authoritative theologian is consequently someone whom experience has shown superabundantly to have had a consistently correct view, with the result that there will be a clear presumption in favour of the fact that what he teaches must a priori at least be taken into account. At this level, then, the authority of one theologian may well be greater than that of "fifty-one percent" (for example, of a series of theological manuals). Moreover, when this is also the church's own view, then the presumption in favour of this author is evidently so strong that the church can regard his inspiration, broadly speaking, as a safe guide in the study of theology, and his fundamental doctrines can be prescribed as a practical norm in the teaching of theology in the church, either by an implicit or by an explicit announcement on the part of the church.

Thus, the "schoolmen" of the church have been Augustine up to the Middle Ages, Peter Lombard from the twelfth century until after the Council of Trent, and Aquinas from about the time of the Council of Trent.[50] The longer the works of a "schoolman" in this sense remain in force as a model in the teaching of theology, the more must be said for the range of his inspiration, but also perhaps for his successors' lack of creativity![51]

[50] For the question of how Aquinas himself should be regarded, according to his own doctrinal principles, as a "theological authority," see M. D. Chenu, "Maître Thomas est-il une autorité?" *RT* 30 (1925), 187–94.

[51] Apart from the works already mentioned, the following have been consulted in connection with the preceding section: I. Backes, *Die Christologie des hl. Thomas und die griechischen Kirchenväter,* Paderborn 1931; G. Bardy, "Sur les sources patristiques grecques de St. Thomas dans la première partie de la Somme," *RSPT* 12 (1923), 493–502; L. Baur, "Die Form der wissenschaftlichen Kritik bei Thomas van Aquin," *Misc. Grabmann,* 688–709; J. Beumer, "Das katholische Schriftprinzip in der theologischen Literatur der Scholastik bis zur Reformation," *Schol* 16 (1941), 24–52; M. D. Chenu, *Introduction à l'étude de St. Thomas d'Aquin,* Montreal and Paris 1950; J. de Ghellinck, "Patristique et argument de tradition au bas moyen-âge," *Misc. Grabmann,* 403–26; J. de Ghellinck, "Pagina et S. Pagina. Histoire d'un mot, transformation de l'objet primitivement désigné," *Misc. Pelzer,* 23–59; H. de Lubac, "A propos de la formule: diversi sed non adversi," *RSR* 40 (1952) (*Mélanges Lebreton* II), 27–40; A. Dondaine, "La documentation patristique de St. Thomas," *RSPT* 29 (1940), 326–7; G. Geenen, "De opvatting en de houding van den H. Thomas v. Aquino bij het gebruik der bronnen zijner theologie," *Bijd.* 4 (1941), 112–47, 224–54; G. Geenen, "Les

TRUTH OR RELEVANCE FOR THE CHRISTIAN LIFE IN SCHOLASTIC THEOLOGY

There has been a tendency in recent years to go back more than in the past to Albert the Great and Bonaventure, in the belief that they represent the substance of the patristic theology, and thus the substance of authentically Christian theology, more excellently than Aquinas, who, it is felt, deviated from the theology of the fathers in favour of a pure and abstract Aristotelian approach. I shall attempt here to clarify only two aspects that are characteristic of the pre-Thomist theology of the so-called *Summa Alexandrina,* of Albert the Great and of Bonaventure, in order to ascertain to what extent these two characteristics are present in Aquinas as well. It should then be possible to establish whether Aquinas really broke with the theology of the fathers or whether he synthesised all these elements in a higher unity.

These two aspects, which I propose to consider briefly here, are the saving aspect and the affective aspect. Both are given considerable prominence in the present renewal of theology, and it is possible that we may learn something from these older theologians here since, to judge from the prologues to the works of Alexander, Albert, and Bonaventure, it is pre-

---

'auctoritates' dans la doctrine du baptême chez St. Thomas d'Aquin. Leur usage, leur influence," *ETL* 15 (1938), 279–329; G. Geenen, "St. Thomas d'Aquin et ses sources pseudépigraphiques," *ETL* 20 (1943), 71–80; G. Geenen, "Saint Thomas et les Pères," *DTC* xv–1 (1946), 738–61; N. Halligan, "Patristic Schools in the Summa," *Thom.* 7 (1944), 271–322 and 505–43; A. Landgraf, "Les preuves scripturaires et patristiques dans l'argumentation théologique," *RSPT* 20 (1931), 287–92; A. Landgraf, "Die Schriftzitate in der Scholastik um die Wende des 12. zum 13. Jahrhunderts," *Bbl* 18 (1937), 74–94; P. Minges, *Über Väterzitate bei den Scholastikern,* Regensburg 1923; B. Paré, A. Brunet and P. Tremblay, *La renaissance du XIIe siècle. Les écoles et l'enseignement,* Ottawa 1933; M. Riquet, "St. Thomas et les 'auctoritates' en Philosophie," *AP* 3 (1926), 117–55; C. Spicq, *Esquisse d'une histoire de l'exégèse latin au moyen-âge,* Paris 1944; C. Spicq, "St. Thomas d'Aquin, exégète," *DTC* xv–1 (1946), 694–738; J. van der Ploeg, "The Place of Holy Scripture in the Theology of St. Thomas," *Thom.* 10 (1947), 398–422; G. von Hertling, "Augustinus-zitate bei Thomas von Aquin," *SBAW* 4 (1904), 535–602.

cisely these two aspects that define theology. For them, theology was not a science—and here I mean a science in the Aristotelian sense[52]—but a "wisdom." Wisdom, too, should not be understood here in the Aristotelian sense, for this would include science,[53] but in the affective sense. It was, for these theologians, *sapientia, sapida scientia,* "a tasteful science"—an "affective science" as Alexander called it, or a *scientia secundum pietatem* ("science in accordance with religion") in the words of Albert. It was something that a Dominican theologian, de Cortenson, later called a "theology of mind and heart." These three great scholastics were not formally concerned with truth in itself, but with the relevance of truth for the life of man. The object of theology was for them not the truth of faith formally, in its intelligibility, but this truth as "scibile secundum quod est inclinans ad pietatem,"[54] that is, truth in its relevance for the Christian life. They did not, in other words, regard the *verum ut verum* (truth precisely as truth), but the *verum sub ratione boni salutaris* (truth as a value in human life), as the object of theology. In concrete terms, this means *Deus beatificans*—the God of our salvation (Albert).

Thus, the aim of theology was not speculation, but instruction in how to live the Christian life. Bonaventure rephrased the question "Is theology both speculative and practical?" more concretely as "Do we practise theology because of an urge for deeper insight, or because we wish to become holier?"[55] According to these theologians, then, theology was

52 In the Aristotelian sense, science is the insight into the connection between principles and the conclusions that are necessarily illuminated by them.

53 In the Aristotelian sense, all that wisdom adds to the concept of science is that the conclusions are being related to the deepest and ultimate principles.

54 Albert, *Summa Theologiae* I, q. 2 (ed. Borgnet, part 31, 11).

55 *In I Sent.*, Proem., q. 3 (ed. Quaracchi, 13): "utrum theologia sit contemplationis gratia an ut boni fiamus" ("whether theology is for contemplative speculation or for us to become good").

directly at the service of the Christian life. The entire study was related to man's destiny, his salvation in and through Christ, and was conducted not rationally but "affectively." That is why the *Summa Alexandrina* saw a gap that could not be bridged between a "rational science" and what he called a "science of salvation"—or, in other words, theology.

Thus we come to the attractive definition of theology according to the *Summa Alexandrina:*

> Theology is the science of understanding the divine substance by means of Christ in his work of reparation.[56]

Theology, in other words, knows God through the mystery of Christ. Because everything in theology is seen, according to the *Summa Alexandrina,* from the aspect of salvation, and so not in an abstract and metaphysical light, but in the concrete light of the history of salvation, therefore Christ is also directly involved in the very definition of theology.

This brief outline of the theological thought of Alexander, Albert, and Bonaventure may serve to sum up the theological situation at the time of Aquinas. It is certainly possible to see in this situation the continuation of a very old patristic tradition. Recent works on the theology of Augustine, for example, confirm this. They emphasise the central importance of the saving aspect, the affective character, in the theological thought of this doctor of the church as well, and the fact that his theology consequently also has a patristic and apostolic and thus, ultimately, a "kerygmatic" orientation. What we have here is, in other words, an authentic Christian inheritance which was treated by Alexander, Albert, and Bonaventure only in a more systematic and consciously reflective way, because at this time a consciously devised methodology

56 *Summa Alexandrina* I, q. I (ed. Quaracchi, 6): "theologia est scientia de substantia divina cognoscenda per Christum in opere reparationis." Or: "scientia de Deo cognoscendo per Christum redemptorem" ("the science of understanding God by means of Christ the redeemer").

had been achieved in theology, a reflection about the theological method as already practised in living experience.

But, as I have already indicated, the charge of breaking with this patristic tradition has been made against Aquinas. He is said to have spurned the warm traditional example of "Christian wisdom" and to have modelled his theology on the cold reason of an Aristotelian science. From the historical point of view, it cannot of course be denied that Aquinas did appeal to the traditional, patristic *sacra doctrina*. This accounts for the fact that he was able to call theology a science in an analogous but real sense, at least formally as far as its reasoning function is concerned. He certainly did not consequently call it a science in respect of everything that it is and does.[57] But this is not our main concern here—what does concern us is the fact that it is not true that the authentically patristic elements were simply banished by Aquinas's vision. I propose to show that he, on the contrary, did not leave out any single essential element. By this I do not mean that he took these elements over eclectically, as, for example, Albert did, but that he accorded a place to them either in theology (the saving aspect) or outside theology, but in immediate association with it (the affective aspect).

The Saving Aspect

According to Aquinas, theology is a science of faith, a reflection about faith, that is demanded by the structure of faith itself. We may say that the life of faith includes not only an element of firm resolution, of repose or settled assent or resolute acceptance of faith, but also an element of reflection which is in motion. The fact that this reflection about faith is not at rest does not in any way invalidate the

57 Theology could be called a science (in the modern sense) in respect of all its functions—that is, a knowledge that is critically justified, methodically conducted, and systematically planned.

resolution of our consent to faith. It is rather the result both of the fact that the datum of faith is not self-evident and of the special nature of the human intellect, which is inclined towards quidditative insight. This natural attitude of the intellect moreover reaches an apogee here, as the "object" is one that at the same time offers itself as the highest value in life—God himself, "the first truth and salvation." That is why, together with the tension of the "natural desire to see God," an unpleasant resentment on the part of the intellect is also revealed in this aspect of reflection—our mind feels itself to have been "made captive" when confronted with the "obscurity" of the datum of faith.[58] Consequently, if it is the purpose of theology to be a reflection about faith, then the structure of faith itself must also be relevant for the structure of theology.

If, then, we consider the material object of our Catholic faith, that is, what we believe, we come to the conclusion that, according to Aquinas, saving truths constitute this object. We have been raised to the level of the supernatural order, that is, to God as the "content of our salvation." In addition, this activity is also raised to this level, so that we may attain this transcendent destiny in a vital way, that is, through activity that is strictly human, but which has been made supernatural. Since the dynamic force of man has an intellectual character, knowledge of this destiny and of the means of attaining it must also already be provided in advance. Consequently, revelation is a necessary element in the supernatural order of salvation. It is the good news of our elevation to a supernatural destiny—God reveals himself as man's supernatural destiny. God reveals himself as God, because he gives himself to us precisely as the content of our

58 Aquinas, *Verit.* q. 14, a. 1: "Intellectus credentis dicitur *captivatus,* quia tenetur principiis alienis et non propriis" ("the intellect of the believer is called 'captive' in that it is bound by principles foreign to it rather than its own").

salvation. He makes himself known to us as our salvation. "Notum fecit Dominus salutare suum." We may therefore say that, according to Aquinas, the real object of our faith is the God of our salvation or, expressed in a different way, "Deus qui sub ratione Deitatis est salus nostra: Veritas prima salutaris"—that is, God as God-for-us.

Aquinas therefore placed the God of salvation, *Deus salutaris,* at the very beginning of the *Summa,* in the first article. As known by us, the God of salvation is, it is true, "plurified" in various conceptual truths.[59] These truths do not, however, thereby lose their saving character—"actus credentis non terminatur ad enuntiabile sed ad rem" ("the act of the believer terminates, not at the object of the profession, but at the reality"),[60] that is, it is not the conceptual ideas that are the aspect of repose in the act of faith, but the reality of salvation. As a result, Aquinas was able to speak in this first article of the *Summa* of saving truths, "truths that are necessary to salvation." He is therefore really writing about God who is God-for-us precisely in his being God. Moreover, if we maintain that this saving aspect should not be included in the object of faith, the question can be raised as to exactly what the criterion should be for the extension of the material object of faith. If our answer is formal revelation, then we are simply shifting the difficulty. What, then, is the criterion by which God reveals certain supernatural truths and not others? For, as Aquinas said explicitly in his commentary on the *Sentences* of Peter Lombard (the writings of Aquinas which are of particular interest for his teaching on faith):

Not everything that, in God's wise knowledge, transcends our human intellect is an object of faith.[61]

59 *Verit.* q. 14, a. 12: "plurificatur per diversa enuntiabilia" ("he is 'plurified' in the various objects of the profession of faith").

60 *ST* II–II, q. 1, a. 2, ad 2.

61 *In 3 Sent.* d. 24, a. 3, sol. 1, ad 3.

Aquinas consequently put the criterion for the extension of the material object of faith in the *beatitudo humana,* man's salvation—for him, it was the relevance for human life, the saving significance of a truth, that decided whether God revealed this truth or not:

> Not everything that, in God's wise knowledge, transcends our human intellect is an object of faith, but only what is necessary to our knowledge of our supernatural destiny and of everything that directs us in a supernatural manner towards it.

All truths of faith are therefore saving truths by the very fact that they are truths of faith. To maintain, as some "kerygmatic theologians" do, that prominence ought only to be given, in faith and therefore in preaching and theology, to those truths that are saving truths and are relevant to human life, and that other truths may be neglected, would be to misjudge the real nature of every truth of faith formally as a truth of faith and thus to betray a too pragmatic, utilitarian conception of value and relevance for life. In Aquinas's view, it was God himself who, by the very fact that he revealed the truths of faith *propter nostram salutem,* for our salvation, determined their relevance. The totality of faith as such has a saving value and, within this totality, so does each separate truth of faith. On pain of falling into error (*ST* II–II, q. 5, a. 3), consent to faith refers to this totality as such, to the entire complex of salvation. One of theology's many tasks must therefore be to attempt to make this saving value and this relevance for life—in the Christian sense of the word—of every separate truth of faith within the totality of faith intelligible. This was clearly expressed by the First Vatican Council:

> When reason illuminated by faith searches with diligence, piety, and prudence, it attains—through the gift of God—a certain un-

derstanding of the mysteries [of faith], and an abundantly fruitful understanding at that: . . . from the interconnection of these very mysteries with each other and with the final end and purpose of man.[62]

According to this council, one of the main functions of speculative theology was to discover the reference towards salvation and modestly to attempt to make it intelligible, as well as to investigate the mutual connections between the mysteries of faith. As I have said, theology is reflection about the data that we accept in divine faith—positive theology attempts to describe these data of faith, in the light of the church's teaching authority, according to their pure factuality, whereas speculative theology attempts to find their aspect of intelligibility. Theology formally considers the "first truth" that brings salvation (and, as it is known by us, this therefore means the "truths that are necessary to salvation"), not as believed in—this is assumed—but as intelligible. This does not, however, mean that the inner reference of these truths of faith towards salvation is thereby set aside —because it is a reflection about the objective, present, and implicit content of faith, theology is at the same time a reflection about the reference towards salvation which is inseparable from the content of faith. Theology is therefore bound to throw light scientifically on the saving value of all the data of faith.

The direct result of this is that Aquinas also regarded both the mystery of the Trinity and what he called the "mystery of Christ's humanity" as the two basic truths on which the totality of faith is founded and in which it acquires its significance (*ST* II–II, q. 1, a. 8), even going so far as to call it "that through which man finds his salvation" (*ST* II–II, q. 2, a. 5). The point at issue is salvation itself, God, and the means to salvation, Christ. All the rest is at the service

62 DS 3016 (= DR 1796). For the Latin text see Chapter 5, *n*. 53 above.

of reflection about "God who in Christ is our salvation." Aquinas's theocentricity is, because of the necessary relationship between salvation and faith, a theocentricity that has its point of support in Christ. In other words, the Catholic doctrine of faith is centred in God, but in and through Christ. "The whole of Christian faith turns around the divinity and the humanity of Christ."[63]

It is thus possible to see that the saving aspect is as essential to Aquinas's theology as it is to the theology of the church fathers. It is not here that Aquinas differs from the fathers, and there is consequently no question of his having broken with patristic theology. A difference does, however, become evident in the interpretation of the *beatitudo* or salvation itself. An urge towards salvation, an *appetitus beatitudinis,* is revealed both in Albert's and in Aquinas's theology. For Aquinas, however, this state of blessedness was to be found formally in the intellect, the will following the intellect in ultimate resignation. Aquinas viewed everything from the vantage point of the beatific vision. According to him, man's spiritual life reached its highest point in contemplation, and he preferred for this reason to stress the contemplative character of faith. Aquinas saw faith as focused on the truth as such, and as becoming effective, practical, and apostolic only by extension. For him, therefore, it had a value in itself, a value that was not dependent even on the moral and apostolic activity aroused by faith. A radiation or extension of faith was, in his view, possible in the practical sphere (the moral and apostolic aspect of faith), because the "first truth," although it was primarily the object of contemplation, was at the same time the "aim of all our desires and activities."[64] This explains Aquinas's threefold repetition of the same outline: (1) as far as *faith* is concerned, "faith

63 *De articulis fidei et Ecclesiae sacramentis,* Proem.

64 *ST* II–II, q. 4, a. 2, ad 3.

is speculative and practical, but above all speculative";[65] (2) as far as connatural *divine reflection* on the basis of the gifts of the Holy Spirit is concerned, "the gifts of the Holy Spirit [i.e., insight, wisdom, and knowledge] are speculative and practical, but above all speculative";[66] and (3) as far as connatural *human reflection* is concerned—in other words, theology—"theology is speculative and practical, but above all speculative."[67] Aquinas thus emphasised the dogmatic character of faith and theology—for him, theology was simply dogmatic theology and only secondarily, by extension, moral theology.[68] He thus established the indissoluble unity of dogma and ethics by showing that moral theology is merely speculation about the mystery of God itself, and thus dogmatic, but with a view to its practical reflections upon human life. Aquinas would therefore have answered the question "Is theology for the purpose of gaining a deeper insight, or for that of becoming good; or, in other words, is it speculative or practical?" as Bonaventure answered it: "For the purpose of becoming good."[69] We practise theology in order to become more holy and to bring those who believe to holiness.

The aim of theology is practical and apostolic, too, and indeed essentially so—but only *extensione,* by "repercussion." It is here that Aquinas differs from Albert and Bonaventure. It is precisely our reflection about the dogmatic truths of salvation, about the *Deus salutaris,* that enables us to appreciate the relevance of the truths of faith for the Chris-

65 *ST* II–II, q. 4, a. 2, ad 3. See also *3 Sent.* d. 23, q. 2, a. 3, sol. 2.

66 *ST* II–II, q. 8, a. 6; a. 3; q. 45, a. 3, ad 3.

67 *ST* I, q. 1, a. 4.

68 *ST* II–II, q. 4, a. 2, ad 3: "habitus speculativus extensione fit practicus" ("the practice of reflection is, by extension, made practical").

69 Bonaventure, *In 1 Sent.*, Proem, q. 3 (ed. Quaracchi, 13): "utrum theologia sit contemplationis gratia an ut boni fiamus seu utrum sit speculativa an practica: . . . etiam ut boni fiamus."

tian life. Action is enlightened and guided by this insight, and our practical, apostolic activity can only gain from it if we respect the distinctive nature of faith and theology, which is in principle *speculativa,* that is, disinterested and contemplative, and not utilitarian and pragmatic. That is why Aquinas stated in the first article of the *Summa* that knowledge—that is, knowledge of God as a value for human life, the knowledge of "those truths that are necessary to salvation"—must be presupposed if this relevance for life is really to be a norm for life.

It is therefore evident that Aquinas fully maintained the saving aspect of the truths of faith and their relevance for the Christian life—values which the whole Christian tradition had always stressed—but that he provided them, with the help of Aristotle, with a different basis.

The Affective Aspect

This is an even more delicate question and, because Aquinas in fact banished the entire affective aspect from his theology, it would seem as if we must decide against him here. In a certain sense, he was very far from being a protagonist of a "theology of mind and heart."

In view of the fact that this affective element forms an essential part of the authentically Christian inheritance, we may say a priori that Aquinas did not simply reject it in his theology which was so closely linked to tradition. It is true to say that there is evidence of a certain lack of differentiation in the theology of an Augustine, an Albert, or a Bonaventure, in the sense that they confused scientific research with insight into faith through the gifts of the Holy Spirit. As a result, theology became, in their case, a *scientia affectionis* ("a science of the feelings"). There is, on the other hand, a striking differentiation in the case of Aquinas. He made a clear distinction between insight into faith *per modum cognitionis* ("by the mode of understanding"), that is, by theology, and insight into faith *per modum inclinationis seu connaturalitatis* ("by the mode of inclination or affinity"), that is, by the affective knowledge of faith as acquired by the saints (*ST* I, q. 1, a. 6, ad 3). He called theology a reflection about faith *per modum cognitionis,* a technical science acquired by analytical and synthetical study (*per studium habetur*). In this way, he rejected the affective aspect as the appropriate theological method of knowing, and thereby allayed the danger of being lured into vague arguments. This, of course, does not in any way mean that he claimed to be able to make everything clear by means of his scientific method. On the contrary, he was the first to recognise that theological insights could only be reached "insofar as such a matter makes this possible."[70]

For Aquinas, then, theology was not a knowledge *per modum affectionis.* He was nonetheless able to preserve this affective aspect by transferring it to the sphere of reflection about faith by virtue of the gifts of the Holy Spirit. In the life of faith as such, he distinguished, apart from an aspect of acceptance (the *adhaesio*), a supernatural aspect of perception and affective judgement (II–II, q. 9, a. 1). This aspect of perception and judgement was, in Aquinas's view, made possible by the fact that faith is at the same time believing in love, *informata caritate,* and that the gifts of the Holy Spirit (insight, wisdom, and knowledge) are only modifications, further refinements of what was already implied, in an embryonic form, in faith. This refined insight into faith by virtue of the gifts of the Spirit is rooted in charity and therefore comes about "in the manner of connaturality and affection" or by means of a kind of sympathy in grace with the content of faith. This results in what Aquinas called "a certain sharp perception of the divine truths,"[71] a divine acu-

70 *ST,* Prologue: "secundum quod materia patietur."

71 *ST* II–II, q. 49, a. 2, ad 2: "quaedam acuta perspectio divinorum."

men, on the basis of the conformity of the will with God —that is to say, a consciousness by virtue of grace.

This entire Thomist doctrine should therefore be seen in the light of Aquinas's teaching about love as the "completion of faith" (*caritas forma fidei*), a doctrine that is occasionally misunderstood. He did not simply call love the final form of faith as a result of his general teaching that "love is the completion of all the virtues" ("caritas est forma omnium virtutum"). He meant much more than this. Mature faith, *fides informata caritate,* was for him not simply faith-plus-love. The relationship between the two was much more intimate—faith itself was inwardly completed precisely as faith, that is, as intellectual consent, and thus as a direct extension of believing. There is no need to examine this more closely here. All that needs to be said is that the impulse of the will is essential to the act of faith and that faith is a fruit of love, but in the intellect—"the assent of the intellect moved by the will" ("assensus intellectus motus a voluntate"). The act of faith is thus inwardly connected with the inclination of the will. Faith will therefore be inwardly more perfect if the inclination of the will is aroused by divine charity.[72]

Unlike the moral virtues (which refer only to the object of *charity,* because they are directed by love not to their own object, but to that of charity, the final aim), faith refers to the object of charity precisely insofar as faith is directed to its *own* object, the "first truth," "for the first truth is connected with the will insofar as it is at the same time an aim" (*ST* II–II, q. 2, a. 2). This brings us once more formally face to face with the first truth that brings salvation. There is consequently a close affinity between faith and love. Of course, faith remains an act of the human spirit which, independent of charity, continues to retain its own and thus supernatural distinction, but which owes its completion in

72 *Verit.* q. 14, a. 5, ad 4; *ST* II–II, q. 4, a. 3.

the intellect itself and thus its inward perfection as faith to charity alone. From the theological point of view, therefore, love is the normal environment of Christian faith. As a result, Aquinas regarded the more pronounced acumen possessed by a believer in a state of grace, and thus in a state of love, as the normal flourishing of the Christian life of faith, and not as a *gratia gratis data.*[73] The fact that people of simple but deep faith display, because they experience faith in an active and powerful way, a spontaneous insight into faith that is not reflective but is nonetheless profound is the experimental proof of this theory. We are thus confronted by a double insight into faith—insight achieved in a connatural divine manner, *per modum inclinationis* (the affective insight) and insight achieved in a connatural human manner, *per modum cognitionis* (theology). Aquinas made a clear distinction between the two (*ST* I, q. 1, a. 6, ad 3), regarding them as specific and different wisdoms. This sharp definition of the limits of each marked a decided advance on the pre-Thomist theology of, for example, Albert and Bonaventure.

On the other hand, however, although they are different, there is a perceptible interrelationship between rational wisdom and affective wisdom in faith. It is therefore important to emphasise that theology, even though its method is undoubtedly strictly technical and scientific, nonetheless to some extent presupposes the affective wisdom in the optimum case. We know that Aquinas regarded theology as a science that was subordinate to faith—"scientia subalternata scientiae Dei mediante fide"—and that this is so because of the structure itself of faith. The First Vatican Council defined the subjective principle of theology as the *ratio fide illustrata,* the intellect formally in its association with faith.

[73] That would be a grace that is not given separately to everyone, but only to certain individuals, and then not for themselves, but for the service of the community.

Now, when faith is fully mature—*informata caritate*—it has, as I have already said, greater perspicacity and a finer insight into faith. If, then, theology (both positive and speculative) is indeed closely and permanently linked with faith because of its subordinate character, it can, in Aquinas's view, only gain immeasurably from this faith's possession of full maturity and extreme acumen by reason of "affective wisdom." And, relying directly on Aquinas's premisses, we have experimental proof of this theory as well. Saints in the strict sense, that is, those men who possessed this affective insight into faith to a very high degree, were also, when they devoted themselves to theology, the greatest theologians. This was clearly so both in the case of the fathers of the church and in the case of the scholastics of the high Middle Ages. Assuming that the natural prerequisites of intellectual, philosophical, and historical formation are already satisfied, the best theologian is the Christian who also possesses this affective wisdom of faith because he actively embodies in a holy life the Christian faith.

We should, however, be careful not to interpret the ability of this affective wisdom to infiltrate into theology that is conducted on a technical basis wrongly. Aquinas had a marked aversion to all forms of vague mysticism that sacrificed technical analysis and synthesis pursued according to the critical method (typified by the constant use of such obscure remarks as "I feel this way about it"). The influence of infused wisdom on theology is purely inspirational. In other words, this wisdom only inspires work in the historical sphere and in the sphere of speculative theology that is closely allied to faith. However important it may be in itself and to the life of the spirit, personal experience of faith based on "feeling" is of no value theologically if it is not justified and made fully explicit at the intelligible level. This also applies, of course, to every science. As Pasteur so rightly said, there is in every science an area of "inspired ideas" and spontaneous insights which are initially not justified but which must, at a later stage, be justified scientifically and intellectually. If this does not take place, then these ideas will never be of any value to the community.

The felicitous influence of this affective knowledge of faith on theology absolves us least of all from the need to analyse accurately and critically. What we certainly do not require is a diluted form of theology, tailored to fit the needs of preachers, an accommodating theology which will suit romantic tastes. Theology is, and will always be, a scientific reflection about faith. This fact, however, need never act as a restraint on the close association of theology with life so long as it follows the structure of faith, which is, after all, already theology in an incipient and spontaneous form. Theology as such is not a pious elevation of the soul, but a science, and consequently technical. It is and must be a science, and must therefore entail all the laborious and nerve-racking process of painful analysis, fair-mindedness, and serious thought, which so often turns counter to man's inclinations, and an almost scrupulous use of methodological precision. Up to a certain point there is, of course, bound to be a tension between every science and life itself, for the simple reason that the scientific process demands a certain distance, a certain detachment from life. Life is after all spontaneous, and science, being reflective, to some extent checks the impulse to live. This is the age-old idea of *primum vivere deinde philosophari,* of living first and only philosophising afterwards, and not one science is exempt from this law, not even theology, which is so closely associated with life. Even theology does not, therefore, coincide entirely with life itself. A certain feeling of "alienation from life," in the sense previously referred to, will inevitably always be present in the work of theology, too. But, although this feeling is inherent in the practice of every science, its manifestation in the sphere of theology is perhaps all the more painful, since a believer—and this the theologian should be above all—is all the more profoundly aware of the fact that the Catholic faith is primarily not a science, but a stimulus to effective, loving Christian life, "by means of which," as Aquinas observed, "we can at last attain to the beatitude of immortal life by rising again."[74] It is only in the case of an insight into faith that has not been acquired scientifically, but is infused wisdom on a basis of supernatural "sympathy," that all alienation from life is overcome.

Let us therefore accept and be loyal to the technical scientific method in the positive and speculative theological study of faith. May this be inspired at the same time by the life of faith as experienced both personally and collectively in the church. But, as we are swept along by the tide of modern life, let us at the same time avoid its being diluted to the level of mere glossy vulgarisation, which may perhaps be appropriate elsewhere, but not in the theological training of the Catholic priesthood. Anyone who has studied the synthesis of faith, in its saving aspect, in a technically scientific way will derive all the more abundant benefit from this study in his apostolic activity, at least as soon as he is able to dissociate himself from this technically scientific element.

I have, then, tried briefly to show how Aquinas did full justice to the patristic elements, but at the same time how these elements underwent a shift of emphasis in his writings, because of his Aristotelian approach and his sharper insight into the structure of faith. It is always instructive to find out how great theologians went to work in their own time, not in order to imitate them, but so that we may also do independently, in our own time, what they did in theirs.

[74] *ST* III, q. 1, Prol.: "per quam ad beatitudinem immortalis vitae resurgendo pervenire possumus."

Table of Original Publications

PART 1

1 REVELATION, SCRIPTURE, TRADITION, AND TEACHING AUTHORITY

First published as "Openbaring, schriftuur, traditie en leergezag," *KT* 14 (1963), 85–99; also included, together with an exchange of views between Catholic and Protestant professors, in *Jaarboek 1962 Kath. Theol. Nederl.,* Hilversum 1963, 137–62.

2 THE LORD AND THE PREACHING OF THE APOSTLES

First published as "De kyriale waardigheid van Christus en de verkondiging," *VT* 29 (1958–9), 34–8.

3 REVELATION-IN-REALITY AND REVELATION-IN-WORD

First published in *LV* 46 (1960), 25–45; and, with a different introduction, as "De dienst van het woord in verband met de Eucharistieviering," *TL* 44 (1960), 44–61.

4 THE DEVELOPMENT OF THE APOSTOLIC FAITH INTO THE DOGMA OF THE CHURCH

First published as "Dogma-ontwikkeling," *Theologisch Woordenboek* I, Roermond and Maaseik 1952, cols. 1087–106.

PART 2

5 WHAT IS THEOLOGY?

First published as "Theologie," *Theologisch Woordenboek* III, Roermond and Maaseik 1958, cols. 4485–542.

6 THE BIBLE AND THEOLOGY
First published as "Exegese, Dogmatik und Dogmenentwicklung," *Exegese und Dogmatik,* ed. H. Vorgrimler, Mainz 1962, 91–114. This version has already been published in English translation as "Exegesis, Dogmatics and the Development of Dogma," *Dogmatic versus Biblical Theology,* trans. Kevin Smyth, Burns & Oates, London 1965, 115–45.

The new English translation by N. D. Smith appearing here is from the Dutch version of the original German: "Bijbel en Theologie," *Exegese en Dogmatiek,* Bilthoven 1963, 92–115.

7 THE PLACE OF THE CHURCH FATHERS IN THEOLOGY
First published as "Kerkvader," *Theologisch Woordenboek* II, Roermond and Maaseik 1957, cols. 2768–72.

8 THE CREED AND THEOLOGY
First published as "Symbolum," *Theologisch Woordenboek* III, Roermond and Maaseik 1958, cols. 4449–60.

9 THE LITURGY AND THEOLOGY
First published as "Lex orandi lex credendi," *Theologisch Woordenboek* II, Roermond and Maaseik 1957, cols. 2926–8.

10 SCHOLASTICISM AND THEOLOGY
The Sources of Theology according to Aquinas:
First published as "Loci theologici" and "Gezagsargument," *Theologisch Woordenboek* II, Roermond and Maaseik 1957, cols. 3004–06 and 1908–20.

Truth or Relevance for the Christian Life in the Scholastics:
First published as "Technische heilstheologie," *OG* 27 (1945), 49–60. It therefore relates to the theology of the inter-war years.

INDEX